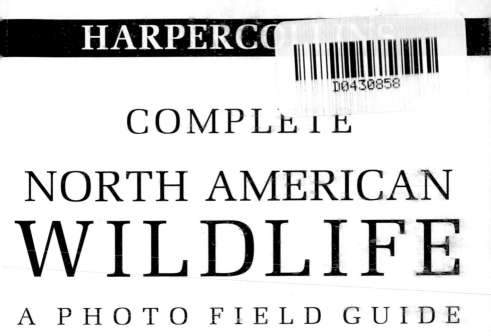

COMPLETE
NORTH AMERICAN
WILDLIFE
A PHOTO FIELD GUIDE

GERARD A. BERTRAND,
JOHN A. BURTON, AND
PAUL STERRY

HarperResource

An Imprint of HarperCollins *Publishers*

HarperCollins books may be purchased for educational, business, or sales promotional use. For information, please write to: Special Markets Department, HarperCollins Publishers Inc., 10 East 53rd Street, New York, New York 10022.

FIRST EDITION

ISBN: 0-06-093393-3

Library of Congress Cataloging-In-Publication Data applied for.

03 04 05 06 07 / 10 9 8 7 6 5 4 3 2 1

All front cover photographs © Nature Photographers Ltd:
Saguaro Cactus—P. Sterry; American Bullfrog—E.A. Janes;
Western Meadowlark—P. Sterry; Sunflower—G. du Feu;
Canebrake Rattlesnake—S.C. Bisserot; Bald Eagle—E.A. Janes.
Back cover and spine photographs © G.A.Bertand

Typeset and designed by D & N Publishing, Hungerford, England
Color reproduction by Colourscan, Singapore
Printed and bound by Imago, Singapore

CONTENTS

INTRODUCTION

The first modern field guide is generally accepted to have been written and illustrated by Roger Tory Peterson and published in 1937. It covered the birds of eastern North America. Since that book was published the number of birders and other amateur naturalists has grown dramatically, and so has the number of field guides that are available, though none offer such a complete view of North American wildlife as does this one. Endangered species conservation is also receiving attention at all levels—from the local city

Glaciated Arctic scenery in Alaska's Glacier Bay National Park.

council through to state, province, and national government. Most visitors to the open countryside and wilderness areas of North America, be they birders, hunters, walkers, botanists or simply tourists enjoying a day out, now have an awareness of wildlife unprecedented in history. Being able to identify an animal or plant and knowing something about it stimulates most people into wanting to know more and, consequently, into taking a keener interest in their natural environment.

Tundra flowers on St Paul Island in Alaska's Pribilofs.

In preparing field guides for North America, there are two fundamental problems: it is a huge area, and people are now very mobile. This book is designed to enable a reader to sample the incredible richness of North America's wildlife and to enable him or her to identify many species, or at least to make an informed judgement as to which group of animals or plants a particular specimen may belong. This book aims to provide enough for readers to learn a little about the species. If they are enthused, it enables their interest to be developed further. The bibliography, internet addresses, and other contact points listed at the back of the book give opportunities for readers to follow up any particular interests.

The area covered by this book, North America north of Mexico, is a vast area, with an incredible diversity of species. A whole library would be needed to identify them all. The emphasis of the book is therefore on the more widespread species and those most likely to be encountered in the more frequently visited parts of the continent. The number of species increases from north to south, which means that in California, Texas and Florida there are many more species than in New England or Alaska.

HOW TO USE THIS BOOK

The layout of the book is such that photographs face the text for each species, with a grid next to each description, which identifies the exact position of the corresponding photograph. The constraints of space mean that the descriptions are concise, but do provide all the necessary information for identification when read in conjunction with the photographs.

THE COMMON NAMES OF SPECIES

The names given to species are sometimes rather variable, but we have tried to give the most commonly and widely used vernacular name. The Latin names (normally italicized) are those used by biologists all over the world. Introduced and standardized in the late eighteenth century by Swedish naturalist Carl Linn/, they are understood by naturalists whatever language they speak. The first of the two names (always capitalized) is the Genus, or group of closely related species, and the second refers to the individual species. Thus *Siala* informs the reader that it is a bluebird and *mexicana*, that it is the Western Bluebird. The Eastern Bluebird is *Siala sialis* and the Mountain Bluebird is *Siala currucoides*. Together with other thrush-like birds the genus *Siala* forms part of the Thrush family (Turdidae).

Despite being much more standardized than the English and other vernacular names, it is often confusing to non-biologists to find that the Latin names may also vary. This is because the names are used to reflect relationships, and naturalists often change their mind about which genus a species should be in. Also the name that was first used takes priority, and in the past, because of delays in communication, naturalists in different parts of the world frequently gave different names to a single species. This meant that later, in cases where such duplication was discovered, more recent names had to be dropped in favor of the earliest recorded.

THE CHOICE OF SPECIES

In the US alone there are approximately 430 species of mammals, 770 birds, 280 reptiles, 233 amphibians, over 820 fish, over 16,000 flowering plants, and even more insects and other invertebrates. New species of mammals and other vertebrates are still being discovered with surprising regularity, and there are doubtless thousands of species of invertebrates still awaiting discovery. The choice of which species to illustrate and describe in this guide is, therefore, based on personal decision. We have illustrated species that are likely to be encountered (over 1,390 in total), are of particular interest, and are fairly readily identifiable. This means that preference has been given to larger, and more abundant species, and proportionately more birds and mammals are described. In order to

make the book attractive to the user, setting a size limit was essential, as was making it affordable. While no two naturalists (let alone three) will ever agree on a particular choice of selection, we do believe that the selection presented fulfills our first and foremost aim—to show beginners the wonderful array of wildlife to be found in North America.

THE CHOICE OF ILLUSTRATIONS

If choosing a selection of species from an area as rich as North America presents a difficult task, then selecting the photos is even more so. It is further complicated by the fact that many species show huge variation depending on the time of year and their particular

Lush, wetland vegetation in a backwater of Florida's Everglades National Park.

range. Consequently we have endeavored to illustrate the most distinct phase possible. This might be the male plumage of birds, plants in flower or in fruit, or the adult of a butterfly. But the observer should always remember that there are not only many similar species, there may be larval, juvenile, and sexual differences to consider also.

The major vegetation zones of North America. Within the broad vegetation types there are numerous pockets and variations, as well as small areas of very distinctive vegetation.

US STATE ABBREVIATIONS

Alabama	AL	Montana	MT
Alaska	AK	Nebraska	NE
Arizona	AZ	Nevada	NV
Arkansas	AR	New Hampshire	NH
California	CA	New Jersey	NJ
Colorado	CO	New Mexico	NM
Connecticut	CT	New York	NY
Delaware	DE	North Carolina	NC
Florida	FL	North Dakota	ND
Georgia	GA	Ohio	OH
Hawaii	HI	Oklahoma	OK
Idaho	ID	Oregon	OR
Illinois	IL	Pennsylvania	PA
Indiana	IN	Rhode Island	RI
Iowa	IA	South Carolina	SC
Kansas	KS	South Dakota	SD
Kentucky	KY	Tennessee	TN
Louisiana	LA	Texas	TX
Maine	ME	Utah	UT
Maryland	MD	Vermont	VT
Massachusetts	MA	Virginia	VA
Michigan	MI	Washington	WA
Minnesota	MN	West Virginia	WV
Mississippi	MS	Wisconsin	WI
Missouri	MO	Wyoming	WY

CANADIAN PROVINCE AND TERRITORY SYMBOLS

Alberta	AB	Nunavut	NU
British Columbia	BC	Ontario	ON
Manitoba	MB	Prince Edward Island	PE
New Brunswick	NB	Quebec	QC
Newfoundland	NF	Saskatchewan	SK
Northwest Territories	NT	Yukon	YT
Nova Scotia	NS		

PLANT AND ANIMAL GROUPS

Scientists and naturalists divide plants and animals into groups, members of which have characters in common with one another. The species included in this book have been organized into these widely accepted groups and the accompanying notes detail their most distinctive features. The colored symbols to the left of the page correspond to those used throughout the book as thumbnail indicators of page subjects.

VERTEBRATE ANIMALS
Animals with backbones, which comprise:

Mammals: warm-blooded animals which have hairy skins, give birth to live young which are subsequently suckled by the mother.

Birds: warm-blooded animals whose skins are covered with feathers, these aiding heat regulation and allowing flight; all birds lay eggs.

Reptiles: cold-blooded animals with scaly skins and which breathe air. The young develop inside eggs which, in some species, hatch within the body of the female.

Amphibians: cold-blooded animals with soft, moist skins capable of absorbing oxygen from water; some also have lungs and can breathe air. Often found on land but most breed in water, laying eggs which grow as larval tadpoles before metamorphosing into miniature adults. Some give birth to live young or lay eggs on land.

Fish: cold-blooded animals that live in water throughout their lives; all the species use gills to extract oxygen from water. In most species, the skin is covered with scales and fins facilitate swimming.

INVERTEBRATE ANIMALS
Animals without backbones, which include:

Sponges: primitive, aquatic animals whose bodies have external vents and are covered in minute pores.

Coelenterates: radially symmetrical, soft-bodied creatures that include sea anemones, jellyfish and freshwater hydras.

Echinoderms: animals which are radially symmetrical, mostly organized into five rays. Some members have bodies protected by a hard shell comprising armored plates with spines. Included in the book are sea urchins, starfishes, and brittlestars.

Mollusks: soft-bodied animals that are found on land, in fresh water, and in the sea. Some mollusks protect their bodies by producing hard shells, while this feature is absent or much reduced in slugs, sea slugs, and octopuses.

Segmented worms: examples of which are found in soil, fresh water, and in the sea. The body is soft, segmented and often bears bristles to aid movements as with earthworms and marine annelid worms.

Arthropods: the most numerous group of animals and one which is characterized by the presence of an external skeleton and paired, jointed limbs. Members include insects, crustaceans, spiders and allies, millipedes, and centipedes. Insect groups dealt with in this book include butterflies and moths, flies, dragonflies and damsel-flies, grasshoppers and crickets, earwigs, mantids, lacewings, bugs, bees, wasps, ants, and beetles; crustacean groups covered include crabs, lobsters, and barnacles; spider allies include scorpions.

HIGHER PLANTS

Distinguished from animals by the presence of the green pigment chlorophyll which is used to manufacture food from sunlight energy, water, and carbon dioxide; oxygen is produced as a by-product of this chemical reaction known as photosynthesis. Higher plants come in all shapes and sizes and are separated into two groups:

Flowering Plants: plants whose reproductive structures are borne in flowers; their seeds are enclosed in structures known as fruits, a term which, for botanists, is not confined to conspicuous and edible forms. Flowering plants covered in this book include deciduous and some evergreen trees, shrubs, and wildflowers.

Grasses, rushes, and sedges are grouped separately.

Conifers: mostly sizeable, evergreen plants whose reproductive structures are borne in cones; the seeds lack a seedcoat.

LOWER PLANTS

These lack the complex reproductive structures of higher plants and are generally smaller and less robust. Among those included in this book are the following:

Algae: primitive aquatic plants. Many are microscopic and not covered in this book but the larger seaweeds are included.

Mosses: primitive land plants which lack roots and whose stems bear simple leaves.

Liverworts: primitive land plants which are usually broad and flattened, anchored to the substrate by root-like structures.

Lichens: unusual organisms that exist as a symbiotic relationship between a fungus and an alga. Usually form encrustations on rock or bark.

Clubmosses: small, simple plants with upright stems which bear numerous narrow leaves. Clubmosses bear a passing resemblance to miniature conifers.

Horsetails: perennial plants that comprise an underground stem or rhizome from which arise upright stems bearing whorls of narrow leaves.

Ferns: easily recognized during their spore-producing stages which are large and robust and have a vascular system and roots.

FUNGI

Although formerly considered to be part of the plant kingdom, many scientists now place fungi in a group separate from both plants and animals. They lack the photosynthetic pigment chlorophyll, which characterizes plants, and are thus unable to make their own food; nutrition is obtained instead from organic matter via the thread-like hyphae, which comprise the bulk of the fungal organism. The familiar mushrooms and toadstools are merely the reproductive structures of the fungi.

NORTH AMERICA: CLIMATE AND VEGETATION

The vast area that North America encompasses inevitably means that there is a huge range in climate and vegetation. From the barren ice fields of Alaska to the lush tropical swamps of Florida and the arid deserts of the Southwest, the range is as great as anywhere else in the world. As well as north–south and east–west vegetation zones, plant and animal life can be separated vertically into zones. At higher altitudes, even as far south as California, the vegetation is more akin to that of the far north. On the higher mountain ranges, the deciduous forest of the lower slopes gives way to conifers. Above the tree line, alpine meadows are eventually replaced by tundra-like habitats, and finally by snow fields that may melt only for a few weeks of the year (or not at all, in the case of glaciers).

The landscape has been moulded by its geological past. The rate of movement of the vast tectonic plates has been measured as 2in a year at Point Reyes in California. This does not sound like a lot, but over a century it is 16ft 6in and over the course of a million years, when time only starts to become geologically significant, it would amount to some 300 miles. These powerful tectonic movements also result in the earth-shattering phenomena that lie along the San Andreas fault. The earthquakes of southern California are bound to recur,

and bound to cause huge damage. The eruptions of Mount St Helens, Mount Lassen and other West Coast volcanoes not only cause local damage, but can also affect the climate of the planet. These movements of the earth are not confined to the west. For instance, if the Boston earthquake of 1755 (8 on the Richter scale) occurred today, it would devastate the city and all its environs. Earth movements on this scale have the power to alter river courses, create lakes, and obliterate forests. Above the earth's surface, North America's moulding has been no less violent. Glaciers have ground away over most of the continent, ablating and accreting throughout the ice ages, leaving behind deposits or scouring rock that make the characteristic landscape of New England and the Midwest. Hurricanes, which rip through many areas with regularity, cause varying amounts of destruction and, from

Organ Pipe and Saguaro Cacti in southern Arizona.

time to time, destroy mature forests and, more recently, human settlements. But it is perhaps fire that has been one of the most significant superficial creators of the landscape. For centuries the wildfires caused by thunderstorms kept the prairies open. Long-needle pine and giant Sequoia are among the trees which are adapted to fire resistance and even the watery swamps of the Everglades were maintained by fire in the dry seasons. Suppression of fire has caused problems through allowing forest litter to accumulate. This means that when a fire does break out, it burns much hotter, killing wildlife that hides in the soil, as well as generating enough heat to destroy even fire-resistant trees and other plants. Water is also one of the most important influences on habitats, defining the vegetation that will grow. But the supply of this vital resource has been changed, mostly by man. Rivers have been channeled and canalized, deserts have been irrigated, rivers and lakes have been polluted and dammed. All of this has a dramatic effect on vegetation and wildlife.

Lush Pacific temperate rainforest in Olympic National Park, Washington State.

HABITATS

In addition to latitude and rainfall, several other factors affect habitats. The most important of these are the underlying geology and altitude, all of which show wide variation in North America.

COASTAL HABITATS

The coasts of North America, stretching from the Arctic Ocean to the Caribbean and the Pacific, are rich habitats for wildlife. While the plant diversity is often relatively low, some animal species are often amazingly abundant.

Seabird cliffs on St Paul Island in the Pribilofs.

Point Fermin Park, California, is good for watching both migrating birds and whales.

A rocky shore on Great Wass Island, Maine.

CLIFFS

In northern parts of the continent, many cliffs are breeding grounds for vast colonies of seabirds. For a brief few months every year, tens of thousands congregate to nest on inaccessible ledges. The flora of such habitats is often interesting, with several species that have become popular as garden plants. The tops of cliffs are generally windswept, with low bushes and shrubs, and other ground-hugging vegetation. Some of the most spectacular cliff habitats are found in the Aleutian Islands and Alaska, but they also are found sporadically south to California. On the east coast, Labrador and Newfoundland have some of the most dramatic cliffs.

ROCKY SHORES

One of the delights of childhood must be exploring rock pools. Here an incredible variety of bizarre creatures lurks within easy reach of the smallest child. The farther north you travel, the greater the tidal fall, and consequently the better the rock pools. Rocky coasts are also the best places for diving and snorkelling outside of coral reefs. Both the North Atlantic and west coasts have rocky shores and generally the farther they are away from towns, the better they are for wildlife.

SANDY BEACHES

While never as rich in wildlife as rocky shores, sandy beaches and sand dunes, though they may look bare, often contain a surprising variety of species. Shorebirds race along the tideline, and beaches are often a good place to search for marine shells and other flotsam and jetsam, such as fish egg cases and dead starfish. The flora of sand dunes is one of pioneering colonizers—plants with long roots that can live in this most extreme of habitats. Unfortunately, sandy beaches are also the most popular with tourists and developers, and in summer it is often difficult to find a beach where the wildlife remains undisturbed. Some of the best beaches are on the Florida Keys and on the Outer Banks.

Look for shorebirds and coastal plants on sandy shores, such as this one at Cape Cod, Massachusetts.

MANGROVES

One of the most threatened habitats worldwide, mangroves are a comparatively rare habitat in North America and are confined to Florida and the southeast. This is one of the most productive habitats, as the roots of the mangroves trap leaves and other organic matter and provide sheltered breeding grounds for fish and a variety of other wildlife.

Mangroves colonizing coastal mudflats in the Everglades National Park, Florida.

INLAND HABITATS

MARSHES AND ESTUARIES
Except in the far north, there are few marshes and estuaries in North America that do not show signs of man. Among the first areas to be settled, they were often drained for grazing and cultivation. But they remain a rich habitat, particularly for attracting birds.

ABOVE: Saltmarsh and mudflats at Cape Cod, Massachusetts.
BELOW: A forest-fringed lake in Baxter State Park, Maine.

Wildlife thrives at the Big Cypress National Preserve in Florida's Everglades.

RIVERS

From the mighty Mississippi to tiny mountain brooks, rivers and streams provide extremely important habitats. For this reason many states have introduced conservation measures which, as well as protecting water supplies, also protect the adjacent flood plains. Cold, fast-flowing mountain streams have an entirely different fauna—including species of trout and other fishes in headwaters, as well as salamanders—from that of slow-moving rivers such as the vast Missouri flood plains. The Everglades are a vast, slow-moving river flowing south from Lake Okeechobee to the sea.

LAKES AND PONDS

Some of the larger lakes were once virtually dead as a result of pollution. However, improvements have been made and Lake Erie, for example, which was once badly polluted, is now quite clean and filled with life. There are still millions of lakes and ponds scattered across North America. These range in size from the Great Lakes on the US/Canadian border, to the prairie potholes of the northern Prairies; and even small ponds which are found in woods and forests. The prairie potholes are extremely important for migrating and breeding ducks and geese, while in the south underground lakes, where no daylight penetrates, provide habitat for blind salamanders and blind fish, as well as unique spiders and other invertebrates.

Although created by accident, Salton Sea, a vast inland lake in California, hosts large numbers of birds.

WOODS AND FORESTS

When the first Europeans arrived in North America they found a world shrouded in forest. The whole of the eastern seaboard was predominantly one large forest, as was much of northern California to Alaska. Even though New England is extensively wooded now, if you look carefully you will see the remains of walls and ditches stretching through the woods, giving an indication that it has all been cleared at some point for agriculture and the forests of today are secondary forest. Although well wooded, the trees are no equals to the giants that were cleared by the European settlers. Gone are the king's trees, great pines taken for masts, and the once abundant American Chestnut, lost to an introduced fungus.

OLDGROWTH FORESTS

North America's oldgrowth forests have almost entirely disappeared from the whole of the east coast, outside the Great Smokies. Significant tracts still survive in the north, but in the west they are all highly fragmented. As might be expected, among the most obvious features of an oldgrowth forest are massive trees, sometimes several centuries old, and an undisturbed forest floor; the accumulation of millennia. The fauna and flora are often dependent on the relatively high humidity, and there are species of birds, such as the ivory-billed

Good oldgrowth forest can be found in the Pacific temperate rainforests of Olympic National Park in Washington State.

woodpecker (now believed extinct), which depend on large areas of very old trees. Forests comprise two main types, with various intermediaries:

DECIDUOUS FORESTS

Deciduous trees shed their leaves in the fall, and in the process create some of the world's most spectacular landscapes. Visitors travel from all over the world to see New England's fall foliage. As the winter approaches, and with the first frosts, the leaves of many of the trees turn shades of brilliant red, yellow, orange and brown. While most trees shed their leaves in the winter, in the southern deserts it is in the hot summers, as they dry out, that the leaves fall.

Oldgrowth forest in Glacier Bay National Park, Alaska.

Stunning desert scenery of the Grand Canyon, Arizona.

Deciduous Cottonwood trees fringe the River Gila in Arizona.

PINEWOODS
Coniferous trees (apart from Larch, which is deciduous) are evergreens, and are generally more abundant in cooler climates. However, several species including Redwoods and Long-needle pine grow in hot habitats. Because conifers retain their leaves all the year round, they are important winter habitats for animals living in the snow-covered north.

DESERT
The American southwest includes some of the most spectacular desert habitats in the world. A desert is usually defined as anywhere having an annual rainfall of less than 10in. However, despite so little rain, some deserts still manage to provide a home for an incredible range of wildlife. After rains, the flowers can be spectacular, and many mammals have adapted to a nocturnal existence, hiding in burrows during the heat of the day and emerging as night falls. Lizards and snakes are particularly well adapted, as are cacti and succulents.

PRAIRIES

The first European explorers to see the Prairies thought of them as a huge desert. Later they were turned into the grain basket of the world. Now, little is left of the original wild prairie, characterized by grasses with flowering plants, that once stretched all the way from Mexico to Canada. Here, herds of Buffalo, Elk, and Pronghorn roamed in their millions. Fortunately pockets of prairie have survived, and the wildlife that was once on the verge of extinction is building in numbers and is easily seen once more.

FARMLAND

Despite popular belief, early native American settlers did not all live in harmony with their environment. While undoubtedly some did, it is

California poppies in the Arizona desert.

Irrigated farmland and sagebrush, Oregon.

generally accepted that all cultures live at the limits of their technology and population. As a result, before the arrival of Europeans, some of the land was over-hunted and, in settled areas, agriculture was impoverishing the soils even then. But with the arrival of European settlers, the whole character of the continent was irreversibly changed. On the whole, the North American agricultural landscape is one of the most biologically sterile environments the world has ever known. Even cities and towns can offer greater biodiversity. Hundreds of thousands of acres of monoculture farming, intensively sprayed with pesticides and herbicides and artificially nourished with chemical fertilizers, leave little room for wildlife. Yet, despite this, some species do manage to cling on.

CITIES AND TOWNS

Modern towns and cities extend for miles and miles, but urban-adapted wildlife manages to survive. Many cities have extremely fine parks, and these can be a real haven for wildlife. Central Park in New York is particularly well known for its spring birds. In the suburbs too, with their hundreds of thousands of bird feeders, a replacement habitat has been developed for millions of birds that might otherwise have nowhere else to live. And gardeners try to eradicate 'weeds', which are in reality only highly successful plants from almost anywhere in the world.

A boating lake in Central Park, New York City.

WILDLIFE MIGRATIONS

Many species are migratory. Birds are probably the best known migrants, with some species travelling from the Arctic, where they breed, to the sub-Antarctic to spend the northern winter months. Even tiny birds the size of hummingbirds may travel thousands of miles. Many mammals are also migrants, including bats and buffalo. Some insects migrate too; perhaps the best known is the Monarch Butterfly, which congregates in huge hibernacula in Mexico and California. There are often other more local migrations. In mountain areas there are altitudinal

Snow Geese on migration.

migrations, when animals descend to lower levels during the harsh winter months. Frogs, toads, snakes, and turtles, all migrate to and from their breeding grounds and their hibernation sites.

THREATS TO THE WILDLIFE OF NORTH AMERICA

Despite the seemingly limitless areas of wilderness in many parts of North America, the greatest single threat to wildlife continues to be the increasing human population. Not only is the population continuing to grow, but so are its aspirations for material wealth. With this comes an increasing use of natural resources, in particular non-renewable energy.

Most people are familiar with the stories of the Buffalo and the Passenger Pigeon, both once so numerous that no-one believed it possible they could become extinct. But the Passenger Pigeon's uncountable flocks will never be seen again. The last Passenger Pigeon died in 1914, and the Buffalo was reduced to a few hundred before any reserves or

The suburbs of Phoenix, Arizona.

breeding programs were developed. Now the causes of endangerment are becoming more insidious: acid rain, pesticide pollution, estrogen mimics, foreign introduced species, atmosphere pollution, release of genetically modified organisms, and a myriad other negative impacts. But perhaps the single greatest threat is the destruction and fragmentation of natural habitats.

At the end of the twentieth century there was a tendency to try and justify conservation in strictly economic terms, but the greatest economic value comes when it is appreciated intrinsically. When nature reserves and national parks become an integral part of the economic structure of our society, we will be prepared to pay for the privilege of seeing spectacular scenery and the wildlife that depends on it.

Even the mighty Everglades are not immune to the pressures of human activity.

OPOSSUM *Didelphis virginiana*   Total length 2ft 9in; tail 12½in
The only marsupial in North America. A cat-sized mammal with a long, mostly naked, prehensile tail. It has prominent bare ears, and a long pointed snout. The fur has a rather grizzled appearance. Has up to 13 young, which the mother carries in her pouch. Feeds on almost any small animals, as well as eggs and fruit. When cornered or attacked, it will feign death ("playing possum"). Nocturnal, it is found in a wide range of mostly wooded habitats. Often encountered as road kill, and in suburban gardens. It is found from Central America, N into the US as far as New England, with isolated populations in the W.

NINE-BANDED ARMADILLO *Dasypus novemcinctus*   Total length 2ft 6in; tail 14in
Unmistakable. The only mammal in North America with a hard shell. It burrows and makes a nest of dried leaves, giving birth to 4 young from a single fertilized egg. Curls up on the approach of danger, and is a frequent road kill. It is found mostly in tillable farmlands. Before European colonization it was confined to TX, but spread E naturally merging with a population introduced to FL which was expanding northwards. Range now extends as far N as GA, SC.

BLACK-TAILED JACK RABBIT *Lepus californicus*   Total length 2ft; tail 4in
A hare with exceptionally long ears-up to 5in. The upper side of the tail and base of the rump are blackish. Feeds on grasses and other vegetation, and is active mostly at dusk and dawn or at night. Can have up to 4 litters of up to 8 young in a year. Found mostly in open, rather dry habitats, including desert, creosote scrub, and sagebrush. Also found in pasture and farmlands, and frequently seen at airports, in W from WA and SD to Baja CA.

SNOWSHOE HARE *Lepus americanus*   Total length 18in
Similar in size to a domestic rabbit. In summer, brown above, whitish below, with long, black-tipped ears. In winter most populations turn pure white, with only the ear tips remaining black. The feet are well furred, and in winter they leave distinctive, large, wide, footprints. Has 2 or 3 litters a year of up to 9 young, and populations can build up very rapidly, but are cyclical, crashing when populations become too numerous every 9 or 10 years. Important prey for species such as lynx, foxes, weasels, owls, and hawks. Widely distributed over N North America from AK to Newfoundland, and S to forested areas of N US.

EASTERN COTTONTAIL *Sylvilagus floridanus*   Total length 18in
Brownish above and whitish below, with a fluffy white underside to the short tail. A prolific breeder, having up to 7 litters a year of up to 7 young. Born in a nest made in dense vegetation, the young are blind and helpless at birth. Widespread and often common over most of E North America. This species is spreading N and gradually displacing the New England Cottontail (*S. transitionalis*).

DESERT COTTONTAIL *Sylvilagus audubonii*   Total length 16in; tail 3in
A typical cottontail, with long ears (2½in) and a fluffy tail. Brown above, with a reddish brown nape. Up to 6 young are born in a fur-lined nest; usually two litters a year. An agile climber, often climbing in sloping trees and bushes. Found in arid habitats feeding on mesquite, grasses, cacti, and other vegetation, throughout central and SW US.

SWAMP RABBIT *Sylvilagus aquaticus*   Total length 21in; tail 2½in
The largest cottontail. Born in fur-lined forms, often in a hollow log or the burrow of other animals, the young (usually 2 or 3) are fully furred and their eyes open soon after birth. A first-class swimmer, which dives to avoid predators, staying submerged with only its nostrils exposed. It feeds on aquatic plants, and also comes on land to feed, often among crops. Found almost exclusively in wet habitats throughout SE US.

MARSH RABBIT *Sylvilagus palustris*   Total length 18in; tail 1½in
Smaller and darker than Swamp Rabbit. To avoid predators it often dives into water and then stays submerged with only the eyes and nose above water. In tall vegetation it often walks on its hind legs. Litters of 2–5 young are born in a domed nest made out of rushes and grasses. Always found close to water, in river valleys, swamps, and around ponds in SE US .

CINEREOUS SHREW *Sorex cinereus* Total length 4in; tail 2in
One of the most widespread shrews in North America. A relatively small species, brown above, gray below, with a distinctive two-tone tail, dark above and pale below. Like all shrews it is voracious, eating its own weight in insects, slugs, spiders, and other invertebrates each day. Widespread in most habitats in N North America, extending S through the Rockies to northern NM.

WATER SHREW *Sorex palustris* Total length 6in; tail 3in
A dark shrew, blackish above, gray below. One of the largest North American shrews, though in the Pacific states an even larger species of water shrew, the Masked Shrew (*S. bendirii*), is found. Distinctive fringes of hair on the hind feet help it swim and run on the water's surface. When diving it appears silvery, due to the air trapped in the fur. Feeds on invertebrates, and has litters of up to 8 young. It is found near water in marshes, streams and rivers, usually in well-wooded areas. Widely distributed, but absent from most of the Plains states and the SE.

 PYGMY SHREW *Sorex hoyi* Total length 4½in; tail 3½in
The smallest mammal in North America, and one of the smallest in the world (weighs less than ⅒oz). Brownish gray above, paler below. It feeds on small invertebrates. Litters of 3–8 are born in late summer. It is fairly rare throughout its range, but is found in a wide variety of habitats, including marshes, meadows, and woods. It has an extensive, if patchy, distribution from AK and Canada, several parts of N US and down the Appalachians to NC.

 NORTHERN SHORT-TAILED SHREW *Blarina brevicauda* Total length 5½in; tail 3½in
The largest North American shrew, it is a uniform dark gray, and has a relatively short tail. Its minute eyes and ears are largely hidden in its fur. It feeds on invertebrates, earthworms, and young rodents; its saliva is venomous and is used to paralyze its prey. It makes a nest, usually under a log, and its litter consists of 3–7 young, born blind and naked. Found in a variety of habitats including woodland, grasslands, and swamps. Often found in cultivated areas. It is relatively abundant and is found over much of NE North America.

 LEAST SHREW *Cryptotis parva* Total length 3½in; tail 1in
A very small shrew, but with a shorter tail than the Pygmy Shrew. It is browner than the other short-tailed shrews. Like other shrews it has a voracious appetite, feeding on invertebrates up to the size of grasshoppers, beetle grubs, and earthworms. It is one of the smallest mammals in North America, weighing around ⅕oz when adult. It is found in woods and fields, but is less common in marshes than other shrews. It is widespread in E US from SD to TX.

EASTERN MOLE *Scalopus aquaticus* Total length 8½in; tail 1½in
A typical mole, with dense velvety dark fur, and large shovel-like forepaws. The eyes are vestigial and covered with skin. It feeds almost exclusively on invertebrates, particularly earthworms. It has a single litter each year of 2–5 young, born naked and helpless in an underground nest. Found in habitats with loamy well-drained soils, often in woodlands, meadows, and grasslands, and also lawns. It is widespread over much of E North America from S Canada to southern TX, with isolated populations in southwest TX and Mexico. There are also other species of mole in W US.

 STAR-NOSED MOLE *Condylura cristata* Total length 9in; tail 3½in
Easily distinguished from other moles by the bizarre cluster of 22 pink tentaclelike projections on the tip of its nose. Like other moles, with short velvety black fur, vestigial eyes, and massive forepaws. It has a relatively long tail, which increases in size, probably to provide a food reserve when it is breeding. It is found close to water in wet meadows, and swims well, often hunting fish when the ground is frozen. Its distribution covers NE US and SE Canada, with isolated populations S to GA.

LITTLE BROWN BAT *Myotis lucifugus*   Total length 3½in; wing span 10in
Breeds in colonies of up to 800, but occasionally up to 30,000, which are found in buildings. Despite the size of some colonies, it is probably declining. It hibernates in caves, and derelict mines and tunnels, and sometimes enters homes in search of an overwintering site. Probably the commonest bat over most of North America, but rarer in the S.

WESTERN PIPISTRELLE *Pipistrellus hesperus*   Total length 3½in; wing span 10in
Even smaller than the Eastern species, weighing about ¼oz. Emerges early in the evening, like the Eastern Pipistrelle, and is very slow-flying. Seen flying in broad daylight more frequently than most other species of bat. Lives in desert and scrub areas, roosting in caves and buildings. Confined to the W of the US.

EASTERN PIPISTRELLE *Pipistrellus subflavus*   Total length 3½in; wing span 10in
The smallest bat over most of North America, also one of the commonest. It emerges earlier than most bats, and can be seen in the evening light, hunting for insects and spiders. Generally found around farmland, open woodland and parks, where it roosts in trees, migrating in the fall to hibernate in caves and mines. It is found in E North America from SE Canada to TX.

SILVER-HAIRED BAT *Lasionycteris noctivagans*   Total length 4in; wing span 11in
Medium-sized, with dark fur tipped with silvery white, giving it a frosted appearance. A slow-flying bat, emerging from its roost early in the evening. Sometimes collides with buildings. Found in woodland, roosting in old woodpecker holes, in hollow trees, and behind bark. It is found over S Canada and US and in fall migrates S.

HOARY BAT *Lasiurus cinereus*   Total length 6in; wing span 15in
A very large bat with distinctive, frosted fur. Ears are rounded and blackish. Has a very obvious white mark on the wrist, and an orange-brown collar. It usually roosts in crevices in trees, or among vegetation, emerging at dusk to feed on moths and other large insects.The most widely distributed bat in North America, found even in Hawaii.

BIG BROWN BAT *Eptesicus fuscus*   Total length 6½in; wing span 13in
Large, with rounded ears and a broad muzzle. Color is variable, but generally dark reddish brown in the E, paler in the W. Fast-flying (up to 40mph). Usually roosts in barns, churches, and other buildings. Breeds in colonies of up to 300. Widespread from S Canada over most of US except S FL and TX.

EASTERN RED BAT *Lasiurus borealis*   Total length 4½in; wing span 13in
One of the few small mammals to show obvious sexual dimorphism—male is more brightly colored than female. Reddish, with white patches on the shoulder, and white tips to the hair. Unusually, this bat gives birth to 4, occasionally 5, young. Found mostly in wooded habitats. Widespread in E from S Canada. It is migratory in N.

TOWNSEND'S BIG-EARED BAT *Plecotus townsendii pallescens*   Total length 4in;
                                                                                                                      wing span 11in
Easily distinguished by its huge ears—up to 1½in long—half of its body length. Ears are curled up when roosting, but extended when active. Emerges after dusk, feeding on moths and spiders which it picks off leaves while hovering. The females gather in nursery colonies of up to 1,000; males are usually solitary. Widely distributed in W of US, with scattered populations in WV and VA.

MEXICAN FREE-TAILED BAT *Tadarida brasiliensis* Total length 4in; wing span 11in
Unlike that of most bats, the tail of this species is not contained within a membrane, but is 1½in long and mouselike. Roosts in caves, often in colonies of 10,000+, but numbers have undergone massive decline in recent years. Mainly tropical, it is found over much of Central and South America, extending as far N as FL and TX.

MAMMALS

AMERICAN PIKA *Ochotona princeps*   Total length 7½in
Short-legged, guinea-pig sized mammal, almost tail-less, with a rounded compact body and
short muzzle. The short, dense fur is grayish or buff, but rather variable. The Pika's most
distinctive character is its voice, often described as a bleat or whistle, and this can often be
heard before the animal is seen. Sun-loving, often basking on rocks. Feeds on vegetation.
3–5 young are born in May or June. Found only in the Rockies from Canada to NM.

WOODCHUCK *Marmota monax*   Total length 2ft 3in; tail 6in
Large, ground-dwelling rodent with a short tail. Coloring is variable, but generally reddish
brown. In fall becomes very fat, and hibernates from October through March. Feeds on
grasses and other vegetable matter. A single litter of 2–6 young is born in April or May.
Found close to burrows, mostly in E North America.

YELLOW-BELLIED MARMOT *Marmota flaviventris*   Total length 2ft 3in; tail 8in
Similar to the Woodchuck, but yellow-brown above, and yellowish below, with a larger,
bushier tail. Feeds mostly on green vegetation. Makes an underground den among rocks
or in a burrow, in which a litter of 5 young is born in March or April. Found in rocky hillsides, in the Rockies from British Columbia S to CA and northern NM.

HOARY MARMOT *Marmota caligata*   Total length 2ft 6in; tail 9in
Similar to the Woodchuck with silver-gray fur, and a black and white face. Hibernates from
October through February or March. A litter of 4 or 5 young is born underground about 6
weeks after the end of hibernation. The mound of dirt from the burrow is often very obvious.
Usually found in mountainous rocky habitats in the N Rockies from ID to AK.

BLACK-TAILED PRAIRIE DOG *Cynomys ludovicianus*   Total length 16in; tail 4½in
A large ground squirrel living in colonies which used to be extensive and highly populated.
The burrows (towns) are guarded by a sentry which stands on a heap of dirt, and yaps at
the approach of danger. A single litter of 4–5 young is born underground in April–May.
Found only on short-grass prairie, feeding mostly on grasses. Now mostly confined to iso-
lated populations in protected areas in the plains of the Midwest from Canada to Mexico.

RICHARDSON'S GROUND SQUIRREL *Spermophilus richardsonii* Length 14in; tail 3½in
Similar to prairie dogs but with a longer tail. One of the most widespread and abundant
mammals within its range. When danger approaches it stands on its hind legs and gives a
whistling warning. It lives in colonies in burrows, feeding on grasses and other vegetation,
as well as insects and even carrion. Gives birth to a single litter of 2–11 young in an underground nest. Hibernates, storing food underground for the winter. Found in the Rockies
from S Canada to CO and NV.

ROCK SQUIRREL *Spermophilus variegatus*   Total length 20in; tail 9in
A large ground squirrel, with a long bushy tail. Usually most active in morning and
evening. Alarm call high-pitched and followed by a trill. Feeds on berries, nuts, cacti, and
fruit. An agile climber, making its den in a burrow under rocks. 2 litters a year of up to 7
young. Often lives among oak and juniper, and is seen sunbathing on rocks. Found in open
rocky gullies, gorges, and canyons in southwest US and N Mexico.

SPOTTED GROUND SQUIRREL *Spermophilus spilosoma*   Total length 10in; tail 3½in
A small, gray-brown ground squirrel with indistinct spots and bold stripes—most ground
squirrels are striped. Black tip to tail. Feeds mostly on seeds, vegetation, and insects. Lives
in burrows under bushes or rocks in relatively arid habitats, often pine woods. Range
extends from MI and SD to TX and NM.

WHITE-TAILED ANTELOPE SQUIRREL *Ammospermophilus leucurus*
                    Total length 9½in; tail 3½in
Like a pale chipmunk, with a characteristic jumping gait, and tail carried over its back. Often
active during the day. Excavates burrows or lives in rock crevices, feeding mostly on seeds
and insects. A single litter of 5–14 is born underground. Found in arid habitats, including
desert and creosote country. Confined to the S Rockies from OR and ID to Baja CA.

EASTERN CHIPMUNK *Tamias striatus* Total length 11in; tail 4in
A very common ground-dwelling squirrel. Very vocal, with rapid trilling calls. Lives in burrows, but is an agile climber. Feeds on nuts, berries, and seeds, as well as insects and other small animals, and stores food for use after emerging from hibernation. Litters of up to 5 are born in May and midsummer. Most common in woodland, around stonewalls, gardens, and similar habitats. Found over much of E Canada and US.

LEAST CHIPMUNK *Tamias minimus* Total length 8½in; tail 4½in
A small, very pale chipmunk Although generally terrestrial, it is an agile climber and sometimes nests in trees, though usually in burrows. Often sunbathes on rocks or branches. High-pitched call is very similar to that of the Eastern Chipmunk. The single litter of up to 7 young is born in May. Found mostly in open habitats, including open pine woods, as well as grasslands, prairies, sagebrush, and desert. Range includes most of S Canada from Ontario westwards, and S into the Rockies.

YELLOW-PINE CHIPMUNK *Tamias amoenas* Total length 9½in; tail 4in
Smaller than the Eastern Chipmunk, and although very similar in markings, more brightly colored, with a heavily striped face. The most widely distributed of about 16 species of western chipmunks, found in the Rockies from N BC to N California.

RED SQUIRREL (CHICKAREE) *Tamiasciurus hudsonicus* Total length 15in; tail 6in
A small reddish brown tree squirrel, which has prominent ear tufts in winter. Often very vocal, making chattering noises. Feeds on pine nuts, berries, and fungi, often leaving abundant remains. It nests in old woodpecker holes or builds a leaf nest, and has 2 litters of 3–7 young in spring and late summer. Found in wooded habitats, particularly coniferous. Very widespread across N North America, being found from AK to E Canada and S down the Rockies and Appalachians.

EASTERN GRAY SQUIRREL *Sciurus carolinensis* Total length 19in; tail 9in
A fairly large squirrel, with a bushy tail, Although mostly gray, it often has a brownish tinge to the back. Feeds on nuts, buds, berries, and also eggs and small animals. It makes a large nest of leaves, or nests in a tree hole, and produces 1 or 2 litters of 2–3 young. Found in a wide range of wooded habitats, as well as parks and gardens. Naturally widespread over E North America from S Canada to E TX, widely introduced elsewhere.

EASTERN FOX SQUIRREL *Sciurus niger* Total length 2ft 3in; tail 13in
The largest North American tree squirrel, with very variable coloring. Some are all black; others brown above, orange below, or gray above and white below. Feeds on nuts, shoots, berries, and also eggs and small animals. Found in wooded habitats, and also swamps. Widespread in E North America, and introduced in several places in W US. Declining over much of its range.

DOUGLAS'S SQUIRREL *Tamiasciurus douglasii* Total length 14in; tail 6in
Very similar to the Red Squirrel, but grayer above and yellowish brown below. It is a very vocal squirrel with a range of trills and chattering calls. Like other squirrels, it often hides food for use in winter. Found mostly in coniferous forests, and the mounds of eaten pine cones are often very obvious. It is confined to W North America, from British Columbia, S to CA, and E to the Rockies.

SOUTHERN FLYING SQUIRREL *Glaucomys volans* Total length 9½in; tail 4½in
A very small nocturnal squirrel. Its fur is soft and silky, grayish above, white below. A fold of skin between the fore limbs and the hind limbs is used to glide from tree to tree. It nests in old woodpecker holes, and also uses nest boxes, and attics. It hoards food for winter use, but also feeds extensively on insects and other small animals. Usually has 2 litters of up to 6 young. Found in woodland. Range extends over most of E North America, and also S into Central America.

BOTTA'S POCKET GOPHER *Thomomys bottae* Total length 12in; tail 3in
One of the most widespread pocket gophers but, like other species, it is rarely seen above ground, and even then only ventures a couple of inches from the entrance to its burrow. Highly adapted for burrowing, excavating soil with its huge front teeth, and carrying it to the surface in its fur-lined cheek pouches. Found in a wide variety of habitats including deserts and meadows, from S Oregon to Canada to E TX.

PLAINS POCKET GOPHER *Geomys bursarius* Total length 14in; tail 4in
Pocket gophers are highly modified for a life spent almost completely underground and are very similar in appearance. This species is one of the more widespread, though it is rarely seen above ground. However, its mounds of dirt are often very obvious—they can be up to 1ft high and 2ft across. It is active all year round, feeding on roots and tubers and other vegetable matter. Does not hibernate, but digs deeper down in winter. Found not only in prairies, but also in tillable land, pastures, and gardens, from E ND, WI, and MN, S to LA and TX.

ORD'S KANGAROO RAT *Dipodomys ordii* Total length 11in; tail 6in
One of the most widespread of the kangaroo rats. Like all the kangaroo rats it is strictly nocturnal and hops on its hind legs, using its long tail to balance. Although active all the year round in the S, in Canada it spends the winter underground, and plugs up the entrance. It feeds mostly on seeds, which it stores underground for winter. Found from S Canada to TX.

WESTERN HARVEST MOUSE *Reithrodontomys megalotis* Total length 5½in; tail 2½in
A small brownish mouse superficially similar to a house mouse, with a long tail. Feeds mainly on seeds and shoots, and makes a store in its nest, which is usually above ground. There are several closely related species of harvest mice, mostly associated with marshes and overgrown grassy habitats such as grassy fields, bramble patches, and overgrown wet areas. This species is widespread in dry habitats in W US and extreme S Canada.

NORTH AMERICAN DEERMOUSE *Peromyscus maniculatus* Total length 8½in; tail 4½in
A very common and widespread mouse, generally rich brown to grayish above, white below, with the tail sharply bicolored, white below. Like most deer mice it has large ears and large eyes. However, it is a very variable species with numerous subspecies described. Feeds on berries, nuts, seeds, and invertebrates. Found in a wide variety of habitats from woodlands to prairies, where it lives in among tree roots and under logs, and sometimes excavates tunnels. Widespread across most of Canada and US except SE US.

WHITE-FOOTED DEERMOUSE *Peromyscus leucopus* Total length 8in; tail 3½in
Very similar to the Deer Mouse. Like most other mice it is active all year, but in winter lives in runs and tunnels beneath snow, and may remain in the nest in extreme cold. Implicated in the spread of Lyme's disease, which is carried by ticks. Range confined to North America E of the Rockies, and mostly S of the Canadian border. There are several other closely related species of *Peromyscus* mice in North America, most with more restricted ranges.

SOUTHERN PLAINS WOODRAT *Neotoma micropus* Total length 20in; tail 7½in
A widely distributed woodrat, also known as a pack rat. It is famous for its habit of building stick houses. These houses can be very large, and are usually placed by a cactus. Generally grayish or dark charcoal above, white below, with a hairy tail. Confined to the Mexican US border area, N to S Kansas and S Colorado.

MAMMALS

AMERICAN BEAVER *Castor canadensis*   Total length 3ft 10in; tail 18in
The largest rodent in North America. Easily recognized by its characteristic flattened tail. Feeds on vegetation. Has 4 or 5 young in a litter. Stores branches underwater for use during the winter to build its lodge, which has an entrance underwater, and also to build dams to adjust the water flow. Confined to slow-moving aquatic habitats. Widespread, and with scattered populations, S from AK and Canada. Absent from most of CA and FL.

MEADOW VOLE *Microtus pennsylvanicus*   Total length 7½in; tail 2½in
A typical vole, and one of the most widespread and abundant within its range. Variable in coloring. Its extensive runs, which often contain little heaps of grass and other stems, can indicate its presence. Found over most of Canada, extending to AK and S to much of N US. A related species, the reddish brown Pine or Woodland Vole (*M. pinetorum*), is found in established deciduous woodlands over much of E North America.

SOUTHERN BOG LEMMING *Synaptomys cooperi*   Total length 6in; tail ¾in
Brown above, grayish below, with a tiny tail and inconspicuous eyes and ears. Lives mostly below ground, digging runs and also using the runs of other mammals. Feeds on grasses, clover, and roots. The name is misleading as it is found mostly in meadows and grassy areas in forests. Populations are highly cyclical. It is found in KS and MB, E to QC and NC.

MUSKRAT *Ondatra zibethicus*   Total length 2ft; tail 12in
A large aquatic relative of the voles. Distinguished from the beaver by its thin, rounded tail. Builds smaller lodges made from aquatic vegetation and does not construct dams. Widespread over most of North America, except the S, and in FL where it is replaced by the smaller Round-tailed Muskrat (*Neofiber alleni*).

BROWN RAT *Rattus norvegicus*   Total length 18in; tail 8½in
Fur often has a characteristic "greasy" appearance. Generally found close to human habitations, in cities as well as farms and suburbs. A pest species found all over the world, the Brown Rat first reached North America during the Colonial War, and has since spread over most of the US, and as far N as S Canada.

BLACK RAT *Rattus rattus*   Total length 17in; tail 10in
The Black Rat originated in Asia, arriving via Europe with the Jamestown colonists at the beginning of the 17th century. Nowhere near as common as *R. norvegicus*, which tends to push it out. Most common around seaports. Still largely absent from the Rockies, the Prairies, and Canada.

MEADOW JUMPING MOUSE *Zapus hudsonicus*   Total length 10in; tail 6in
An agile mouse with a very long tail. Can jump up to 4ft in a single bound. When disturbed it makes several leaps then freezes. Omnivorous, also eats underground fungi. Unlike many other rodents it does not hoard food, but accumulates fat and hibernates. It is found in damp habitats such as woodland, marshes, and overgrown fields, mostly across much of Canada, S AK and S to GA and OK.

NORTH AMERICAN PORCUPINE *Erithizon dorsatum*   Total length 3ft; tail 11in
Unmistakable. The quills (up to 30,000) are only loosely attached to the skin, and when cornered or attacked, very easily become embedded in the attacker. Exclusively vegetarian, feeding on leaves, shoots, and bark. Arboreal, descending to the ground only to walk between trees, or to find a den. Found in W US from AK across Canada, and S to PA.

COYPU *Myocastor coypu*   Total length 4ft; tail 18in
An aquatic mammal imported from South America in the 20th century and raised on fur farms. In the 1940s some escaped in LA and spread very rapidly. A prolific breeder, and although the gestation period is long (over 4 months), the young are active and swim within 24 hours of birth. Widespread in LA and elsewhere.

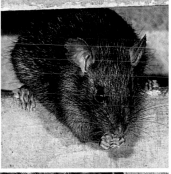

BLUE WHALE *Balaenoptera musculus*   Total length 90ft
The largest living animal, but most are now under 80ft. Like most other baleen whales it is a plankton feeder, engulfing fish and plankton near the surface. It has been hunted to the verge of extinction but has now been protected for many years and may be recovering. Although it is very rare, it is regularly seen off the Pacific and rarely off the Atlantic coasts.

NORTHERN MINKE WHALE *Balaenoptera acutorostrata*   Total length 30ft
The smallest and one of the fastest of the "rorqual" whales. It has bright white bands on its flippers. This is the species most likely to be seen on whale-watching excursions because of its abundance and wide distribution.

SEI WHALE *Balaenoptera borealis*   Total length nearly 60ft
A large whale, most easily distinguished from other baleen whales by its dorsal fin, which is further forward than in other species. Found in the Pacific and Atlantic Oceans, it is very similar to Bryde's Whale (*B. edeni*), which lives in warmer waters.

FIN WHALE *Balaenoptera physalus*   Total length 78ft
One of the largest whales, surpassed only by the Blue Whale. Like other baleen whales it is a fast-swimming species, with a very streamlined shape. It is dark colored, whitish below, and has a small dorsal fin, well back towards the tail. Identified by prominent white streaking on the back, and a high straight spout. Tends to surface exposing the head and blowhole, then blowing and exposing the back and fin as it dives. It is one of the more frequently seen whales, particularly off the Atlantic coast of New England and Canada. It migrates from warm subtropical waters to the Arctic for the summer, returning S in the fall, and on migration often comes close to shore.

HUMPBACK WHALE *Megaptera novaeangliae*   Total length 40ft
A large, slow-moving whale, with characteristic long, narrow flippers—the longest of any whale. The dorsal fin is small, but distinct. Very acrobatic, often leaping out of the water—breaching—and also slapping the surface with its flippers or tail. These whales are found in all oceans, but are much depleted as they were one of the easiest species to kill. However, they are believed to be increasing and are among the easiest to see, particularly on migration, when they are often in shallow coastal waters of CA and New England.

SPERM WHALE *Physeter catodon*   Total length up to 50ft
A massive whale with a huge head. Male much larger than female. The jaw is long and narrow, the back lacks a dorsal fin, but has a series of bumps, and the blowhole points forwards. Before diving this whale may blow up to 20 times, and it can descend to depths of over 2½ miles. It feeds almost entirely on squid, and lives in groups of 20–30. Where the whales are protected they can often be approached. It can be seen in almost all deep oceanic waters, moving to warmer tropical waters to breed.

NORTHERN BOTTLENOSE WHALE *Hyperoodon ampullatus*   Total length up to 32ft
A small whale with a bulbous head, and a very small dorsal fin set well back. Once very common, this species was easy to hunt and numbers are now much depleted. It lives in groups of up to 10 and is often very tame. It feeds on squid, as well as fish such as Herring. It is confined to the N Atlantic.

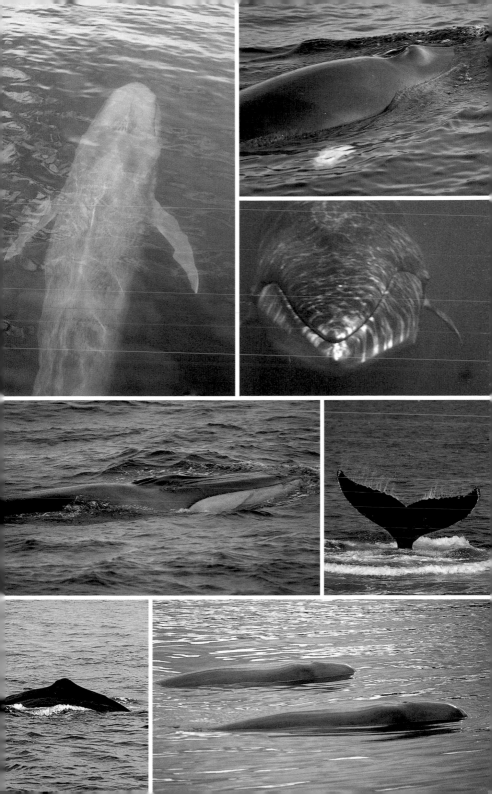

MAMMALS

KILLER WHALE *Orcinus orca*   Total length 31ft
A very distinctive medium-sized whale, with a very large, pointed dorsal fin, and a characteristic black and white pattern. Carnivorous, preying on seals, young whales, sea lions, birds, as well as squid and fish. Hunts in groups ("pods") of up to 25, and is an extremely effective predator. These whales often tear young whales, larger than themselves, to pieces, and will play with baby seals for some time before eating them. Found in all oceans, and frequently comes close to shore.

SHORT-FINNED PILOT WHALE *Globicephala macrorhynchus*   Total length 22ft
A medium-sized whale, generally black all over, except for a pale strip down the center of the underside. The front of the head has a characteristic dome, known as the "melon". Mostly nocturnal, feeding on squid. Almost invariably found in "pods", often of up to 200 individuals. Has a wide range in the Atlantic Ocean, mostly in deep water. It is found N to New England and is also widespread in the Pacific.

NARWHAL *Monodon monoceros*   Total length 16ft
Generally larger than the Beluga, and heavily dappled dark gray, but its most distinctive feature is the single long tusk carried by the male. This can be up to 10ft long, and in medieval Europe was prized as the unicorn's horn. The Narwhal is found in almost exactly the same area as the Beluga.

BELUGA *Delphinapterus leucas*   Total length 15ft
An unmistakable species, also known as the white whale, since the adults are milky white. The new born young are pinkish brown, becoming dark gray before turning white as adults. Lives in groups, which sometime aggregate into several hundreds. It is still hunted by native Americans, although commercial hunting has now stopped. Often found close to pack ice, where it feeds on fish and crustaceans. It is confined to colder waters of the Arctic of Canada and AK, no longer being seen in the waters of New England.

SHORT-BEAKED COMMON DOLPHIN *Delphinus delphis*   Total length 8ft
One of the smaller dolphins, with a prominent beak, and variable gray, white, and buff-yellow on the sides. The back and dorsal fin are black. Feeds on fish, and often gathers in large numbers: up to 1,000 or more on rich feeding grounds, and over 100,000 have been recorded. They also ride the bow wave of boats regularly. Large numbers are drowned in fishing gear, particularly those involved in the tuna fisheries, since they often associate with tuna. This dolphin lives mostly in deeper waters, but often comes close to both coasts. More rarely it will swim up estuaries and rivers.

BOTTLENOSE DOLPHIN *Tursiops truncatus*   Total length 13ft
A fairly large dolphin, with a prominent beak, it is bluish gray, paler below. The most familiar dolphin, frequently exhibited in aquaria and dolphinaria. It feeds in small schools, mostly on fish. It is widespread in both the Pacific and Atlantic Oceans, and because it has never been hunted in vast numbers (although it is still killed in some coastal fisheries), it remains fairly numerous. The Pacific population is often regarded as a separate species, *T. gilli.*

HARBOR PORPOISE *Phocoena phocoena*   Total length 5ft
A small compact cetacean, with a small dorsal fin. Usually seen in small groups (10–15), swimming near the surface ("porpoising"). Feeds mostly on fish such as herring, as well as squid and crustaceans. These porpoises are still hunted by native Americans, and are drowned in gill nets, seines, and trawls. Formerly very widespread and abundant in coastal waters, and although still found along both Atlantic and Pacific coasts, the species is not as common. Two other closely related species are also found in Pacific waters.

DALL'S PORPOISE *Phocoenoides dalli*   Total length 7½ft
A distinctive black and white porpoise. Most of the body is black, with a pure white belly and white edges to the fin and tail flukes. It is only found off the W coast, from AK to CA.

46

WALRUS *Odobenus rosmarus*   Total length 11ft
A very large seal, with bare skin, which is usually pinkish or brownish, but can be reddish when sunburnt. Male is much larger than female, but both sexes carry tusks (the males' are larger). The tusks are used for gouging up mollusks on the sea bed. During the breeding season, walruses gather in large colonies on beaches. They have been extensively hunted in the past (mostly for their ivory), and are still hunted by native Americans. Found all around the North Pole, and those found in Alaskan waters are larger than those in the N Atlantic.

HARBOR SEAL *Phoca vitulina*   Total length 5ft 6in
A small seal, with very variable coloring and markings, but generally grayish blue above with dark blotches. The pup is born in early summer, and is well developed and able to swim within a few hours of birth. Feeds mostly on fish, as well as mollusks, crustaceans, and squid. Some populations have declined, and the species is very vulnerable not only to oil spills and other pollution, but also to disturbance. However, the Harbor Seal is recovering and is still common in many parts of its range. It is generally confined to coastal waters, rarely venturing into deep waters, but often traveling inland up rivers. Found in both Atlantic and Pacific waters, with some populations in land-locked lakes.

RINGED SEAL *Phoca hispida*   Total length 5ft
A very small seal, usually grayish above marked with pale oval rings, with darker centers. It lives close to the ice, often keeping a breathing hole clear, and feeds on fish and plankton. The single white-coated pup is born in a den which the mother excavates in the ice in spring. This seal is found all around the North Pole, and as far S as Labrador and Newfoundland in the E and Point Barrow in AK.

GRAY SEAL *Halichoerus grypus*   Total length 7ft 6in
A large seal, usually grayish or blackish, with darker and paler blotches. It breeds in small colonies, and the single white-coated pup is born in late winter. Gray seals feed on fish, and are often accused of damaging fisheries. They do indeed steal from nets, and often damage nets. Numbers have declined greatly, mostly due to persecution by fishermen. Where the seals are protected from persecution and disturbance they generally increase rapidly. Found in the Atlantic from Newfoundland S to New England, where it occurs mostly in coastal waters.

HARP SEAL *Phoca groenlandica*   Total length 6ft 6in
A medium-sized seal, which often has a dark harp-shaped marking on the back of the male. Feeds on fish and crustaceans. The white-coated pups are born in late winter, and have been hunted commercially in large numbers. Although their numbers may have been reduced, like other seals they are likely to recover well when protected. Normally confined to Arctic waters of the Atlantic, breeding on the pack ice in large numbers.

NORTHERN ELEPHANT SEAL *Mirounga angustirostris*   Total length 21ft
The male is the second largest seal in the world, weighing up to 5,000lb, but the female is less than 11ft long. The name comes from the male's trunklike snout, which is inflated during the breeding season. At one time the Northern Elephant Seal teetered on the verge of extinction, having been slaughtered for its oil. By 1911 there were probably as few as 20 surviving. Under protection, numbers have recovered: by the 1980s there were 70,000, and in 2000 over 100,000. This is one of the most easily seen seals, in the parts of southern CA where it breeds. Breeding is mostly on small offshore islands, but the smell of the colonies is noticeable on the mainland.

GRAY WOLF *Canis lupus*　　　　　　　Total length 6ft 6in; tail 18in
Similar to a large dog. Usually grayish, but can be almost pure white or blackish, with a long, usually black-tipped, tail. Can be confused with Coyote although Coyote is smaller. Wolves live in packs of usually fewer than 10. Vocal, with a range of howls, yelps, and barks. Confined to AK, Canada, and N US states around the Great Lakes and Rockies.

COYOTE *Canis latrans*　　　　　　　Total length 4ft 4in; tail 15in
Also known as the Prairie Wolf. Resembles a small wolf, and has spread into areas once occupied by wolves. Range extends S into Mexico and N to AK and S Canada, and E to New England. The range continues to expand, and coyotes are often found in suburbs.

RED FOX *Vulpes vulpes*　　　　　　　Total length 3ft 3in; tail up to 18in
Variable in color, but usually reddish brown above, with black on the back of the ears and on the paws. The underparts and tail tip are white. Very adaptable, found in a wide range of habitats. Widespread and often abundant over most of North America except the SW. Its range has expanded greatly, partly due to the introduction of European Red Foxes in the S.

ARCTIC FOX *Alopex lagopus*　　　　　　　Total length up to 3ft; tail 13in
Small with very variable coloring and relatively small ears. Most are brownish or bluish brown in summer, and turn white in winter, while some are dark bluish in summer, paler in winter. The Arctic Fox has a litter of about 6 young (can be up to 25). Unusually among smaller mammals, it is often migratory, or wanders over large distances. Confined to the N of Canada and AK.

GRAY FOX *Urocyon cinereoargenteus*　　　　　　　Total length 3ft 6in; tail 17in
Colorful, with grizzled gray fur above, and orange on the sides and under the tail. Relatively arboreal. Feeds on a wide range of small animals, fruits, birds' eggs, and carrion. Has a single litter of up to 7 cubs. Widespread and often common, although seldom seen by day.

SWIFT FOX *Vulpes velox*　　　　　　　Total length 2ft 3in; tail 13in
Small, sandy-gray with very large ears and a black-tipped tail. Emerges at dusk to feed mostly on rodents and rabbits. A single litter of up to 6 cubs is born in spring. Confined to short-grass prairies and similar open habitats, in S Canada to N TX and W NM.

BLACK BEAR *Ursus americanus*　　　　　　　Total length 6ft; tail 6in
Usually dark brown, and some are "cinnamon," but can be very pale or bluish; there is sometimes a white patch on the chest. Diet varied. Found principally in forests, often near meadows and farmlands. Hibernates in caves, hollow trees or among tree roots. The most common and widespread bear in North America, although absent from most of the Prairies and the SE.

GRIZZLY BEAR *Ursus arctos*　　　　　　　Total length up to 7ft; tail 3in
Large, with the largest individuals being found in the NW of its range. Omnivorous, food varies seasonally. Cubs (1–4) tiny at birth, weighing less than 1lb. Hibernates underground or in a hollow tree. Once found over most of the Rockies, S into Mexico, now confined to the AK and Canada with scattered populations in NW US.

POLAR BEAR *Ursus maritimus*　　　　　　　Total length 8ft; tail 5in
Huge and unmistakable, white or yellow-white, can weigh up to 1,400lb. Swims and preys mostly on seals, particularly Ringed Seal, but also eats carrion, birds, and eggs, and grass and berries. Litters of 1–3 tiny, helpless young, are born every 2–4 years in a den in snow, in mid-winter. Confined to the Arctic, living on pack ice or in coastal regions.

NORTHERN RACCOON *Procyon lotor*　　　　　　　Total length 2ft 6in; tail 16in
Familiar mammal, grayish with a banded tail, and "robber's mask" face pattern. It occurs in almost all habitats, and is found in most towns, where it often raids garbage. A true omnivore, eating almost anything edible. A single litter of up to 8 is born in late spring. Found over much of North America.

RINGTAIL (CACOMISTLE) *Bassariscus astutus*   Total length 2ft 6in; tail 17in
Rather like a slender cat, grayish yellow above, buff below with a long, distinctively banded, bushy tail. A very agile climber, making its den among rocks or in a hollow tree. It is generally nocturnal, and when attacked or cornered emits a foul-smelling scent from its anal gland. Feeds mostly on insects, small mammals, fruit berries, reptiles, amphibians, and also scorpions. A litter of 2–4 young is born in late spring or summer. Widespread in Central America, its range extending N to southwest OR, OK and KS.

AMERICAN MARTEN *Martes americana*   Total length 2ft 1in; tail 9in
A large relative of the weasel with dark glossy brown fur above, paler below, often orange or buff on the throat. It is very arboreal, living in coniferous forests, hunting squirrels, mice, and birds, as well as feeding on fruit and insects. The den is usually in a hollow tree, or in an old birds' nest, and 1–5 young are born in spring. Found mainly in the N of the continent, ranging S to NY and New England in the E, and from AK through the Rockies, to northern CA.

FISHER *Martes pennanti*   Total length 3ft 4in; tail 16in
A large relative of the weasel, slightly larger than the closely related Marten. It is also darker, and lacks a pale throat patch. It feeds on a wide variety of animals including porcupines, hares, rodents, and birds' eggs, and fruit and berries. A litter of 2–5 young is born in a den, usually among rocks or in a hollow tree. Found in a wider variety of habitats than the Marten, but generally confined to mature forests and woodlands. It has a similar range to the Marten, but not as far S, and is absent from AK.

ERMINE *Mustela erminea*   Total length 13in; tail 3½in
Ermine was originally the name for the white winter coat of the short-tailed weasel. In the northern parts of its range it turns completely white except for the black tip of the tail. It is a voracious predator, feeding mostly on mice, but also mammals up to the size of baby cottontails. It kills with a bite to the base of the skull or neck, and often drinks the blood of its prey. Very vocal, and can also be attracted by "squeaking" or by using bird calls. Its fur was traditionally used for trimming robes of the European nobility.

LEAST WEASEL *Mustela nivalis*   Total length 8in; tail 1½in
One of the smallest carnivores in the world, it preys on small mammals (and also birds and other animals) and can pursue mice down their holes. It is brown above and white below, but in the N of its range it turns completely white in winter. Unlike the other weasels it lacks a black tip to its tail. It is widespread across N North America (and also the Old World).

LONG-TAILED WEASEL *Mustela frenata*   Total length 22in; tail 6in
A medium-sized weasel, easily distinguished from other weasels by its long tail. It feeds mostly on mammals, including squirrels, rabbits, and small rodents, but also often takes poultry. It is found in a wide range of habitats, from forests and marshes to grasslands and tillable land, though usually close to water. It occurs over most of North America from S Canada to TX, and is also found in Central and South America.

MAMMALS

BLACK-FOOTED FERRET *Mustela nigripes*　　　　Total length 22in; tail 5½in
Very similar in appearance to the domestic ferret, with a raccoonlike face mask. It is totally dependent on prairie dogs, living in their burrows and preying on them. It also feeds on other small mammals as well as birds and invertebrates. It has 3–5 young in a litter born in an underground den. Saved from the brink of extinction by captive breeding, the Black-footed Ferret has been reintroduced into several protected areas. It appears to be thriving, and is once more breeding in the wild. It once was found from S Canada throughout the Plains to TX.

WOLVERINE *Gulo gulo*　　　　Total length 3ft 6in; tail 10in
A large weasel superficially resembling a small bear, and with a rather shambling gait. It is a voracious predator, tackling prey up to the size of deer and young moose, giving rise to its other name of "glutton." It also follows trappers to steal their catches. It marks any uneaten food with a foul-smelling scent to deter other scavengers. It also feeds on fruit and other plant matter. Up to 5 cubs in a litter are born in a den among rocks, in a burrow, or under a bush. Now mostly confined to the Arctic regions, but once more widespread in the Rockies.

AMERICAN MINK *Mustela vison*　　　　Total length 2ft 4in; tail 9in
A large weasel, generally uniform dark brown or blackish, often with a white spot on the chin and throat. Very aquatic, never found far from water, and it preys mostly on fish, amphibians, and water birds, but also feeds extensively on land. In the water it is very agile and easily confused with an otter. A single litter is born in spring, with up to 8 kittens. The Mink has been domesticated to provide furs, and is still extensively trapped, particularly in Canada. It has been introduced into Britain and other parts of Europe. It is found over most of Canada and the US, but is absent from the drier regions of the SW.

AMERICAN BADGER *Taxidea taxus*　　　　Total length 2ft 9in; tail 6in
A very heavily built member of the weasel family with a characteristic black and white face pattern. The legs are short, and the paws have long powerful claws. It is normally nocturnal, particularly close to human habitations. It feeds on almost any small animal, including ground squirrels, mice, gophers, prairie dogs, as well as frogs, ground-nesting birds, and also invertebrates. Up to 5 cubs are born in an underground den in spring. It ranges over much of North America W of the Great Lakes and S to Mexico.

EASTERN SPOTTED SKUNK *Spilogale putorius*　　　　Total length 22in; tail 8½in
A small black skunk with rows of large spots that often form incomplete stripes. When cornered or attacked it stands on its forepaws and sprays a foul-smelling scent at the intruder—it can reach over 12ft away. It is an omnivore, feeding on carrion, fruit, small mammals, lizards, and insects. A litter of 4–5 young is born in spring, usually in an underground den. It is found in a wide range of habitats including woodland and farmland, and often takes over disused woodchuck burrows. It is a frequent road kill. Found over much of E US, but absent from New England and the Atlantic coast.

STRIPED SKUNK *Mephitis mephitis*　　　　Total length 2ft 6in; tail 15in
A very familiar mammal, but usually seen (and smelled) dead by the roadside. It is black with white stripes extending from the head to the rump. Feeds on almost any small animal, as well as fruit and other plant matter. It carries rabies in many areas, but the risk to humans is generally much lower than that posed by domestic dogs. Found in a wide range of habitats, including farmland, desert, suburban gardens, and woodlands. It is very widespread and is found throughout most of the US, and much of Canada.

RIVER OTTER *Lontra canadensis*　　　　　　　Total length 4ft; tail 18in
A large, slender, aquatic mammal, nearly always seen in or close to water. It is brown above, whitish buff below, with a long tapering tail. Feeds on fish and other aquatic animals, including crayfish, mollusks, mammals, frogs, and water birds. A litter of up to 6 young is born in an underground den, usually among tree roots, close to water. The River Otter is found in rivers, estuaries, lakes, and ponds, and although once common over most of the continent it is rare or extirpated in many areas.

SEA OTTER *Enhydra lutris*　　　　　　　Total length 5ft 6in; tail 14in
A large, almost entirely marine otter. Feeds by diving among kelp to gather abalone, urchins, and other shellfish which it crushes with stones on its chest. The single young is born at sea, and the otters sleep at sea, using kelp as an anchor. Found only in or close to the sea, on the W coast. Rarely comes to the shore, but normally remains within about a mile of the coast. Sea otters can survive among high waves and storms. Although once widely distributed, there are now two main populations, in southern CA and in AK.

JAGUAR *Panthera onca*　　　　　　　　　Total length over 7ft; tail 2ft
A large, heavily built cat, generally nocturnal, shy and very difficult to see. Feeds on Peccary and other mammals and large birds. The Jaguar can be found in a wide range of habitats from tropical rainforests to scrubby hillsides. Widespread in South and Central America, it once occurred in SE US, through TX and perhaps as far N as AR. It still is found in Mexico, and there are occasional sightings in TX, NM, and AZ. With strict protection it is possible that a small population could survive.

PUMA *Puma concolor*　　　　　Total length up to 8ft 2in; tail up to 2ft 11in
Also known as the Mountain Lion or Cougar, the Puma is a predator of large mammals, including deer and peccaries as well as domestic livestock, and even humans (although rarely adults). It usually kills large prey by crushing the throat. The Puma is found in a wide variety of habitats, and although almost exterminated from New England and much of the E US by the end of the 19th century, is beginning to make a comeback under protection. It has the widest distribution of any native mammal in the Americas, being found from AK to Tierra del Fuego.

OCELOT *Leopardus pardalis*　　　　　Total length up to about 4ft; tail up to 15in
A medium-sized spotted cat. Fur color varies from yellowish golden to grayish with black-bordered brown spots (very variable in shape), which often have a tendency to form rows. The Ocelot is very agile, often climbing and preying on birds, but also feeding on reptiles, mammals, and even fish and frogs. Often hunts in pairs. Mostly found in Central and South America, with a small population in TX and adjacent states.

BOBCAT *Lynx rufus*　　　　　　　　　Total length up to 4ft; tail 6in
Fairly large, with a short "bobbed" tail. Coloring variable but usually yellowish brown, with black barring and tip to the upper side of the tail, and blackish barring on the legs. The back and sides are covered with indistinct spotting. Usually spends the day hidden in its den, and feeds mostly on hares, cottontails, squirrels, and other small mammals. It also occasionally raids poultry and other domestic stock. Widespread over North America, from S Canada to Mexico.

CANADIAN LYNX *Lynx canadensis*　　　　　Total length up to 3ft 6in; tail 5in
Similar to the Bobcat, but with longer fur, less distinctly spotted. Prominent ear tufts. The tail tip is black above and below. Less vocal than the Bobcat, but has a piercing scream and a catlike wail. The Lynx lives mostly in dense forest and preys mostly on the Snowshoe Hare, and also on other small mammals and birds. Large well-furred paws help it to run in thick snow. Range confined to the N.

MUSTANG *Equus caballus*   Total length 7ft 10in
A feral horse descended from horses introduced by the Spanish and other European colonists, which have reverted to a wild state. Mustangs are indistinguishable from domestic ponies. Together with burros (feral donkeys) they have now become a significant factor in the ecosystem in some parts of the W US. However, because of a lack of predators in much of their range, it is believed that they are degrading much of their habitat.

WILD BOAR *Sus scrofa*   Total length 6ft; tail 12in
Superficially very similar to the Peccary, but much larger, with the male (boar) weighing up to 400lb. It can also be distinguished by its heavily striped piglets. The Wild Boar builds a nest and has litters of 4–12 young. In some areas it has interbred with escaped (feral) hogs, to which it is very closely related. A native of Europe that has been introduced into many parts of the US and Hawaii.

COLLARED PECCARY *Pecari tajacu*   Total length 3ft 6in; tail 2in
Also known as the Javelina, the Peccary is superficially similar in appearance to the domestic hog, but with a very small tail and a pale "collar." It feeds on a wide range of fruit, such as prickly pears, squashes, also tubers and roots, as well as snakes, lizards, mice, and ground-nesting birds. In the fall it often eats acorns. It breeds in most months of the year, and has litters of 2–6. Peccaries are often gregarious, and in the past were found in herds ("sounders") of 1,000 or more, although at present groups of more than 30 are unusual. It is found in S AZ, S TX, and S NM, and S to South America.

WAPITI *Cervus elephus*   Total length 9ft 6in; tail 8½in
Also known as the Elk, this large deer can be distinguished from White-tailed and Black-tailed Deer by its larger size and generally much darker fur coloring. The male has large, branching antlers, and a shaggy throat. During the rut (late fall) the male has a short call also described as a resonant belch. The powerful "bugling," which ends in a shrill whistle and a series of grunts, can be heard for a considerable distance during the fall. Although often found in wooded areas, the Wapiti was once abundant in the Prairies. Widely distributed in the Rockies and N across Canada, its range in the E US is more restricted, but it is beginning to spread again.

WHITE-TAILED DEER *Odocoileus virginianus*   Total length 6ft 6in; tail 12in
The young fawn of the White-tail is Walt Disney's Bambi, and is heavily spotted. Adults are reddish brown above, and white below in summer, grayish in winter. The inside of the ear and the underside of the tail are white. When alarmed, the deer flashes its white rump patch and the underside of its tail as it bounds away. Where they are not hunted, these deer are often seen by day. They range over most of the US except the SW, S Canada, and S through Mexico to Brazil.

MULE DEER *Odocoileus hemionus*   Total length 6ft 6in; tail 9in
Similar to the White-tailed Deer, the Mule Deer is best distinguished by its black-tipped tail. It also has rather large ears and antlers in which both the main beams branch. It is active in the early mornings and evening, and although it rarely forms large herds, families stay together in small groups. The newborn young are hidden in dense vegetation for the first month after birth. Found mostly in well-wooded areas or habitats close to forests or woodlands, and in mountainous areas migrates to lower altitudes to avoid snow. Confined to W North America.

CARIBOU *Rangifer tarandus*   Total length 6ft 9in; tail 8¾in
Known in the Old World as the Reindeer, the Caribou is adapted to living in extreme conditions. Unusually among the deer family, both sexes carry antlers, although those of the female are smaller than the male's. Caribou are very gregarious, often forming large herds. Most populations are migratory, some covering several hundred miles between their summer and winter feeding grounds. Confined to Canada and the N of the US.

MOOSE   *Alces alces*   Total length up to 9ft; tail 6in
The largest deer in the world, standing up to 7ft or more at the shoulder and weighing up to 1,400lb. Easily recognized by its distinctive long-legged build and large muzzle. Despite its size it is capable of galloping at speeds of more than 30mph. The male has massive spreading antlers, which can be over 6ft across, and a roaring bellow in the rutting season. Moose are solitary most of the year, but occasionally groups are found near water, particularly when trying to escape black fly. They are generally considered potentially dangerous, particularly when they have calves; they may charge intruders and even vehicles. Found in N North America from New England to AK, and S through Rockies to CO and UT.

PRONGHORN   *Antilocapra americana*   Total length 4ft 6in; tail 6½in
Superficially deerlike, however not closely related to either deer or sheep, but in a family of its own. It is rather stocky, with very distinctive horns unlike any other species, which are shed at the beginning of winter. One of the fastest mammals on land (up to 70mph), it has a cruising speed of about 30mph, but is a very poor jumper and consequently Pronghorns are often killed when they collide with fences. They are confined to open habitats, and once formed huge herds migrating in the Prairies. By the 1920s there were fewer than 20,000, but they are now much recovered. Widespread in W North America from S Canada to N Mexico.

AMERICAN BISON   *Bison bison*   Total length 12ft; tail 18in
The Bison (also known as Buffalo), is a massive relative of domestic cattle, with dark brown shaggy fur. The calf is active within hours of birth, following the herd with its mother. Although generally known as a plains-dwelling species, some populations lived in woodlands. Once one of the most numerous mammals in North America, and found from S Canada to Mexico and east to VA, the Bison came close to extinction at the end of the 19th century. Numbers have slowly rebuilt, and there are now numerous herds in national and state parks, as well as on private ranches.

MUSK OX   *Ovibos moschatus*   Total length up to 8ft; tail 6½in
A close relative of sheep, the Musk Ox is easily identified by its size, long wool, and distinctive down-curving horn shape. It grazes on grasses, lichens, willows and sedges. The animals live in small herds (up to 100) and, when attacked, form defensive circles to protect their calves. This defense, evolved to deal with wolves, makes the Musk Ox easy prey to hunters with rifles. It was hunted to the edge of extinction, but protection combined with reintroductions has allowed it to recover slowly. Mostly found in open exposed habitats. Confined to the extreme N of Arctic Canada, and there are semi-domesticated herds in AK.

BIGHORN SHEEP   *Ovis canadensis*   Total length up to 6ft; tail up to 5in
A powerfully built sheep, the male has massive curled horns, the female short spikes. Generally brownish, paler in desert areas. These sheep spend most of the year in herds of up to 10, but may aggregate in herds of 100 or more, led by a female in winter. During the rut the males charge and clash horns at over 20mph, with a sound that can be heard over a mile away. Confined to the Rockies, from S Canada to N Mexico, and usually found in areas undisturbed by man.

DALL'S SHEEP   *Ovis dalli*   Total length 5ft; tail 4½in
A very pale, almost white sheep. In the S of the Dall's range it is darker (often nearly black), and known as the Stone Sheep. The male has massive curled horns, the female only small spikes. Very similar to the Bighorn, which is found further to the S. In winter the sheep gather into large herds, and during the rut the rams charge head on and clash horns, the sound of which can be heard from more than a mile away. Found in AK and W Canada.

MOUNTAIN GOAT   *Oreamnos americanus*   Total length 5ft 9in; tail 8in
Easily identified by its yellowish white fur. Mainly active in early morning and evening, and also on moonlit nights. The single kid (rarely 2 or 3) is born in May or June. During summer it moves to higher altitudes, and is normally found in very steep, precipitous habitats. Accidental falls are one of the main causes of mortality. Confined to the higher altitudes of the N Rocky Mountains and Sierras.

COMMON LOON   *Gavia immer*   Total length 2ft 8in
Large, swims low in the water. Large, pointed daggerlike bill. Breeding adult has a distinctive black head and neck with a barred collar. The call is a plaintive yodeling wail, which can be heard all year. An expert diver, feeding on fish. Breeds on northern lakes and ponds. Migrates S in winter.

RED-THROATED LOON   *Gavia stellata*   Total length 2ft
Smaller and slimmer than the Common Loon, with a gray head, rusty throat patch, and black and white markings on the neck and shoulders; in winter it is dark gray, paler below. Like other loons, builds its nest at the water's edge from mud and vegetation. Breeds in the high Arctic, migrating to the Great Lakes and coastal waters for the winter.

HORNED GREBE   *Podiceps auritus*   Total length 14in
An elegant waterbird, with a thin pointed bill. The breeding adult is spectacularly plumaged with orange-golden cheeks and tufts, contrasting with the black head and chestnut body; gray and white in winter. Breeds over most of NW North America, and migrates to winter along the Pacific and Atlantic coasts.

EARED GREBE   *Podiceps nigricollis*   Total length 13in
A medium-sized grebe, which usually swims with its bill pointed upwards. Breeding plumage is brownish black, with golden-orange tufts on the cheeks. Nests in colonies on lakes and ponds in W North America from Canada to TX; winters further S.

PIED-BILLED GREBE   *Podylimbus podiceps*   Total length 13in
The most widespread of the grebes. Brownish with a large head and short stubby bill, which in the breeding season has a dark band on it. Appears tailless. Breeds on lakes and ponds over much of North America, winters S into Mexico and Central America.

RED-NECKED GREBE   *Podiceps grisegena*   Total length 18in
A large, long-necked grebe with a characteristic long tapering bill, which is yellow with a black tip. In breeding the neck is orange-red. It is the most loonlike of all the grebes, but when flying it has white wing patches (all loons lack patches). It breeds in Canada and AK, and in a few northern states; winters at sea on both coasts.

GREATER SHEARWATER   *Puffinus gravis*   Total length 18in
A large ocean bird which has a black cap and dark brown back, with a whitish band on the neck and a white base to the tail. It has a typical shearwater flight on stiff wings, often held at right angles to the sea, skimming close to the waves. Found in the Atlantic in summer and fall. Breeds on islands in the eastern Atlantic and Mediterranean.

SOOTY SHEARWATER   *Puffinus griseus*   Total length 17in
An abundant, large shearwater. Dark above and below; underside of wings pale. Feeds on crustaceans and fish at the surface of the sea. Can dive underwater and swim for food. Breeds south of the equator, spending the spring and summer in waters of the Atlantic and Pacific oceans.

FULMAR   *Fulmarus glacialis*   Total length 18in
A gull-like member of the shearwater family, with a short, tube-nosed bill. Color varies from almost white to very dark. Typical stiff-winged flight. Often seen close to the shore. It usually breeds on cliffs with other seabirds. Found in northern waters of the Atlantic and Pacific, moving south in winter.

LEACH'S STORM PETREL   *Oceanodroma leucorhoa*   Total length 8in
A very small seabird, rarely seen from shore. At sea, flutters erratically across the tops of waves, often with feet dangling. It is dark, with a white rump and a forked tail. The only other petrel commonly seen in the Atlantic is Wilson's, which has yellow webbing in the feet. Nests in rock crevices and burrows, and returns to its nest at night. Found in both Atlantic and Pacific waters.

AMERICAN WHITE PELICAN *Pelecanus erythrorhynchus*   Total length 5ft
A very large waterbird, with a huge wingspan—up to 9ft. Adult is white with black flight feathers. During the breeding season it has a small crest and a fleshy protuberance on the bill. The long bill has a pouch beneath, used to scoop up fish. Winters on coasts and on freshwater lakes and estuaries. Breeds in Great Plains and Rockies from Canada to CA.

BROWN PELICAN *Pelecanus occidentalis*   Total length 4ft
Smaller than the White Pelican, and mostly brown with gray back. During the breeding season the adult has an orange-yellow head and the front and back of the neck is rich chocolate. Brown Pelicans are frequently seen flying, and feed by diving on fish. Almost exclusively marine, found on both coasts. Formerly threatened, now recovered.

MAGNIFICENT FRIGATE BIRD *Fregata magnificens*   Total length 3ft 4in
A very large thin seabird, with huge narrow pointed wings, and long, deeply forked tail. The bill is long with a hooked tip. Frigate birds seldom settle on the sea. They are piratical, chasing other seabirds to force them to drop prey, which they then swoop and catch. Largely tropical, they nest in mangroves, trees, and bushes, usually on islands.

GANNET *Sula bassanus*   Total length 3ft
A diving seabird with a long pointed bill, a pointed tail and narrow pointed wings. Adult is white with black wing tips, with orange tinge to head, the young ones are dark brownish gray, with white speckling, and gradually become white until mature in the third year. When feeding on fish, gannets dive head first at great speed from a considerable height. Found in the N.

GREAT CORMORANT *Phalacrocorax carbo*   Total length 3ft
A large waterbird with yellowish bill and yellow throat patch. Adult has only a small amount of white around throat and on flanks, but young have a dirty white belly and are brownish elsewhere. Characteristic silhouette in flight, humped, tapering to the front and back with head held low. Found on coasts or estuaries. Breeds in Canada; winters S to the Carolinas.

DOUBLE-CRESTED CORMORANT *Phalacrocorax auritus*   Total length 3ft
The most widespread cormorant in North America, and the most common. Black, and during the breeding season has white tufts above the eye (the tufts are darker in eastern populations), with an orange throat pouch. Immature birds are brown, with whitish bellies. Breeds on sea coasts and also inland lakes and reservoirs; increasing and spreading.

PELAGIC CORMORANT *Phalacrocorax pelagicus*   Total length 2ft 2in
The smallest cormorant found on the W coast. Like other cormorants it is predominantly black, with conspicuous white patches on the flanks. The breeding adult has a dark red face, a small tufted crest, and some fine white on the neck. Young are dark brown. Breeds colonially in coastal areas from CA to AK.

ANHINGA *Anhinga anhinga*   Total length 2ft 10in
Known as the Snake Bird or Darter, this species is unmistakable with its long, snakelike neck, and long pointed bill. When swimming it sits very low in the water and dives by slowly submerging. It spears its fish prey and usually comes to the surface to toss it into the air and swallow it. Characteristic of southern swamps and ponds.

GREAT BLUE HERON *Ardea herodias*   Total length 3ft 10in
A large heron, mostly bluish gray, with a black stripe on the head ending in a small plume. In south FL the population is white. In flight the neck is folded, and the bird often makes a harsh croaking call. Nests in the tops of trees, over water, or on islands, building a platform of sticks. One of the most widespread and common herons.

GREEN HERON *Butorides virescens*   Total length 18in
A small heron that looks dark when flying. Underparts are a rich reddish brown; the wings and back are dark greenish and blue-gray. Young birds are much browner, with pale streaking below. Usually solitary, perched along ponds and streams. Nests in bushes. Feeds by spearing fish and other aquatic animals.

LITTLE BLUE HERON *Egretta caerulea* Total length 2ft
A medium-sized heron. Adult a dark slaty blue with a bi-colored bill. Young birds are almost pure white. Eats fish, frogs, and insects, feeding in ponds, marshes and salt marsh. Breeds widely in the E with scattered breeding colonies in the W. Once in trouble from hunting, has recovered and is still spreading N.

CATTLE EGRET *Bubulcus ibis* Total length 20in
A small, white heron often tinged on the head with yellow-cream. In the breeding season the bill is bright orange-yellow, but yellow the rest of the time. Nests in colonies with other egrets and herons. The Cattle Egret was an Old World species which colonized North America in the 1950s. Now found throughout the US into Canada and still expanding.

SNOWY EGRET *Egretta thula* Total length 2ft
A medium-sized heron, pure white with a thin black bill, black legs and bright yellow feet. During the breeding season it has plumes on the head, neck, and back, for which these birds were once hunted. The young can be confused with those of Little Blue Heron. Nests colonially in bushes and trees, and feeds on aquatic animals. Found widely over the US in the breeding season, and in winter in southern wetlands.

GREAT EGRET *Egretta alba* Total length 3ft 3in
A large white heron with long head plumes during the breeding season. The legs are black and the bill is yellow. Feeds on fish, reptiles, amphibians, and other aquatic species. Outside the breeding season it is found mostly in frost-free coastal areas. Found worldwide. Common in wetlands over most of the US but sparse in the Rockies.

BLACK-CROWNED NIGHT HERON *Nicticorax nycticorax* Total length 2ft
Squat gray, black, and white bird. Flies on rounded wings with neck tucked in and legs barely showing beyond its tail. Often makes a low, croaking call in flight. Most active by night, emerging at dusk to fly to feeding areas. Hides in trees by day. Feeds on amphibians and other aquatic prey, also young of other species of heron. Widespread over US and N to S Canada.

LOUISIANA HERON *Egretta tricolor* Total length 2ft 3in
Formerly known as the Tricolored Heron. Upper parts mostly dark, slaty blue with a contrasting white belly. Young birds have extensive chestnut, on the neck and wings. Like most herons, feeds on aquatic animals. Found in marshes, estuaries, and mangroves. Occurs in coastal areas of the E, but occasionally inland and in CA.

YELLOW-CROWNED NIGHT HERON *Nyctanassa violacea* Total length 2ft
Similar to the Black-crowned, but with no black on the back, yellow crown, and black and white facial pattern. Juveniles have longer legs than Black-crowned. Habits similar. Call is higher and shorter. Range is mostly E of the Rockies.

WOOD STORK *Mycteria americana* Total length 3ft 4in
A large wading bird with black flight feathers and tail, and a stout, black, slightly downcurved bill. Nests colonially in tall trees and feeds by standing motionless in shallow water by the back or edge of pools. A strong flier, often gliding and sailing in high thermals. Breeds in FL and SE, but can be found N to ME and W to CA.

AMERICAN BITTERN *Botaurus lentiginosus* Total length 2ft 4in
A secretive heron that hides in thick vegetation when alarmed. Often stretches with its bill pointing up, relying on camouflage to escape detection. Predominantly brown with extensive spots and streaks. Slow, flapping flight. Characteristic breeding call a deep boom which carries widely. Decreasing because of wetland loss. Widespread over most of US and S Canada.

GLOSSY IBIS *Plegadis falcinellus* Total length 2ft
Easily distinguished from herons by its dark, glossy coloring and long downward-curving bill. Active and sociable, feeding in small flocks while wading through shallow pools or damp meadows. Flies with neck outstretched and legs trailing; short glides alternate with several rapid wing flaps. Confined to E coastal areas from S Canada to MS.

TUNDRA SWAN *Cygnus columbiana*   Total length 4ft 4in
A smaller version of the Trumpeter Swan, having a black bill often with a yellow spot. Swims with a straight neck. Call is a loud yodel, often uttered in flight. Feeds on aquatic vegetation. Breeds in the high Arctic of Canada and AK, migrating S to winter in the W Rockies and on the E coast.

TRUMPETER SWAN *Cygnus buccinator*   Total length 5ft
One of the heaviest flying birds. Similar to the Whistling Swan, but larger, and with a more restricted range. Loud, musical honking call. Once on the verge of extinction. Now widespread in W North America from AK to CA and throughout much of the Rockies.

MUTE SWAN *Cygnus olor*   Total length 5ft
Bill is orange-red and black. When swimming it holds its neck in a curve. Makes hissing noises at nest intruders and has a trumpeting call, rarely heard. Feeds mostly on aquatic vegetation. A European species, now widespread and common in many parts of the NE, particularly in town parks and on golf courses. Now controlled.

CANADA GOOSE *Branta canadensis*   Total length 3ft 9in
All Canada Geese have the distinctive dark head and neck with a pure white chin patch. Size variable, with particularly small birds breeding in the high Arctic. Voice variable, from a high cackle to low honk. The most widespread and familiar goose in North America.

SNOW GOOSE *Chen caerulescens*   Total length 2ft 2in–2ft 9in
A goose with variable plumage, found in two principal forms. One is pure white with black flight feathers; the young are pale buff and whitish. The other form, the "Blue Goose", has a gray-brown body tinged with bluish on the upper wings; the young are dark brown. Breeds in the high Arctic, and migrates S to feed on farmlands.

BRANT GOOSE *Branta bernicla*   Total length 2ft
A relatively small thickset goose, which is dark above, with an almost black head and neck, with some white on the neck. In the W this bird has a dark belly. Found in estuaries or at the coast feeding on aquatic plants, or grazing on grasses and crops. Breeds in the high Arctic of Canada and AK, migrating S for winter.

WHITE-FRONTED GOOSE *Anser albifrons*   Total length 2ft 4in
A medium-sized goose, mostly grayish brown, with orange feet. The pink bill is surrounded by pure white, from which it takes its name. Often found in flocks of several thousand, particularly in protected wetlands. Breeds in the high Arctic and migrates south to CA and the Gulf states in winter.

MALLARD *Anas platyrynchos*   Total length 22in
One of the most familiar of all ducks. Iridescent green head and brown chestnut breast separated by a narrow white band easily identifies the male; female is mottled brown. Feeds on aquatic vegetation by tipping up, "dabbling." The Mallard is the ancestor of the farmyard duck, with which it freely interbreeds. Widespread over most of North America.

BLACK DUCK *Anas rubripes*   Total length 23in
The same size as the Mallard and similar to the female Mallard. Speculum is plain blue (Mallard is blue with white edges). Hybrids occur. Found in almost any marsh or pond, particularly salt marsh. Confined to North America E of the Rockies, S to Gulf of Mexico.

GADWALL *Anas streptera*   Total length 22in
Similar in size to the Mallard. Both sexes have white on the inner wing feathers which is visible even when they are swimming. The male is gray with characteristic black feathers above and below the tail. The female is similar to the female Mallard, but easily identified in flight by the white wing patches. Found on ponds and in marshes throughout the US from S AK and Canada.

PINTAIL *Anas acuta*   Total length 22in–2ft 4in
Elegant duck with a long, slender neck, and long pointed tail; sits high in the water. Male has a chocolate head and upper neck, contrasting with white lower neck, long black-and-white plumes on lower back. Female mottled brown. Found on shallow ponds and in marshes, breeding in most of northern half of North America from AK to NF, and wintering as far S as Mexico.

GREEN-WINGED TEAL *Anas crecca*   Total length 17in
A small dabbling duck. Male has buff patch on tail, green wing patch, rufous and green head. Female mottled brown with green on the wing. Widespread, breeding over most of Canada and northern states. Migrates S in winter.

BLUE-WINGED TEAL *Anas discors*   Total length 15in
A small dabbling duck. Male has a grayish, blue-tinged head with a prominent white, crescent-shaped face patch. Female mottled brown with blue wing patch in flight. Breeds in most areas except high Arctic; winters in S US and Mexico.

CINNAMON TEAL *Anas cyanoptera*   Total length 16in
A small dabbling duck. The male is easily identified by rich cinnamon coloring, but the female is virtually indistinguishable from the female Blue-winged Teal. Cinnamon Teal is confined to western North America, breeding as far N as S Canada; most migrate, to winter S of the US border. Year-round resident in CA.

AMERICAN WIGEON *Anas americana*   Total length 21in
An abundant and widespread duck recognized in flight by the large white patch on the fore-wing. Black rump bordered by white, white forehead with green patch from eye running across the head, white belly. Feeds on aquatic and terrestrial vegetation, commonly grazing on land. Breeds across Canada to AK and into northern states. Winters on both coasts and at inland reservoirs and lakes into Mexico.

SHOVELER *Anas clypeata*   Total length 20in
Distinguished by a long spatulate bill in both sexes. Female drab; male distinct with dark green head, white belly, and chestnut sides. Feeds in shallow water, skimming the surface with its bill. Most common in W North America, breeding from AK to CA. Also breeds on the Prairies and scattered to the E coast, where it is increasing.

WOOD DUCK *Aix sponsa*   Total length 18in
One of the best known ducks, the male's plumage is exceptionally colorful; the female has spotted flanks and white around the eye. Nests in a tree hole 20ft or more above the ground. The young hatch and tumble to the ground, "parachuting" on their downy feathers. Frequently uses special nest boxes. Found over most of North America from S Canada southwards, except the Rockies.

REDHEAD *Aythya americana*   Total length 19in
A small diving duck with a red head, black chest, and gray back. Male bill blue-gray with a black tip. Female uniform soft brown. The Redhead is widespread but decreasing and is a species of conservation concern. Breeds in the prairies of the W and in AK. Winters on both coasts and on freshwater reservoirs, ponds, lakes, and rivers.

RING-NECKED DUCK *Aythya collaris*   Total length 17in
A small, handsome diving duck with a peaked head. The male is mostly black, with gray sides separated from the back of the neck by a white crescent. Bill is blue and white with black tip. Female is brown with white eye ring. Found on freshwater ponds and small lakes. Widespread, breeding mostly in Canada, wintering S.

CANVASBACK *Aythya valisineria*   Total length 21in
One of the largest diving ducks, bigger and whiter than Redhead. Sloping forehead and bill are distinctive. Gregarious, often concentrating in large rafts in bays and estuaries. Breeds from N states to AK. Winters S and E.

GREATER SCAUP *Aythya marila*   Total length 18in
Male is distinguished from Ring-necked Duck by its gray back. Female has an extensive area of white around the bill. Found in fresh and salt water; feeds on mussels and other mollusks. Often seen in large flocks resting on the water in rafts in winter. Breeds in N Canada and AK, wintering in coastal waters further S.

COMMON GOLDENEYE *Bucephala clangula*   Total length 18in
In flight this diving duck has a characteristic whistle created by the wing feathers. Male has black head with an oval white spot and a black and white body. Female gray with a rich brown head. Nests in tree holes close to lakes and ponds. Winters on both coasts. Breeds below the tree line from AK to Newfoundland, wintering S across most of the US.

BUFFELHEAD *Bucephala albeola*   Total length 13in
Small, compact with a large head. Male has a large white patch on the head; female and immatures grayer with less white. Nests in tree holes in N woodlands and forests. In winter found on open water almost anywhere in the US.

LONG-TAILED DUCK *Clangula hyemalis*   Total length 22in
Male identified by its long tail, clearly visible when flying. Breeding male predominantly black, brown, and white. Female mostly white and brown. Nests in high Arctic tundra. Winters on sea coasts, rivers, and estuaries, and also on the Great Lakes.

HARLEQUIN DUCK *Histrionicus histrionicus*   Total length 17in
Male is patterned with contrasting patches of chestnut, blue, gray, black, and white. Female is brown with a white spot on the head. Breeds along fast-flowing streams and rivers, mostly in Canada and AK. Winters along both coasts, preferring rocky areas.

RUDDY DUCK *Oxyura jamaicensis*   Total length 15in
Small, sits high in the water with tail held stiffly upright. Male mostly chestnut with a white face and a bright bluish bill. Female and immatures duller with a white face. Nests in thick vegetation. Breeds throughout W US and Canada; winters in S and E.

COMMON EIDER *Somateria mollissima*   Total length 2ft
A large duck with a sloping forehead and pointed bill. Male has sharply contrasting black and white plumage. Female has rich browns with intricate darker patterning. Nest is lined with down from the breast which is still harvested in some places: eiderdown makes the finest duvets and quilts. Feeds on mussels and other mollusks. Nests in colonies in far N, expanding S to New England. Winters on E coast and AK.

WHITE-WINGED SCOTER *Melanitta fusca*   Total length 21in
A large duck with white patches on the wing clearly visible in flight. Male is almost black with a small patch of white behind the eye, and orange on the bill. Female is dark brown. Feeds on mussels. Breeds close to lakes and ponds, in Canada and AK. Winters at sea on both coasts and also on reservoirs, lakes, and estuaries.

BLACK SCOTER *Melanitta nigra*   Total length 19in
A medium-sized black sea duck with a bright yellow-orange knob on the bill. Female dark brown with a light cheek and brown cap. Feeds on mussels and clams. The smallest and most coastal scoter. Winters at sea on both coasts.

HOODED MERGANSER *Lophodytes cucullatus*   Total length 18in
Round, slightly crested head with a thin bill. Male has black and white; female is dull brown with a brown crest. Breeds near ponds, rivers, and other waters close to woodlands. It is found widely in the E, less common in the W. Migrates S in winter.

COMMON MERGANSER *Mergus merganser*   Total length 2ft 1in
Large with a long, thin, red bill with a hooked tip. Male's glossy green-black head contrasts with mostly white body. Female and juveniles have red-brown heads. Nests in tree holes in woodlands. Winters on lakes and rivers. Breeds from AK to NF, wintering further S.

TURKEY VULTURE *Cathartes aura*   Total length 2ft 3in
Large (wingspan nearly 7ft), black bird, with pale gray on underwings and tail. Head has bare, red skin in adult but is gray in young birds. In flight, wings held in a shallow "V". Wonderful flier, often seen soaring. Feeds by scavenging on rubbish dumps, roadkills, and carrion. Widespread over most of North America and expanding N into Canada.

BLACK VULTURE *Coragyps atratus*   Total length 2ft 1in
Smaller than the more common Turkey Vulture, black with bare black head, grayish white on underside of the wings. Often seen with the Turkey Vulture, and feeds on a similar diet, but also found in swamps. Range more restricted than that of the Turkey Vulture; found in E US and W to south NM, but spreading.

MISSISSIPPI KITE *Ictinia mississippiensis*   Total length 15in
A medium-sized bird of prey with long wings and a slightly forked tail. Adult gray, with blackish tail and wings, pale gray head, and pale gray wing patches. Eyes red. Young brown with heavy streaking. Often colonial, feeds on large insects such as grasshoppers and locusts captured on the wing. Rapidly expanding range; frequents golf courses. Confined to SE US from W NM to VA. Isolated population in AZ.

SWALLOW-TAILED KITE *Elanoides forficatus*   Total length 2ft
A beautiful bird of prey with a long, deeply forked tail. Blackish above, white below with white head. Very agile, swooping on insects, lizards, birds, and other small animals. Gregarious, often seen in groups. Breeding in the deep south, it migrates to S America in winter.

GOSHAWK *Accipiter gentilis*   Total length 2ft
Medium-sized, round-winged when soaring, with long tail. Female one-third larger than male. Adult uniform gray above; dark brown in females and immatures. Prominent pale stripe above the eye. Found in coniferous forest and woodland. Captures birds up to the size of small ducks, and mammals such as rabbits. Widespread in Canada and N US.

SHARP-SHINNED HAWK *Accipiter striatus*   Total length 12in
Smallest of three Accipiters, best distinguished by shorter, square tail, gray above, rufous below. An expert hunter and flyer, feeding almost exclusively on songbirds. Fairly common in mixed woodlands. It is found over most of North America either breeding or migrating.

COOPERS HAWK *Accipiter cooperi*   Total length 18in
Midway in size between Sharp-shinned Hawk and Goshawk, it is similar in general shape, but has a longer tail than Sharp-shinned and lacks the white eyebrow of the Goshawk. Found in open woodlands preying on songbirds and small mammals. Breeds across N US, Canada, and AK; migrates S in winter.

RED-TAILED HAWK *Buteo jamaicensis*   Total length 19in
The most common large hawk. Very variable in plumage, but most adults have a broad red tail. Feeds on small mammals, birds, reptiles, and carrion. Found in all open habitats from deserts to open woodlands. Often soars, and is also seen perched along roadsides or on telephone poles. Breeds throughout the US and most of Canada.

BROAD-WINGED HAWK *Buteo platypterus*   Total length 16in
Medium-sized, broad, rounded wings when soaring. Adult dark brown above, rufous, brown barring below and broad bands in tail. Young streaked below. Widespread and abundant over E US and Canada. Migrates in large flocks to Central and S America.

RED-SHOULDERED HAWK *Buteo lineatus*   Total length 18in
Medium-sized, with characteristic broad, rounded wings, and a pale patch at the base of the flight feathers from below. Adult has a reddish shoulder patch and a rufous chest. Feeds on insects, snakes, birds, and other small prey. Favors damp woodlands. Common in E US and Canada, in CA and OR.

ROUGH-LEGGED HAWK *Buteo lagopus*   Total length 22in
Large. Identified by the dark "wrist" patches on the underside and white rump. Dark birds occur. Wings in "V" formation in flight. Hovers. Found in open habitats where it feeds on rodents and birds. Breeds in far N above tree line; migrates to N US in winter.

MARSH HAWK OR NORTHERN HARRIER *Circus cyaneus*   Total length 2ft
Large, long-tailed, with white rump; owl-like facial disc. Male gray above and white below. Female and young brown. Prefers open areas including marshes, heaths, and fields. Hunts low with wings in a "V". Prey includes small animals, rodents, snakes, and waterbirds. Nests on the ground. Widespread.

GOLDEN EAGLE *Aquila chrysaetos*   Total length 3ft
A large, dark brown eagle with a golden brown head. Flight feathers spread when soaring and wings in a "V". Feeds on rodents, rabbits, other medium-sized mammals, and carrion. Nests on cliffs. It is found mostly in or near mountains and wilderness. Widespread over much of North America; generally low density.

OSPREY *Pandion haliaetus*   Total length 2ft
Dark chocolate-brown above, whitish below. Hovers before diving into water to capture fish which it then carries to a perch to devour. Rarely seen far from water. Nest of sticks close to water. Once declining, now widespread through reintroduction.

BALD EAGLE *Haliaeetus leucocephalus*   Total length 3ft
Large, blackish brown, white head and tail. National bird of the US. Found near water, builds large stick nests in tall trees. Feeds on fish in summer; scavenges in winter. Canadian populations migrate S in winter. Declining population in S is now recovering; widespread.

PRAIRIE FALCON *Falco mexicanus*   Total length 18in
Slightly smaller than the more widespread Peregrine. Like a pale Peregrine but with black armpits from below. Feeds on small mammals and birds. Found in open habitats including prairies, deserts, canyons, and open areas in mountains. Nests on ledges on rocky cliffs. Confined to W North America, S to Mexico.

PEREGRINE FALCON *Falco peregrinus*   Total length 20in
Characteristic hooded appearance, gray above, barred below; young browner. Large, wingspan over 3ft. Fast-flying with pointed wings and narrow tail. Knocks birds such as ducks out of the sky by hitting them at high speed.

MERLIN *Falco columbarius*   Total length 12in
Small, fast-flying. Gray above, streaked below, banded tail. Feeds mostly on small birds, but also takes insects. It is found in a wide range of habitats in winter, including sea coasts, woods, and forests. Nests in Canada, AK and S into the W.

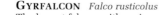

AMERICAN KESTREL *Falco sparverius*   Total length 10in
Small, beautiful. Adult male with blue-gray wings, reddish brown above, rufous, black-tipped tail, white, streaked below. Head gray, brown, and white, black stripes in the face. Females browner. Seen by roadsides perched on telephone wires. Feeds on a wide range of small animals.

GYRFALCON *Falco rusticolus*   Total length 2ft
The largest falcon, with a wingspan up to 5ft. It is found in several color phases including gray and pure white with black spotting. Slower flying than Peregrine; can hover. Feeds on larger birds up to the size of geese, and rabbits and other mammals. Found on the high tundra of AK and Canada, and occasionally S to the lower states.

RUFFED GROUSE *Bonasa umbellus*   Total length 17in
A plump, chickenlike bird, gray or rufous above with a mottled dark neck and black bars on the sides. Male has ruff of feathers on the neck raised in courtship display. Wings fanned to produce a drumming sound as part of courtship. Often over N US and Canada in deciduous woodland: fairly common.

BLUE GROUSE *Dendragapus obscurus*   Total length 16in
In display the blue-gray male is spectacular with reddish comb, fanned tail, and exposed bare neck sacs. Low, muffled booms accompany courtship. Female closely barred with brown. Nests on the ground. Found in W North America from Canada to CA in coniferous forests.

RING-NECKED PHEASANT *Phasianus colchicus*   Total length 21in
Male is generally brightly colored with a bare, red face, green head, and white neck ring. Body is metallic bronze with brown and black spots. Female is dull brown, like many gamebirds, with a long tail. Generally runs or flies short distances before gliding down. An Old World species, extensively introduced as a gamebird, now widespread across the US and Canada.

GREATER PRAIRIE CHICKEN *Tympanuchus cupido*   Total length 17in
A barred, brownish chickenlike bird of the Prairies. Sexes superficially similar, but in courtship display the male inflates large, bright yellow-orange neck sacs and erects its crest while making a low, booming call. Flies with few rapid wing beats, then glides. Widespread in eastern and Midwestern grasslands; now rare.

SHARP-TAILED GROUSE *Tympanuchus phasianellus*   Total length 17in
Chickenlike bird with spotted, not barred, underside. Male has purplish-pink neck sacs, inflated during courtship; call is low "coo-oo". Feeds on insects, buds, and seeds. Nests on the ground. Widespread over much of the N Prairies to AK.

SAGE GROUSE *Centrocercus urophasianus*   Total length 2ft 4in
A large grouse with a black belly and long, pointed tail feathers. Larger courting males puff out the white breast feathers and fan and raise the tail while making a loud, popping sound. Nests on the ground. Found in sagebrush habitats. Resident in W US, N to SK. Declining throughout range.

BOBWHITE QUAIL *Colinus virginianus*   Total length 10in
A small, compact quail which runs on the ground. Takes its name from its call, a whistled "bob-white." Nests on the ground. Found in open woodlands, hillsides, farmland and similar open habitats. Widespread resident over most of the E half of the US.

CALIFORNIA QUAIL *Callipepla californica*   Total length 10in
Like the Bobwhite in habits, with distinct head plume on both sexes. Male is gray, white and black on the head and neck. Large coveys found in winter. Nests on the ground. Confined to CA, nearby states and Mexico in chaparral, open woodland, farmland and scrub near fresh water.

WILD TURKEY *Meleagris galloparva*   Total length 4ft
Similar to the farmyard Turkey (and descended from it), but more slender and with iridescent plumage. Female smaller than male. Male's gobbling call carries over a mile. Feeds on the ground on nuts, berries, and small animals; prefers to run not fly. Roosts in trees at night. Nests on the ground. Widespread natural range, but introduced for hunting.

SANDHILL CRANE *Grus canadensis*   Total length up to 4ft
A large, long-legged bird. Wingspan up to 7ft. Uniform gray with bald, red face and crown. Young birds brown. Nests on a large mound of vegetation on the ground in a marsh. Breeds on tundra, prairies, and marshes, mostly in Canada and AK, with a few populations in the N US. Winters in C and the Gulf states. Resident populations in FL and MS.

SORA *Porzana carolina* Total length 8in
Small, plump, gray and brown with a short, yellow bill. In breeding, black on the face, throat and breast. Difficult to see, hides in dense vegetation. Call a high-pitched, descending whinny and a sharp "kek." It is found in wetlands, brackish marshes, tidal creeks, rice and grain fields. Nests on the ground in marshes. Winters in Gulf states and CA.

PURPLE GALLINULE *Porphyrula martinica* Total length 14in
A bright purple waterbird with a greenish purple sheen, red bill, and long, yellow legs with unwebbed toes. Young are brown but, like adult, white under the tail. Walks on surface vegetation hunting aquatic invertebrates. Nests on vegetation floating in reeds. Found in freshwater lakes and swamps; common within range. Breeds along Gulf states and N to S Carolina. After breeding season, can turn up almost anywhere.

AMERICAN COOT *Fulica americana* Total length 15in
Often seen with ducks. Uniform gray-black with a white bill; red forehead in breeding. At close range toes are lobed. Omnivorous, feeding on invertebrates and vegetation. Nests on the edge of ponds in dense vegetation. Found on large ponds, lakes, and reservoirs, often in large flocks in winter. Breeds over most of North America from Canada S. Declining.

MOORHEN (COMMON GALLINULE) *Gallinula chloropus* Total length 14in
Blackish gray with white under tail and on the flanks, bright red forehead and bill, and long yellow legs which dangle in flight. Young brown. Favors dense vegetation in wetland habitats. Widespread breeder in the E to S Canada; more scattered in W. Declining.

AMERICAN OYSTERCATCHER *Haematopus palliatus* Total length 18in
A large, easily identifiable shorebird with black and white plumage and a large, bright orange-red bill, and pink legs. Call is loud and piping. Feeds on marine mollusks and other invertebrates. Strictly coastal; found on beaches, estuaries and mud flats on the Atlantic and Gulf coasts. On the Pacific coast it is replaced by the Black Oystercatcher.

SEMI-PALMATED PLOVER *Charadrius semipalmatus* Total length 7in
Distinguished from Snowy by its dark back. It is named from the small amount of webbing between the toes. Its call is a piping "tsee-wee." Feeds along the tideline on invertebrates. Breeds in the high Arctic of Canada and AK. Winters on southern shores and estuaries. Moves inland on migration. Abundant and widespread.

KILLDEER *Charadrius vociferus* Total length 10in
A large plover with double breast band, and a loud, piercing "kill-deer" call. Adult Killdeer performs a "broken wing" act to lure intruders from near nest. Nests in pastures and other open, grassy habitats, plowed fields, marshes and even gravel driveways. Nest is a simple scrape. Breeds over almost all of North America except the high Arctic.

AMERICAN GOLDEN PLOVER *Pluvialis dominica* Total length 10in
In breeding plumage the male is spectacular: jet black on the underside and face, bordered with white and spangled golden on the back and top of the head. Female is duller. Outside breeding, adult and juvenile lack the black belly and white markings. Breeds in the high Arctic of Canada and AK; winters in South America. Seen on migration on the E coast in fall. In spring, flies up the Mississippi Valley.

BLACK-BELLIED PLOVER *Pluvialis squatarola* Total length 11in
Distinguished from the Golden Plover in flight by its black "armpits." During breeding season the male has a jet black belly, face and neck, a white crown, and black and white back and wings. Outside breeding, both sexes lack black belly and are grayer overall. Nests on the tundra. Winters on mudflats, saltmarshes, estuaries, and similar open wetland habitats on both coasts and S to the Pacific and Atlantic coasts.

RUDDY TURNSTONE *Arenaria interpes* Total length 9in
A spectacular shorebird in breeding plumage, otherwise drab. Breeding adult has colorful plumage of chestnut, black and white; female duller. In flight distinctive black and white wing, rump and tail markings are seen. The Black Turnstone of the Pacific coast is similar. An active forager, usually in small flocks, overturning shells, driftwood and seaweed for crustaceans and other invertebrates. Nests on the Arctic tundra; winters on both coasts.

AMERICAN WOODCOCK *Scolopax minor* Total length 11in
A squat, round-bodied bird with an exceptionally long bill and large eyes. Plumage a mixture of browns and grays, for camouflage on the forest floor. Nocturnal and secretive, flies at dusk to feed in marshes and pastures, along the margins of ponds and rivers. Often seen when flushed. Found in E North America from S Canada to TX.

COMMON SNIPE *Gallinago gallinago* Total length 10in
A long-billed, short-legged wading bird with brown, white, and cream camouflage markings. Often feeds or roosts in dense vegetation; when accidentally flushed, flies with characteristic zig-zag flight uttering a rasping call. During breeding season male winnows, flies high and dives with outer tail feathers spread, making a low, hollow whistle. Breeds over most of N US and Canada, wintering further S.

LONG-BILLED CURLEW *Numenius americanus* Total length 2ft
Recognized by its exceptionally long, downward-curving bill which makes up over one-third of the bird's total length. Adults brown and cinnamon. In flying, the distinctive cinnamon-brown underwing is visible. Noisy, with loud musical "cur-leew" call. In winter found on fields, marshes, pastures, mudflats, and tidal estuaries. Winters S to CA, Mexico, and coastal TX. Breeds in W US and S Canada Prairies. Decreasing.

WHIMBREL *Numenius phoeopus* Total length 17in
Somewhat like the Long-billed Curlew, but the bill is proportionally shorter and the head is striped. Flight call a series of 6 or 7 short whistles at the same pitch. Breeds in the high Arctic tundra; winters S to both Atlantic and Pacific coasts in marshes, tidal mudflats, and other wetland habitats. The only curlew common on the Atlantic coast.

SPOTTED SANDPIPER *Actitis macularia* Total length 7in
A common brown-backed shorebird seen singly along streams, rivers, and creeks, and edges of wetland pools, around ponds, lakes, and reservoirs. Numerous black spots on white chest and belly. Forages with constant, characteristic bobbing movement. Flies stiff-winged, uttering a shrill "tweet-tweet" call note. Breeds over most of N North America. Winters in CA E to FL and S.

WILLET *Catroptrophorus semipalmatus* Total length 15in
A relatively large shorebird, fairly heavily built with long, straight bill. Nondescript until it takes flight and shows unmistakable black and white wings. Name from loud call, "pilly willy willet." Two populations: western birds are larger with a longer bill and nest in wetlands in the Prairies from Canada to NV; they winter in CA. Eastern birds nest along the Atlantic coast from Newfoundland to TX. Widespread but not abundant.

GREATER YELLOWLEGS *Tringa melanoleuca* Total length 14in
A medium-sized, fairly abundant shorebird, heavily spotted, with long yellow legs and a long, thin, slightly upturned bill. Similar to the Lesser Yellowlegs and most easily distinguished by call. One of the most familiar shorebirds seen on migration in any suitable habitat. Nests across Canada to AK. Winters S on both coasts.

RED KNOT *Calidris tenuirostris* Total length 10in
In breeding a rich, reddish below, gray above, spangled with brown and black. In winter, uniform gray. Short, black bill, black legs and feet. On passage congregates in large roosting and feeding flocks. Feeds on mudflats and sandy beaches, on horseshoe crab eggs. Nests in high Arctic, migrates to Central and S America.

PURPLE SANDPIPER *Calidris maritima*   Total length 7in
Small, dark, with a slender, down-curved bill. Spotted in breeding, uniform purple-gray in winter. Feeds among seaweed-covered rocks on rocky shores and jetties. Breeds in the high Arctic; winters on the Atlantic coast of Canada, S to NY.

PECTORAL SANDPIPER *Calidris melanotus*   Total length 9in
Medium-sized with prominent streaking on the breast, separated from the belly in a clean line. Found on both coasts, but more often in wet meadows, mudflats, estuaries, and salt-marshes. Nests in the tundra of Canada and AK, winters in S America.

LEAST SANDPIPER *Calidris minutilla*   Total length 6in
Tiny, with a thin, down-curving bill, yellow-greenish legs, and buff breast. Flight call is a thin "kreeet." Breeds across Arctic tundra. Passage migrant on both coasts; winters in frost-free coastal areas.

SANDERLING *Calidris alba*   Total length 8in
Small, pale with black bill, legs and feet. Feeds on small invertebrates uncovered by the receding waves. Common on Atlantic and Pacific coasts in winter in small flocks along the edge of the surf. Breeds in the high Arctic in tundra habitats.

DUNLIN *Calidris alpina*   Total length 8in
Small, with slightly down-curved bill. Distinctive black belly and red back in breeding plumage; gray with black in winter. Flight call is rasping "chee-it chee-it." Common. Usually in small flocks, with other shorebirds. Breeds in the high Arctic, wintering on frost-free marshes, mudflats, coasts, and other wetlands.

STILT SANDPIPER *Calidris haemantopus*   Total length 8in
Slender, long-legged, with slender bill, slightly down-curved at the tip. Generally grayer in fall. In breeding, dark bars on the belly, white eyebrow, and reddish brown cheek patches. Rare on migration in W; most often seen on E coast in fall. Breeds in the Arctic tundra; winters in marshes, mudflats, and ponds of S FL, TX and Central and South America.

MARBLED GODWIT *Limosa fedoa*   Total length 18in
A large shorebird, with a long, upturned bill, flesh-colored at the base and blackish at the tip. On breeding, buff-brown with fine, black barring on the underside; in winter, uniformly lighter brown. Call is "godwit-godwit." Nests in grassy meadows in the N Prairies, usually close to water. Winters on both coasts on seashores, estuaries, and mudflats.

AMERICAN AVOCET *Recurvirostra americana*   Total length 18in
A graceful, elegant shorebird with a long, slender upward-curving bill, long bluish legs and black and white plumage, but ochre on the head and neck in breeding. Feeds wading in shallow water, sweeping the bill from side to side. Nests in loose colonies inland in the W. Winters south on both coasts. Fairly common in range.

BLACK-NECKED STILT *Himantopus mexicanus*   Total length 14in
Unmistakable. A large black and white shorebird with exceptionally long pink legs and a long, needlelike black bill. Nests on dry ground in marshes or near water. Widespread, though patchy breeding distribution extends N into Canada in the Prairies. Winters in CA and the Gulf of Mexico and S. Seen in many coastal areas on migration.

WILSON'S PHALAROPE *Phalaropus tricolor*   Total length 9in
A delicate, colorful shorebird with a slender bill. Female is more brightly colored than male. Male incubates the eggs. Non-breeding plumage is gray above, whitish below. Feeds on land and also in water, swimming in a tight circle, stirring up mud. Breeds in prairies and other wetland habitats from S Canada with scattered outlying populations.

GREAT BLACK-BACKED GULL *Larus marinus*   Total length 2ft 6in
A huge gull with a wingspan of over 5ft. Adult black on the back, attained by fourth year. Immatures mottled brown on back and belly, gradually becoming white on the belly and black on the back. Feeds on offal from fishing fleets; scavenges at landfills. Nests in colonies and is a major predator of other seabirds. Range eastern.

HERRING GULL *Larus argentatus*   Total length 2ft
A large, widespread gray-backed gull with black and white wingtips.Sometimes difficult to identify because its plumage is variable; takes four years to molt into its final adult plumage. Many closely related species. Most common in the E, becoming less common further W. Breeds from AK to Newfoundland and S to the Great Lakes.

RING-BILLED GULL *Larus delawarensis*   Total length 18in
A medium-sized gull similar to the California Gull but smaller, and has a yellow bill with a black band around the tip.Takes three years to molt into adult plumage. Nests on islands in lakes and ponds across North America in a belt running from the Rockies of northern CA to Newfoundland.

LAUGHING GULL *Larus atricilla*   Total length 17in
A relatively small gull which, as a breeding adult, has a black hood, dark red bill and black legs. The immatures are brown, taking three years to molt into adult plumage. Call is a penetrating "ha-ha-ha-ha-ha-haa-haa-haaaa." A common gull from Nova Scotia to TX, and uncommon on the W coast where there are scattered breeding colonies.

CALIFORNIA GULL *Larus californicus*   Total length 21in
Very similar to the Herring Gull but smaller. Like many other gulls, the California Gull takes four years to acquire adult plumage. Omnivorous but during breeding eats mostly insects. Nests in colonies. Breeds inland on the Great Plains and Rockies, wintering on the Pacific coast.

BLACK-LEGGED KITTIWAKE *Rissa tridactyla*   Total length 17in
The adult is recognized in winter by its small size, white head, yellow bill, and black wing tips, a "dipped in ink" appearance. It is a pelagic bird, coming to land during storms or in the breeding season, when it nests on narrow ledges on steep cliffs. On both coasts the breeding colonies often contain several thousand pairs.

GULL-BILLED TERN *Sterna nilotica*   Total length 14in
A fairly large tern, distinguished from gulls by its forked tail clearly visible in flight, black cap (not hooded like some gulls), and a more pointed black bill. Feeds on insects and small fish, skimming the water with a graceful, swallowlike flight. Often common, it breeds in coastal colonies from the mid-Atlantic to TX. Northern populations migrate S in winter.

COMMON TERN *Sterna hirundo*   Total length 15in
An elegant seabird with a long, forked tail, pointed wings, and a black cap which extends down the neck. It has a slender, orange-red bill, often dark-tipped. Feeds primarily on fish, but also insects during breeding season. Breeds in large colonies in coastal areas and inland from the Atlantic to the Rockies. Further N it is replaced by the Arctic Tern.

CASPIAN TERN *Sterna caspica*   Total length 21in
The largest tern in North America, with a massive red bill, black feet and legs. During the breeding season the adult has a black cap. Confused with the Royal Tern which has a slimmer, orange bill. Nests in small colonies on beaches and islands, or in marshes. Summer breeders are found on both coasts and inland.

BLACK TERN *Chlidonias niger*   Total length 10in
A small tern often seen in freshwater marshes and around ponds and rivers. The breeding adult is black with gray wings and tail, but outside the breeding season the adult and young have extensive white, particularly on the underside. Nests in small colonies, often on islands in marshes. A widespread summer breeder across W Prairies to New England and SE Canada.

BIRDS

PARASITIC JAEGER *Stercorarius parasiticus*   Total length 20in
Jaegers are parasitic seabirds that chase gulls and terns to make them disgorge their prey.
Superficially like a dark brown gull. Two color phases: one is white on the underside,
with white patches at the base of the flight feathers, the other uniformly dark. Nest is a
shallow depression on the ground close to gull colonies in the Arctic. Found in the high
Arctic.

LONG-TAILED JAEGER *Stercorarius longicaudis*   Total length 22in
Similar to the Parasitic Jaeger, and also found in two color forms, but easily distinguished
by its long central tail in summer. Nests on dry ground in the Arctic tundra and migrates
to the southern oceans in winter. Seen offshore on migration, but only very rarely inland.

BLACK SKIMMER *Rynchops niger*   Total length 18in
A large tern, unusual because its lower mandible is considerably longer than the upper. The
wings, back, and cap are black. Feeds with the orange and black lower mandible trailing in
the water as it flies close to the surface, dipping to snap up fish. Mainly tropical, but widespread, in CA and the Gulf of Mexico from TX to FL, spreading N to New England.

RAZORBILL *Alca torda*   Total length 17in
A penguinlike seabird which is normally found only in and close to the sea. Similar to the
Common Murre, but has a broader bill. Makes no nest but lays its single, conical egg on a
bare ledge. Breeds on rocky cliffs on Atlantic coasts from N Canada and Greenland S to
New England; also found in the Old World.

COMMON MURRE *Uria aalge*   Total length 17in
Similar to the Razorbill, but with a pointed, more slender bill. Nests on cliffs, often with
Razorbills and other seabirds. Feeds on fish under water, using its wings to "fly." It is
found widely throughout the N hemisphere in both Pacific and Atlantic waters. In the Old
World it is known as the Guillemot.

RHINOCEROS AUKLET *Cerorhinca monocerata*   Total length 15in
The largest auklet, it is a fairly uniform gray with a large head and a yellowish "horn" at the
base of the bill. It also has two whitish plumes on either side of the head. Nests in burrows
on islands. It is confined to Pacific waters and breeds from the Aleutians and AK south to CA.

TUFTED PUFFIN *Lunda cirrhata*   Total length 15in
A thickset bird with spectacular, massive orange bill and long, pale orange plumes on
either side of the head. The rest of the plumage is black, with a white face. In winter it
loses its plumes and is a uniform dark gray with a pale cheek. Breeds along the Pacific
coast from CA to AK, nesting colonially in burrows on offshore islands.

PIGEON GUILLEMOT *Cepphus columba*   Total length 14in
Mostly black, with white wing patches in the breeding season, the Pigeon Guillemot has a
slender, pointed black bill. Mostly white in winter, this common species breeds in crevices
on rocky cliffs and on pilings. Like most auks, can be found inland after ocean gales. Confined to coast of western North America, from AK and Aleutians S to CA.

THICK-BILLED MURRE *Uria lomvia*   Total length 18in
One of the largest of the murres, it is similar to both Razorbill and Common Murre, but
with a bill intermediate between the two. Nests on cliffs where the single, conical egg
spins in a circle in the wind. Found in northern waters of both Atlantic and Pacific oceans,
breeding in Canada and AK and wintering offshore further S.

ATLANTIC PUFFIN *Fratercula arctica*   Total length 12in
The adult is usually described as comical or clownlike during breeding when it has a brightly
colored bill and contrasting black and white plumage. Feeds on small fish, such as sand eels,
and often returns to its breeding burrow with a row of fish dangling from its bill. Winters at
sea, usually well offshore, particularly in rough weather. Confined to Atlantic coast from
Canada to New England.

ROCK DOVE *Columba livia*   Total length 13in
The ancestor of a wide range of domestic pigeons, this species is variable in plumage. Introduced from Europe, it is now established over most of North America. In some places it has reverted to its natural habitat of rocky cliffs and canyons.

COMMON GROUND DOVE *Columbina passerina*   Total length 6in
Tiny, plump with a short tail. Feathers on head and breast look scaly; in flight the wings are reddish brown. Call is a monotonous, repeated "woo-woo." Range from Mexico N to FL and adjacent states in the E and CA in the W. Declining.

MOURNING DOVE *Zenaida macroura*   Total length 12in
Widespread and abundant, one of the largest doves. Buff, with black spots on the upper parts of the wings. Long, tapering tail. Nests in trees, buildings, and other structures; common at feeders. Wide range of habitats from S. Canada to Mexico.

MONK PARAKEET *Myiopsitta monachus*   Total length 12in
The native Carolina Parakeet is extinct in the wild; however, several exotic parakeets have been introduced, including the Monk Parakeet from S America. Builds nest of twigs. Widespread in scattered colonies from TX to FL and N to Boston; still spreading.

ROADRUNNER *Geococcyx californianus*   Total length 2ft
A large, terrestrial relative of the cuckoos. Brown and white with a shaggy crest, large bill and long tail. Rarely takes flight, avoiding intruders by running. Feeds on lizards, snakes, large insects, small mammals, and birds. In deserts and other habitats from S CA to AR.

YELLOW-BILLED CUCKOO *Coccyzus americanus*   Total length 12in
Brown above, creamy white below, long tail with prominent white spots on the underside. Bill and skin around the eye are yellow, unlike the related Black-billed Cuckoo. The most widespread cuckoo in North America. Winters into Central America.

BARN OWL *Tyto alba*   Total length 18in
A very pale owl, often almost pure white on the underside, with a heart-shaped face. Generally nocturnal, but can also be seen hunting by day, particularly after bad weather. Calls include blood-curdling screeches and screams as well as a hissing screech. Hunts rats. Nests in holes or buildings. Often found around human habitations and farms. Widespread from S Canada to Mexico, but absent from SE US.

EASTERN SCREECH OWL *Otus asio*   Total length 8in
A very small owl with prominent ear tufts. It is found in two main color forms: a reddish brown form which is most common in the south of its range and a grayish form which is commoner in the north. Nests in old woodpecker holes and other cavities in trees. Widespread E of the Rockies. In the W replaced by the Western Screech Owl.

GREAT HORNED OWL *Bubo virginianus*   Total length 2ft 10in
A massive owl with long ear tufts, a well-defined facial disc, and yellow-orange eyes. Mostly nocturnal, but often seen by day roosting in trees. Call is a deep, repeated "hoot." Feeds on animals up to the size of rabbits and skunks. Found throughout North America.

SNOWY OWL *Nyctea scandiaca*   Total length 2ft
North America's largest owl. Old males are often almost pure white; immatures and females have varying amounts of gray and black. Feeds on lemmings, hares and grouse. In winter found in open country, often at the coast. Breeds in high Arctic.

BURROWING OWL *Athene cunicularia*   Total length 9in
Small, diurnal, often seen on the ground or perched on fence posts. Brown, heavily spotted with white, comparatively long legs. White eyebrows give it a fierce expression. Feeds mostly on insects. Found in open prairies and deserts, and on golf courses and parks. Confined to Great Plains and the Rockies from S Canada to Mexico; also Florida.

BIRDS

SAW-WHET OWL *Aegolius acadius*   Total length 8in
Smaller than the Screech Owl and lacking any ear tufts. It is reddish brown above with white spots, and white below with reddish brown streaks. Very vocal in spring, making a monotonous "too-too-too-too-too" whistle, repeated endlessly up to 130 times a minute. Strictly nocturnal. Feeds on mice, voles, and nocturnal insects. Breeds across S Canada, S to NY, and throughout the Rockies. Some populations move S.

WHIP-POOR-WILL *Caprimulgus vociferus*   Total length 10in
Nocturnal bird which emerges after sunset to feed on moths and night-flying insects. Mottled and barred plumage provides camouflage by day. Owl-like face and large eyes, with long, narrow wings, long tail and great agility in flight. Nests on ground in open woodlands in E North America.

COMMON POORWILL *Phalaenoptilus nuttallii*   Total length 7in
A small nightjar with a short, rounded tail, and short, rounded wings. It takes its name from its call, described as a whistled "poor-will." Settles on the ground making short sallies to catch passing insects. Found in open sagebrush and chaparral habitats; usually seen by roadsides hunting for insects. Some hibernate rather than migrate. Widespread summer migrant to W US and into extreme S Canada.

COMMON NIGHTHAWK *Chordeiles minor*   Total length 10in
Large with long, pointed wings and a long, narrow tail. In flight there are clear white bands on the wings. Nests on the ground or on flat roof tops. Found in open woodlands, on plains, on golf courses, and in cities. Often seen feeding over towns, calling in early evening. The most widely distributed nightjar in North America.

CHIMNEY SWIFT *Chaetura pelagica*   Total length 5in
A cigar-shaped, fast-flying bird with wings held stiff. Nests in chimneys, on cliffs, in barns, or in hollow trees. Noisy in flight. Widespread summer breeder over most of North America E of the Rockies. In the W replaced by the similar, but smaller and paler, Vaux's Swift.

BLACK-CHINNED HUMMINGBIRD *Archilochus alexandri*   Total length 3in
In sunlight, dark metallic green above, whitish on the belly, black throat with violet sheen (often difficult to see). The male's display flight is a swooping arc, and the wings whirr. Found in drier mountain habitats including deserts, but near water. The most common and widespread hummer in the W, from S TX to S Canada.

RUBY-THROATED HUMMINGBIRD *Archilochus colubris*   Total length 3in
Male has a bright, metallic red throat; female is whitish on underside. Wings make a characteristic whirr as it darts back and forth; hummingbirds actually fly backwards for short distances. A familiar garden bird easily attracted to feeders or garden flowers. The only hummer found over most of E North America.

BROAD-TAILED HUMMINGBIRD *Selasphorus platycercus*   Total length 3in
Similar to Ruby-throated Hummingbird, but male is easily distinguished by the high-pitched trilling sound made by its wings. Metallic, rose-red throat, iridescent green back. Widespread in the Rocky Mountains in clearings, meadows, and open woodlands.

RUFOUS HUMMINGBIRD *Selasphorus rufus*   Total length 3in
A distinctive hummer, rufous on the tail and back. The adults have varying amounts of metallic green on the back, and the adult male has a metallic, orange-red throat. Almost identical to Allen's Hummingbird. A summer breeder as far N as AK. Winters in Mexico and Central America.

BELTED KINGFISHER *Ceryle alcyon*   Total length 13in
A robust bird with a long, daggerlike bill, striking blue-gray and white plumage; the female has a broad, rusty-orange band on the belly. Both sexes have a shaggy crest. Always found close to water, where it fishes from a perch, or hovers over the water and dives.The only kingfisher likely to be seen in most of North America.

NORTHERN FLICKER *Colaptes auratus*   Total length 12in
A large woodpecker found in two color forms: the eastern Yellow-shafted Flicker is yellowish on the underside of the wings; the western Red-shafted Flicker is tinged orange-red under the wings. Nests in tree holes in open woodlands, cacti, telegraph poles, and in nest boxes. Widely distributed over most of North America from AK to Newfoundland.

PILEATED WOODPECKER *Dryocopus pileatus*   Total length 17in
The largest surviving woodpecker in North America. Mostly black with white; male has a red-crested crown. Nests high in trees, excavating a hole up to 2ft deep in dead wood. Residents of dense, mature woodlands over most of North America.

RED-BELLIED WOODPECKER *Melanerpes carolinus*   Total length 9in
Heavily barred above with a red head and nape, grayish white on the underside tinged with red; the rump white in flight. Eats mostly insects, but comes to bird feeders in suburban gardens for suet and seed. Nests in tree cavities up to 1ft deep. Breeds over most of E US. In recent years its range has expanded northward.

DOWNY WOODPECKER *Picoides pubescens*   Total length 6in
Abundant, small, widespread. Black and white with a bright red patch on the back of the head of the male. Common in woodland, regular visitor to feeders, especially for suet. Very tame. Shares most of its range with the Hairy Woodpecker.

HAIRY WOODPECKER *Picoides villosus*   Total length 9in
Similar to the Downy Woodpecker, but larger with a longer bill. Darker in W with fewer spots. Male drums on branches of dead trees as part of its territorial display. Feeds on grubs of wood-boring insects. A common visitor to feeders during the winter months, attracted to suet and peanuts. Resident over most of North America, except extreme N and S TX.

RED-HEADED WOODPECKER *Melanerpes erythrocephalus*   Total length 9in
Distinctive, with bright red head and neck, pure white belly, black wings with white patches, and black tail. Widely distributed over most of E US and S Canada. Northern populations migratory. Declining.

WILLIAMSON'S SAPSUCKER *Sphyrapicus thyroides*   Total length 9in
Male mostly black, with white rump, white wing patches, yellow belly, dark red chin, white stripes on the side of the head. Female barred black and white on back, wings, and breast; yellow belly. Drills evenly spaced rows of holes for sap, and feeds on insects attracted by the sap. Fairly common in dry pine forests in the Rockies.

YELLOW-BELLIED SAPSUCKER *Sphyrapicus varius*   Total length 8in
Mostly black and white, with red forehead and throat, and whitish yellow underside. White wing patches and rump are clear in flight. The only sapsucker found in the E. Common summer visitor to deciduous woods from AK to Newfoundland, S into N US and Appalachians.

HORNED LARK *Eremophila alpestris*   Total length 6in
Sparrow-sized, usually seen on the ground in open places. Brown body with dark streaking. Head has variable vibrant black and yellow markings, but mostly with black "horns" above the eyes. Nests in open areas. Breeds widely from the tundra to TX.

EASTERN KINGBIRD *Tyrannus tyrannus*   Total length 8in
Large flycatcher. Slaty black head and upper parts, white below, with a white tip to the tail; red patch on the top of the head difficult to see. Common perched high around farms, in woodland clearings, and over water. Nests overhang water. Widespread over much of E North America. Summer breeder, winters in Central and South America.

SCISSOR-TAILED FLYCATCHER *Tyrannus forficatus* Total length 13in
A spectacular flycatcher with a very long, deeply forked tail. Underside is salmon; head pink and shoulders gray, with back, wings and tail black. Young birds lack long tail feathers. Found in open countryside, often around farms, ranches, and other human habitations in TX and adjacent southwestern states. Winters in Central America.

LEAST FLYCATCHER *Empidonax minimus* Total length 5in
The smallest of 11 species of *Empidonax* in North America. Often difficult to identify. Generally olive, brownish, or greenish above, whitish or yellowish below with pale bars on the wings. Hunts flying insects from a perch. Call is a "chebek," repeated. Breeds in open woodlands from AK to Nova Scotia, S to northern states.

WESTERN WOOD PEEWEE *Contopus sordidulus* Total length 6in
A rather nondescript flycatcher. It is mostly a dull brown, with blackish wings and tail, a whitish chin and under-tail, and faint wing bars. Its call is a nasal "peewee" or "peeeer." It is a summer visitor to the W of the continent from S AK to CA; it winters in N South America.

TREE SWALLOW *Tachycineta bicolor* Total length 6in
A small swallow, glossy blue-green (appearing black) above, and pure white below, with a short, slightly forked tail. Has characteristic, graceful flight, usually in wide circles, consisting of short wing flaps followed by a glide. Nests in tree holes or nest boxes. Widespread summer breeder over most of North America, below the treeline of the Arctic; winters in Mexico and Central America.

BANK SWALLOW *Riparia riparia* Total length 4in
The smallest swallow in North America, dark brown above, white below with a narrow brown band across the chest. Nests colonially, often in large numbers, in burrows it excavates in sand banks. A widespread breeder nesting over much of the US. Also widespread in the Old World where it is known as the Sand Martin.

ROUGH-WINGED SWALLOW *Stelgopteryx serripennis* Total length 5in
A rather nondescript swallow, gray-brown above and dirty white below, with a slight fork in the tail. Nests in burrows or crevices close to water, under bridges, or on river banks. It is found throughout most of the US and S Canada.

VIOLET GREEN SWALLOW *Tachycineta thalassina* Total length 5in
Glossy black, with violet and green sheen on the upper parts in certain lights. Underparts pure white with white on the cheeks and white patches on the sides of the rump. A hole nester, with up to six white eggs. A summer visitor to the W of North America as far north as AK.

BARN SWALLOW *Hirundo rustica* Total length 7in
A swallow with a deeply forked tail with long streamers, a blue chest band and reddish throat. The young lack the tail streamers. Builds mud nests in barns and other buildings, particularly near cattle. Widespread over most of the continent (also widespread in the Old World).

PURPLE MARTIN *Progne subis* Total length 8in
A large, dark swallow. Male is uniform purplish blue, female and young are gray below. Declining, probably due to loss of nest holes in old trees and competition from house sparrows and starlings. Adapts well to artificial nests. Widespread, being found mostly in E US and Canada with scattered populations in the W.

CLIFF SWALLOW *Petrochelidon pyrrhonota* Total length 5in
Somewhat like a Barn Swallow but has a shorter, slightly forked tail and a pale rump. A colonial nester on cliffs, under bridges, and also adapted to buildings. Nest is made from pellets of mud lined with grasses and feathers. Up to 6 creamy white eggs. Widespread over most of the continent.

GRAY JAY *Perisoreus canadensis*   Total length 11in
A variable species. Most of the underparts are gray, with varying amounts of gray on the head and a short, black bill. Usually very tame and often found in campsites. Found in coniferous forests across Canada and the US, and further S in the Rockies.

BLUE JAY *Cyanocitta cristata*   Total length 11in
Has distinctive "jay-jay-jay" call. Omnivorous, and well-known as a nest predator. Nest of twigs is lined with fibers and grasses. Lays up to 6 freckled eggs. Widespread in woodlands and suburbs. A familiar visitor to feeders over most of North America E of the Rockies.

STELLER'S JAY *Cyanocitta stelleri*   Total length 11in
Named after the Russian naturalist who identified the jay on the Bering Sea Expedition. Sooty black head and large crest. Darker but similar in shape to the Blue Jay, which it replaces in the far W from S AK to CA. A coniferous forest species.

BLACK-BILLED MAGPIE *Pica pica*   Total length 22in
A long-tailed relative of the crow, mostly black and white with green and blue iridescence on the wings, white shoulder patches, and a white belly; bill is heavy and black. A closely related species, the Yellow-billed Magpie, is confined to central CA. Widespread over most of W America from AK to E CA and E to the Great Plains.

COMMON RAVEN *Corvus corax*   Total length 2ft
A massive, all-black crow, with a large bill, shaggy throat, and a wedge-shaped tail when seen in flight. Call is a resonant croak. Nests on cliffs and in trees in a variety of habitats, including mountains, canyons, tundra, and desert. It is resident widely across Canada and AK, including the extreme N; also found down the Rockies and Appalachians.

AMERICAN CROW *Corvus brachyrynchos*   Total length 18in
Call is a nasal "caw." A scavenger that often feeds on road kills. Found in a wide range of habitats, including suburbs and town parks. The most familiar and widespread crow, residing over most of the continent.

FISH CROW *Corvus caurinus*   Total length 16in
Smaller than the American Crow, it is most easily identified by its call which is a fairly high-pitched "kaar." Nests in trees, often in small colonies. Generally found near water, in marshes, along rivers, estuaries, and the seashore. Confined to E US from New England to NE TX.

WESTERN SCRUB JAY *Aphelocoma californica*   Total length 11in
A large blue jay with a long tail, gray underside and a whitish throat. Often stores acorns for winter. It is found in SW US and adjacent Mexico. Closely related species are found in AZ, Santa Cruz Island and in FL, in mostly dry habitats.

PINYON JAY *Gymnorhinus cyanocephalus*   Total length 11in
A uniformly blue jay, with white streaking on the throat, and a long pointed bill; the young are grayer. Feeds on insects, fruit, berries, and seeds, in particular the seeds of pinyon pine. Gregarious outside the breeding season. Nests in colonies. It is found throughout the Rockies in the pinyon pine–juniper zone.

CLARK'S NUTCRACKER *Nucifraga columbiana*   Total length 12in
Named after the explorer of the American West. A noisy and often conspicuous bird. Pale gray with a white outer tail, and black wings with white patch. Most common near the treeline in coniferous forests. Populations can build, and erupt into lower elevations, but found mainly in the mountains of the W.

TUFTED TITMOUSE *Baeolophus bicolor*   Total length 6in
Uniform gray with orange-buff on flanks and a noticeable crest. Dark forehead in most of US; Mexican ssp. is found in S TX. Common in suburban gardens, city parks and feeders. In W more uniformly gray. Widespread over E North America in a wide range of habitats. Juniper and Oak Titmouses also may be found.

BUSHTIT *Psaltriparus minimus*   Total length 4in
Similar to chickadee, but with a proportionally longer tail. Coloring is variable, but generally grayish, with green wings; some populations have blackish faces, others greenish, and some have pink on the flanks. It is found from SW Canada to CA, TX, and Mexico, where it may be seen in noisy, active, fast-moving foraging flocks.

BLACK-CAPPED CHICKADEE *Poecile atricapillus*   Total length 5in
In winter, found in mixed flocks. Nests in holes. Common in woodland forests, but also common in suburbs and many other habitats. The most familiar and widespread chickadee in North America; found from AK to Newfoundland and S to AZ and NC.

MOUNTAIN CHICKADEE *Poecile gambeli*   Total length 5in
Very similar to the Black-capped Chickadee, but with a distinctive black stripe through the eye. Like other chickadees, nests in holes. Gregarious outside the breeding season, forming flocks mixed with other species such as nuthatches and kinglets. Found in coniferous forests of the W, from S Canada to S CA and northwest TX.

WHITE-BREASTED NUTHATCH *Sitta carolinensis*   Total length 5in
A small woodpeckerlike bird that can face downward on trees as well as up. Pointed bill, pure white face, throat and chest, but often has rusty tinges on the belly. Gray back with back of head and neck black. A woodland bird that also frequents suburban gardens and feeders. Common in deciduous woods over much of North America.

RED-BREASTED NUTHATCH *Sitta canadensis*   Total length 4in
Similar in shape and behavior to the White-breasted, but with prominent black stripe running through the eye, white eyebrows, rusty-buff belly. Loud, nasal call. A coniferous forest species more widely distributed than the White-breasted, breeding as far N as S AK and Newfoundland, moving S in winter and often seen at suburban feeders near conifers.

PYGMY NUTHATCH *Sitta pygmaea*   Total length 4in
A small, chickadeelike nuthatch with a black cap, a white spot on the nape, and a short, pointed bill. Nests in cavities which it excavates in dead wood, or uses a woodpecker hole. It is found in yellow pine and other coniferous forests. Confined to the W, from S BC to CA and Mexico. Similar species in southeastern conifers.

BROWN CREEPER *Certhia americana*   Total length 5in
A well-camouflaged, small brown bird, appearing almost mouselike as it runs up trees. It has a long, slender, downward-curving bill. Feeds spiraling up a tree, searching for insects and spiders, then flies to the base of another tree. Call is high pitched "tsee-tsee-tsee." Nests behind loose bark. In winter, often mixes with flocks of chickadees and nuthatches. Widespread from S Canada to N Mexico, breeding in N and Rockies and wintering more widely.

AMERICAN DIPPER *Cinclus mexicanus*   Total length 7in
A chunky, short-tailed bird almost always seen in or close to fast-flowing rivers and streams. Adult is a uniform sooty gray; young is browner, with a yellowish bill. Feeds on insects, crustaceans, and other aquatic life, wading among torrents and using its wings to swim under water. Territorial, and when disturbed will fly up or down stream, finally returning to its territory. It is confined to W North America from AK through the Rockies.

HOUSE WREN *Troglodytes aedon*   Total length 4in
Closely barred brown, with a long tail which it cocks up. A loud and constant singer at the nest site. Usually builds nest in a cavity, including holes in walls, using a variety of plant material, feathers, paper, etc. Normally has two broods. A common breeding bird over much of S Canada and the US N of FL and TX; migrates S for winter.

WINTER WREN *Troglodytes troglodytes*   Total length 4in
The smallest wren, with a short tail often held upright. It builds a domed nest, laying 5–8 eggs. Migratory over most of its range, it nests in a broad band across Canada and S into the Rockies and Appalachians. A winter visitor over most of E and S US. Also found in Eurasia.

MOCKINGBIRD *Mimus polyglotta*   Total length 10in
White outer tail feathers and wing patches obvious in flight. Imitates other birds' songs and calls and even telephones. Wide range of habitats, expanding N into Canada.

CATBIRD *Dumetella carolinensis*   Total length 8in
A relative of the Mockingbird. Uniform dark gray, black cap and tail, and rufous under the tail. Frequently cocks its tail, giving a catlike mewing call which it intersperses in its song. Excellent mimic. Skulks in thick vegetation. Widespread over E North America.

BROWN THRASHER *Toxostoma rufum*   Total length 11in
Fairly large, thrushlike bird with a downward-curving bill. Rich brown above, creamy below with extensive streaking. Call note is a harsh "chack." Song a more musical version of the related Catbird's. Usually seen on ground, often noisily feeding among dead leaves under bushes. Found in E North America from S Canada to TX. Northern populations migrate.

SAGE THRASHER *Oreoscoptes montanus*   Total length 8in
Paler than Brown Thrasher, with a stubbier bill. Builds nest low down in a dense bush, rarely above 3ft. Summer migrant confined to the W, breeding in sagebrush habitats from S Canada to CA and AZ; winters in similar habitats further S into Mexico.

ROBIN *Turdus migratorius*   Total length 11in
Familiar garden bird. Chest and belly rusty, red-brown in male, more orange in female; both sexes have whitish throats. Juvenile heavily spotted on the underparts. Builds a bulky nest of fiber, rag, twigs, and grasses. Favors open woodland habitats, parks, and suburban gardens. Breeds over most of North America from the tundra to the S.

HERMIT THRUSH *Catharus guttatus*   Total length 6in
Small, grayish brown bird. Underside spotted, tail rufous. Distinctive song is clear and flutelike with phrases repeated several times. Most common with conifers. Widespread summer breeder in N; winters over much of the US into Mexico.

VEERY *Catharus fuscescens*   Total length 7in
Warm brown above, pale below, with indistinct spotting on the throat and breast. Song is a series of descending "veer-veer-veer-veer" notes. Builds nest on or close to the ground. Widespread breeder in damp, deciduous woodlands in S Canada, N US, and further S in the Appalachians and Rockies.

WOOD THRUSH *Hylocichla mustelina*   Total length 7in
Rich, reddish brown above, cream below, clear, dark brown spots. White eye-ring can be seen up close. Powerful, musical song often sung in the evening. Favors damp mixed woodlands, but during fall and spring migrations is found in a wide variety of habitats. Widespread summer breeder E of the Rockies from SE Canada to E TX; rarely seen elsewhere.

GOLDEN-CROWNED KINGLET *Regulus satrapa*   Total length 4in
Tiny, greenish, golden-orange crown bordered with black, and white eye-stripe. Call thin and high. Usually seen flitting around the tops of conifers. Widespread, summer visitor to Canada and mountain areas of US; winters widely in the US, often mixing with chickadees.

EASTERN BLUEBIRD *Siala sialis*   Total length 7in
Male is deep blue above, red on throat and belly, and white under the tail; female grayer. Nests in old tree holes; readily uses nest boxes. Male Western Bluebird (*S. mexicana*) is a darker blue with a blue throat. Mountain Bluebird (*S. currucoides*) is pale blue on the underside, sky-blue above. Found in open woodlands, gardens, farmlands, and similar habitats, in E North America from S Canada to TX. Northern populations migrate S in winter.

BLUE-GRAY GNATCATCHER *Polioptila caerulea*   Total length 4in
Tail longer than that of Kinglet. Male soft blue-gray above, whitish below, tail blackish with white outer tail feathers; female is paler. An active, scolding species usually heard before seen. Cocks tail up over back. Summer visitor over much of US as far N as New England.

WATER PIPIT *Anthus spinoletta*   Total length 6in
Small bird, streaked buff-brown, spotted below. Seen on the ground or flying off with a "pip-pit" call. Nests on the ground. Undulating flight. Breeds on the tundra and high in the Rockies, wintering in open areas in S US and Mexico and coastal areas.

CEDAR WAXWING *Bombycilla cedrorum*   Total length 7in
Plumage warm, pale brown, yellow on the belly. Distinctive crest. Black face mask, tail tipped bright yellow. The young are heavily streaked. Gathers in large flocks in winter. Feeds extensively on fruits and berries, in summer eats flowers and insects. Widespread over N US and S Canada, migrating S in winter.

BOHEMIAN WAXWING *Bombycilla garrulus*   Total length 8in
Larger than the Cedar Waxwing, more black on the chin, yellow on the wing feathers as well as red, and a prominent white wing bar. Nests in conifers. Irruptive and, every few years, found much farther afield. Breeds in W North America and Canada.

NORTHERN SHRIKE *Lanius excubitor*   Total length 10in
Small predator with hooked bill and black face. Gray above, whitish below, black wings and tail. Hunts large insects, mice, and birds; sometimes stores prey items impaled on thorns or barbed wire. Often seen perching in open habitats. Breeds in far N, winters over S Canada and N US.

LOGGERHEAD SHRIKE *Lanius ludovicianus*   Total length 9in
Smaller than the Northern Shrike and generally darker, with a less distinctively hooked bill. Somewhat similar to Mockingbird, but with smaller white patches on the wings. Found in open habitats, hunting from a prominent perch for insects, birds, lizards, and mice. Its range is constricting S over much of the US.

BLUE-HEADED VIREO *Vireo solitarius*   Total length 5in
An attractive bird with white wing bars, bluish gray head, and prominent white spectacles. Widespread over much of Canada below the treeline and S through the Appalachians. Winters in the SE coastal states of the US and the Caribbean.

RED-EYED VIREO *Vireo olivaceus*   Total length 6in
The most common vireo. Blood-red eye can be clearly seen at close quarters. Builds a round nest of spider webs suspended in a horizontal fork of a bush or tree. Feeds on insects. It is found in woodland over much of North America; scattered in the SW.

BLACK-AND-WHITE WARBLER *Mniotilta varia*   Total length 5in
Plumage is unlikely to be confused with any other warbler. Behaves more like a creeper or nuthatch. Nests on the ground close to trees. Nest is cup-shaped, lined with fine grasses and hair. Common in summer over most of North America in deciduous woods E of the Rockies.

AMERICAN REDSTART *Setophaga ruticilla*   Total length 5in
The male is black with orange patches on the side of the tail and wings, and a white belly; female is mostly gray with yellow patches. Bird often flares its wings and tail to expose color patches. A summer breeder over much of North America, it is common in open woods and secondary forests.

NORTHERN PARULA *Parula americana*   Total length 4in
Breeding male is blue-gray above, with a yellow throat and belly, a dark band across the breast, two prominent white wing bars, and white around the eye. Female and immatures grayer. Nests in damp woodlands. Cup-shaped nest is lined with plant down and fine fibers. Summer visitor to E North America from SE Canada to TX.

MAGNOLIA WARBLER *Dendroica magnolia*   Total length 5in
Male mostly black above with a gray crown, white eye stripe, and yellow rump. Underside yellow with black streaks on the lower breast and white on the wings. Female and young are less contrasting and more heavily streaked. Breeds across the N of US and much of Canada. Seen during migration over most of the US E of the Rockies.

BLACKPOLL WARBLER *Dendroica striata*   Total length 5in
Similar to Black-and-white Warbler (*Mniotilta varia*), but with a solid black cap; does not creep on branches. Call high and insectlike. Feeds on insects. Seen during spring migration over much of E North America. Breeds in spruce forests in Canada and AK.

PROTHONOTARY WARBLER *Protonotaria citrea*   Total length 5in
Large, beautiful species of wet woods and swamps. Adult male is bright yellow, olive on the back, and blue-gray on the wings and tail. Female similar with duller head and neck. The only warbler that commonly nests in holes in trees. Widespread over E US.

NORTHERN WATERTHRUSH *Seiurus novaboracensis*   Total length 5in
Small, usually seen in dense undergrowth near water. Walks (does not hop), bobbing its tail. Nests among tree roots, under fallen logs, or in decayed stumps. Call a distinctive, metallic "chink". Widespread on migration, breeding in extreme N of US, Canada and AK.

OVENBIRD *Seiurus aurocapillus*   Total length 6in
Thrushlike, ground-dwelling warbler distinguished by an orange patch on crown and head stripes, and a distinct white eye ring. Forages on the ground in leaf litter. Call is a distinctive "teach'er-teach'er-TEACHER." Breeds in woods in North America E of the Rockies.

BLACK-THROATED BLUE WARBLER *Dendroica caerulescens*   Total length 5in
The male is mostly dark blue above, with a black throat, white belly, and white patch on the wings; the female is olive above, paler below with a white eye stripe. Breeds in deciduous woods and forests, often low down. Nest in a tree fork, at a height of less than 3ft from the ground, building a bulky cup-shaped nest of twigs, bark, and leaves. Breeds NE US and SE Canada; found on migration in SE US.

COMMON YELLOWTHROAT *Dendroica dominica*   Total length 5in
Male is distinct with a large, black mask and yellow throat. Female is plain olive above with pale yellow throat. Call is a "whitchity, whitchity, whitchity." Common in wide variety of habitats from woods and roadsides to marsh edges. Widespread summer breeder to much of E US, but rare in Canada and a winter visitor to most of FL.

BLACKBURNIAN WARBLER *Dendroica fusca*   Total length 5in
The attractive male has an orange head and chest with black cheek patch; upper parts black, wide white wing patch and white on the tail. Female and young duller. Breeds in conifers over S Canada, NE US and Appalachians, often elsewhere on migration.

WILSON'S WARBLER *Wilsonia pusilla*   Total length 5in
The male is yellow with a solid black cap; both sexes olive on the back and dark in the wings. Nests on the ground in alder and willow thickets and open areas with dense undergrowth and boggy habitats. Breeds over most of Canada, S into the Rockies and W to CA and CO. Seen on migration in most parts of the US.

PRAIRIE WARBLER *Dendroica discolor*   Total length 5in
Yellow with olive back, dark wings and tail. Male has black streaking on yellow sides and black on the head. In E US and SE Canada it is one of the commonest breeders in a wide range of habitats from mangroves to open woodlands.

YELLOW WARBLER *Dendroica petechia*   Total length 5in
An all-yellow warbler with olive wings and tail. The male has streaks on the breast; female and young are paler with olive on the upper parts. Song is often transliterated as "sweet, sweet, sweet, I'm so sweet." One of the most widespread warblers in North America.

BOBOLINK   *Dolichonyx oryzivorus*   Total length 7in
Breeding male mostly black with straw-colored back of the head, white on back, upper tail and rump. Call note "pink" in flight and "bob-o-link." Nests on ground in shallow scrape lined with grasses. Breeds in open grasslands of N US and S Canada.

WESTERN MEADOWLARK   *Sturnella neglecta*   Total length 9in
Identified by yellow breast and large black "V" on the chest. Ground-dwelling, but frequently seen perched on posts, telephone poles, or wires. Range extends E to Great Lakes where it overlaps with similar eastern species. Western is paler with a flutelike song.

RED-WINGED BLACKBIRD   *Agelaius phoeniceus*   Total length 9in
Adult male black with red shoulder patches edged with yellow; female and immature browner and streaked.Breeds in marshes, wet meadows, and swamps. Loud and obvious at breeding sites. Widespread over most of North America.

ORCHARD ORIOLE   *Icterus spurious*   Total length 7in
Adult male chestnut-brown below, black above and on the chest, white wing bar. Female and young yellowish. Feeds on insects, fruit nectar, and blossoms. Nests in open woodlands, orchards, mesquite, and scrub. Breeds in E US and SE Canada.

BREWER'S BLACKBIRD   *Euphagus cyanocephalus*   Total length 9in
Male glossy black, green sheen on the body, purple sheen on the head; female and young brown. Nests in small colonies, often near water. Winters in large mixed flocks. Widespread over W US and Canada, breeding E to the Great Lakes.

COMMON GRACKLE   *Quiscalus quiscala*   Total length 13in
Male large, black, long-tailed; female dark brown and black. Male has bronze iridescence in E, purple in S. Tail keel-shaped. Abundant, comes to feeders on migration. Widespread E of Rockies from S Canada to TX. Larger Boat-tailed Grackle (*Q. major*) is found in SE; Great-tailed Grackle (*Q. mexicanus*) in TX and SW.

BROWN-HEADED COWBIRD   *Molothus ater*   Total length 8in
Male has bright red eye and brown head on a black body; female light brown. Common in farmlands, marshes, and suburbs. Brood parasite: lays eggs in the nests of other birds, leaving its host to rear its young. Comes to feeders. Widespread from YT to NF and S through US.

EUROPEAN STARLING   *Sturnus vulgaris*   Total length 9in
Plumage black with light spots (more prominent in fall); bill bright yellow in breeding. Young birds are grayer. Aggressive, and often competes with native birds for nest holes. Omnivorous. Introduced from Europe, now widespread.

WESTERN TANAGER   *Piranga ludoviciana*   Total length 7in
Highly colored and mainly tropical, a few species of tanager migrate to North America to breed. Western Tanager mostly yellow; breeding male has bright, orange-red head and throat, black wings and tail. Breeds in coniferous forests from Canada to AZ.

SCARLET TANAGER   *Piranga olivacea*   Total length 7in
Male is bright scarlet with black wings and tail; the female, young, and fall males are olive. Breeds in E US and Canada north of SC where it forages in deciduous canopies. Winters in tropical forests of Central America.

SUMMER TANAGER   *Piranga rubra*   Total length 8in
Male red, bill yellow, darker wings and tail. Forages in canopy of deciduous woods. Feeds on insects. Winters in South and Central America. Breeds from CA, E to NJ.

CARDINAL   *Cardinalis cardinalis*   Total length 9in
Male bright red with darker wings, a black face, and red crest. Female and young brownish, with red on wings and tail. Comes to feeders for sunflower seeds. Common over much of US; absent in the W. Range has expanded N due to climate change.

ROSE-BREASTED GROSBEAK *Pheucticus ludovicianus*   Total length 8in
Attractive, with a large triangular bill. Mostly black and white, adult male has uniform black upper parts as well as rose-pink breast and underwings. Seen on migration to Central America and Caribbean; breeds in deciduous woodlands of the E.

EVENING GROSBEAK *Coccothraustes vespertinus*   Total length 8in
Striking, with heavy bill and white patches on the blackish wings prominent in flight. Male yellowish and dark brown, female grayer, and the young more buff. Resident over much of N US and Canada, S through the Rockies, but can erupt S and E in large numbers.

INDIGO BUNTING *Passerina cyanea*   Total length 5in
Darker and smaller than Blue Grosbeak. Found in open scrub and woodland edges. Widespread over most of North America E of the Rockies and N to S Canada.Related Lazuli Bunting is found in the W and has an orange breast and white on the wings.

PAINTED BUNTING *Passerina ciris*   Total length 5in
Male is purple, green, and rose-red all year. Female and young are much duller. Breeds in TX and adjacent states, and also in the coastal areas of the Carolinas to GA. Some winter in S FL and come to feeders, but most winter in Central America.

BLUE GROSBEAK *Guiraca caerulea*   Total length 7in
Male is a spectacular indigo blue, larger than Indigo Bunting with a heavier bill. Female and young buff-brown. Summer visitor to much of the US, except NW and S FL, in dense thickets, vines, and low trees. Winters in Central and South America.

PURPLE FINCH *Carpodacus purpureus*   Total length 6in
Male rose-red (rather than purple), female and young brown-streaked. Sharp "zit" call in flight. Found in a range of woodland edge habitats high in conifers or in deciduous forests. Breeds across Canada and US, also along coastal areas to CA.

HOUSE FINCH *Carpodacus mexicanus*   Total length 6in
A small streaked finch, the male has a bright orange-pink breast and forehead; in the SW this can be yellowish instead. Resident, often associated with humans. Originally confined to arid habitats in W, introduced to E US in the 1940s where it spread rapidly. Now widespread and often abundant, found over almost the entire US and S through Mexico. Resident Purple Finch is declining where the two species overlap.

COMMON REDPOLL *Carduelis flammea*   Total length 5in
Streaky, breeding male has a pink breast; both sexes have pinkish red on the forehead; tail is forked. In winter gathers in large flocks, feeds on the ground in open areas often in mixed flocks. Irruptive. Breeds close to Arctic Circle. A winter visitor as far as S Canada and NE US.

PINE SISKIN *Carduelis pinus*   Total length 5in
Small, heavily streaked, with a forked tail, thin bill, and wide yellow wing bar. Often mixes with goldfinches and, like the Goldfinch, has a bouncing flight. Breeds in northern conifer forests, migrates S in winter. Found over most of the US.

AMERICAN GOLDFINCH *Carduelis tristis*   Total length 5in
Breeding male spectacular bright yellow with black crown, black wings and tail, duller in winter. Often abundant, feeding in flocks and visiting feeders. Particularly fond of thistle seeds. Widespread from S Canada and most of US, moving S in winter.

RED CROSSBILL *Loxia curvirostra*   Total length 6in
Crossed tips of the bill clearly visible at close range. Male variable, a rosy red or scarlet; female (and some males) yellowish and the young streaked. Feeds on pine nuts. Found across S Canada and N US down through the Rockies to Mexico.

RUFOUS-SIDED TOWHEE *Pipilo erythrophthalmus*   Total length 7in
Long-tailed, usually seen on the ground. Female is brown where the male is black, with orange-rufous sides and white belly. It is found over most of E North America. Replaced in W by the Spotted Towhee, male with extensive white spotting on back.

SAVANNAH SPARROW *Passerculus sandwichensis*   Total length 5in
Variable, but with distinctive, streaky head and yellow above eye when breeding. Widespread and common on ground in tillable fields, marshes, barren ground, and beaches. Breeds over most of N US and Canada, N to the high Arctic; winters in S US and Mexico.

GRASSHOPPER SPARROW *Ammodramus savannarum*   Total length 5in
Flat head, with a pale, buffish stripe bisecting the crown, a complete eye ring, and a short tail. Usually found in colonies. Nests on the ground. Found in open, grassy habitats including prairies and pastures. Widespread over US and N to extreme S of Canada. More scattered in W. Declining over most of its range.

DARK-EYED JUNCO *Junco hymenalis*   Total length 6in
Variable, known by a wide range of names including Slate-colored, Oregon and Pink-sided Junco. Generally dark on head and breast, with pale bill; back dark slate or brown. Nests on or close to the ground. Common winter feeder throughout its range. Widespread, breeding from AK, Canada, and New England; winters S in US.

AMERICAN TREE SPARROW *Spizella arborea*   Total length 6in
Male has rufous crown, gray head and neck, and a black spot on the breast. Female also has a black spot, but is streaked. Comes to feeders. Nests in shrubs and on the ground, on the edge of the tundra in N of Canada and AK. Winters S of Canada in small flocks.

WHITE-THROATED SPARROW *Zonotrichia albicollis*   Total length 6in
Handsome, with conspicuous black and white head stripes and distinct white throat patch. Long, musical call of two or three long followed by three short whistles is a sure sign of spring. Found close to the ground in brush and thickets. Comes to bird feeders. Common; breeds over most of Canada, winters in the S and E US. Rare in W.

FOX SPARROW *Passerella iliaca*   Total length 7in
Relatively large and chunky, variable in coloring from dark gray to rufous, heavily spotted and streaked below. Distinct red tail. Usually solitary, comes to feeders. Many subspecies and geographical variations. Fairly common. Breeds mainly in Canada and AK; winters in SE US and far W coast in undergrowth, thickets, and brush.

SONG SPARROW *Melospiza melodia*   Total length 6in
Streaked above and below with white chin bordered by black throat stripes and large central breast spot. The loud song is a pleasant background sound in spring. Comes to feeders. Found in hedgerows, forest edges, brush piles, and marshes. The most common and widespread sparrow.

LAPLAND LONGSPUR *Calcarius lapponicus*   Total length 6in
Sparrowlike, with a long hind claw visible only at close range. Breeding male has a jet-black face, and neck and breast edged with white. Winters in open habitats of much of the US, breeds in high Arctic close to the snow line.

SNOW BUNTING *Plectrophenax nivalis*   Total length 6in
Plump, sparrowlike bird, pale in winter; appears mostly white in flight. Breeding male has black on back, wings, and tail. General plumage snowy white. Usually found in flocks, often mixed with Longspurs. Nests in high Arctic; winters south to S Canada and N US.

STINKPOT *Stenotherus odoratus*   Total length 5½in
Small, with a large head, pointed snout, and two pairs of barbels under the chin. Found in slow-moving rivers, ponds, and swamps with muddy bottoms. Feeds on the bottom on crustaceans and mollusks. Widespread over much of E North America from S Canada to TX.

SPINY SOFTSHELL *Trionyx spiniferus*   Total length 20in
Large, pancakelike shell, soft rather than horny. Muddy colored with black spots. Neck is long and flexible, snout elongated. Found in rivers and streams with sandy or muddy bottoms, also lakes and ponds. Range SE US, N to Great Lakes; introduced into several other areas, including CA, AZ, and NJ.

SMOOTH SOFTSHELL *Trionyx muticus*   Total length up to 14in
Smooth shell is covered by soft leathery skin. Olive brown with darker spots. Aquatic, found in rivers with muddy or sandy bottoms, where they feed on small invertebrates, fish, and amphibians. Widespread in the rivers of the Great Plains, from ND south to TX.

LOGGERHEAD *Caretta caretta*   Total length up to 4ft
Marine turtle with heart-shaped shell, forelimbs modified into paddles. Feeds on a wide variety of marine animals including echinoderms, crustaceans, mollusks, and seaweed. Found in warmer waters of Pacific and Atlantic. Like all species of marine turtle its numbers are seriously depleted.

GREEN TURTLE *Chelonia mydas*   Total length up to 5ft
Large marine turtle, with a dark olive shell. This was the species most prized for its flesh and for making turtle soup. Small numbers still nest in FL; outside the breeding season, they are found further N, as far as New England. Like all other species its populations are seriously depleted and it is threatened over most of its range.

COMMON SNAPPER *Chelydra serpentina*   Total length up to 18in
Large freshwater turtle with a powerful head, hooked jaws, and a long tail. Weighs up to 50lb. Feeds on a wide variety of plant and animal matter. Often basks at the water surface. Found in a wide range of habitats, including rivers, ponds, and marshes. Locally common in E North America from TX to S Canada, but declining in many areas.

ALLIGATOR SNAPPER *Macroclemmys temmincki*   Total length 2ft 6in
Very large, up to 200lb, distinguished from the Common Snapper by three ridges down the back of its shell. It often feeds by lying submerged using its tongue as a lure to attract fish. Unlike Common Snapper it rarely basks, and only surfaces to breathe. Range mostly confined to the Mississippi drainage, but also further E.

WOOD TURTLE *Clemmys insculpata*   Total length 9in
Distinctive carapace, with distinct growth ridges. Underside orange and black. Aquatic in spring, often basking close to water. In summer may wander into woodlands, but returns to hibernate underwater. Northerly distribution from S Canada to N VA.

CHICKEN TURTLE *Deirochelys reticularia* Total length 10in

Long-necked, with characteristic striping on the neck. The rear of the thighs are also striped with pale and dark stripes. Widely distributed from VA to TX; generally in ponds, lakes, and swamps, not rivers or flowing waters.

EASTERN BOX TURTLE *Terrapene carolina* Total length 8in

Domed carapace; lower shell (plastron) is hinged so it can be closed to create a boxlike protection. Feeds on a wide variety of fruit, invertebrates, and fungi. Terrestrial, found in forests and meadows from ME to FL and west to TX. A closely related species, the Western Box Turtle (*T. ornate*), is found in the Midwest, S to Mexico.

MAP TURTLE *Graptemys geographica* Total length 10½in

Olive in color, with an intricate pattern of pale lines, which gradually fade in older animals. Female larger than male. Very aquatic, in ponds, lakes, rivers, streams, where it feeds on hard-shelled invertebrates, including mollusks, crayfish, insects and their larvae, as well as plants and carrion. Found S and E of Great Lakes, with scattered populations in E.

PAINTED TURTLE *Chrysemys picta* Total length 10in

Shell is relatively flat, generally dark olive or blackish on the carapace, with red or yellow markings around the edges, and yellow or red stripes on the neck and legs. Attractive; hatchlings often sold as pets. Found in slow- moving rivers, lakes, and ponds, with muddy bottoms. Widespread, from the Canadian border S to GA and LA.

SLIDER *Chrysemys scripta* Total length 11in

Olive with some yellow on the carapace, yellowish stripes on neck, and a prominent yellowish spot behind the eye. Similar in habits to the Painted Turtle and often basks in large numbers. Closely related to the Painted Turtle, but with a more southerly distribution, from VA to TX and Mexico

COOTER *Chrysemys (= Pseudemys) floridiana* Total length 15½in

Carapace brownish with yellowish markings, neck and legs are striped. They often bask in large groups, sometimes mixed with other species. Found in ponds and lakes, also slow-moving rivers and canals. Widespread, often common over E coast states, from New England to TX, more widely distributed in the Mississippi Basin.

DESERT TORTOISE *Gopherus agassizi* Total length 14½in

Domed carapace, with short stumpy legs. Mostly vegetarian, feeding on grasses, fruits, and other vegetation. Terrestrial, confined to arid habitats with creosote bush, cacti, and other desert plants, from S CA and NV to Mexico. An endangered species. Closely related species found in FL and TX.

GOPHER TORTOISE *Gopherus polyphemus* Total length 14½in

Dome-shelled terrestrial turtle with elephantine hind feet and more shovel-like fore feet. Confined to FL and adjacent states in dry habitats, usually with sandy well-drained soils where they excavate burrows, in which they spend the heat of the day. The tunnels are often long; the record is 47½ft. Threatened by loss of habitat, and by collecting for the pet trade.

TEXAS BANDED GECKO *Coleonyx brevis*　　　　Total length 5in
This lizard is pinkish, banded with brown. Pattern very distinct when young, gradually becoming less distinct with time. The scales are very fine, and the toes slender (no pads, unlike some geckos). When alarmed, it squeaks. The female lays a clutch of 2 eggs. Nocturnal, and often seen on highways, feeding on insects. Spends the day hiding in rock crevices, under logs. Confined to S TX, NM, and adjacent Mexico.

SOUTHEASTERN FIVE-LINED SKINK *Eumeces inexpectatus*　　　Total length 8½in
A dark skink with five pale stripes on the back, which gradually fade with age; older adult is a uniform brown, the male has an orange-brown head. Young are brightly marked, with a blue tail. Often burrows, but is also a good climber. The female lays a clutch of up to 11 eggs which she guards. This species is poisonous to domestic cats. Found in damp woods, meadows, and also drier habitats over E US from MD to FL and LA.

WESTERN SKINK *Eumeces skiltonianus*　　　　Total length 9½in
Similar to *E. inexpectatus*, but the striped pattern is more persistent. Like many other skinks, the young are more brightly marked and have blue tails. Active by day, feeding on invertebrates. The female lays a clutch of up to 6 eggs, in a burrow or under a rock, which she guards. The Western Skink lives in mostly rocky habitats, in woodland or grassland, hiding under logs and stones, or in leaf litter. Found from S BC to Baja CA, and E to N AZ.

DESERT NIGHT LIZARD *Xantusia vigilis*　　　　Total length 5½in
Despite its name, active during the day, and may also be active at night. Although common within its range, its secretive nature makes it difficult to see. Feeds on termites, ants, and other insects. The female gives birth to up to 3 live young, in late summer. The most widespread of the three species of Night Lizard. Confined to a relatively small range in the deserts and other rocky, arid habitats of CA and adjacent states, and Mexico, with isolated populations in AZ.

GILA MONSTER *Heloderma suspectum*　　　　Total length 2ft
Unmistakable, heavily built lizard. One of only two venomous lizards known, though rarely fatal to humans. It has small beadlike scales, and is strikingly patterned with black and orange, pinkish, or yellowish. Feeds on small birds, rodents, and lizards. Unlike snakes, it poisons its prey by chewing. The female lays up to 5 eggs, in fall or winter. Generally nocturnal, hiding by day in burrows and under rocks. Confined to desert areas in the extreme SW of the US and adjacent Mexico.

ALLIGATOR LIZARD *Gerrhonotus (= Elgaria) multicarinatus*　　Total length 18in
Large, and closely related to the legless glass lizards. Diurnal and agile, climbing in bushes where it preys on small vertebrates or large insects. When captured, it is aggressive and bites hard; sheds its tail very readily. The female lays up to 3 clutches of up to 40 eggs during the summer. Found in well-vegetated habitats, including grasslands, woodland, and other moist habitats, in coastal CA, OR, and WA. Range overlaps that of the Northern Alligator Lizard.

SIX-LINED RACE RUNNER *Cnemidophorus sexlineatus*　　　Total length 10½in
Brownish with creamy paler stripes on the sides; despite the name some populations have seven stripes. Young have bluish tails. Small and fast-moving. Active in the morning, often hiding during the heat of the day. In the northern parts of its range and at higher altitudes it hibernates, as do some other lizards in the W. The female lays two clutches of up to 6 eggs. Closely related species of race runner are all female (parthenogenetic), and reproduce asexually. Found in dry open habitats, including prairies and open woodlands. Often abundant, with a wide distribution over much of the Rockies and E US, and S to Mexico.

GREEN ANOLE *Anolis carolinensis* Total length 8in
A long-tailed, slender lizard, usually bright green. However, it can change its color very rapidly to brown, and various shades of green or brown. The male has a pinkish throat flap. Seen on trees and fence posts; at night it shows up bright yellowish in torchlight. Widespread over S US from VA to TX. Several other species have been introduced from the Caribbean into FL.

CHUCKWALLA *Sauromalus obesus* Total length 16½in
One of the largest lizards in North America. Heavily built, dark slate gray, blackish at the front, becoming reddish or yellowish towards the tail. Female and young are often banded with grayish or yellowish. Strictly vegetarian. Confined to rocky desert areas of the SW.

LONG-NOSED LEOPARD LIZARD *Gambelia wislizenii* Total length 15in
Fairly large with prominent eyes. Coloring is variable, but usually has well-defined black spots on a pale gray or buff background; the color becomes paler as the lizard warms up. Agile and fast-running, often hiding around bushes, and darting out after insects and small lizards. Confined to arid habitats in SW.

COLLARED LIZARD *Crotaphytus collaris* Total length 14in
Most of the body and tail is bluish green, heavily spotted, usually with dark bands, and a series of light and dark bands around the neck. The pregnant female has orange spots on her sides. She lays up to 12 eggs in sandy soil, under stones, or in a burrow. Feeds on flowers, insects, and lizards. Found in arid rocky areas, forests, and limestone hills of the SW.

SIDE BLOTCHED LIZARD *Uta stansburiana* Total length 6in
Variable, but often distinctively marked. It normally has a characteristic blue or blackish spot on each side, behind the forelimb. Terrestrial, rarely climbs. Feeds almost entirely on insects. In the N torpid in winter, but in the S active year round. Wide though patchy distribution in arid habitats.

EASTERN FENCE LIZARD *Sceloporus undulatus* Total length 7½in
One of the most widespread lizards, and also one of the most variable in pattern and coloring. Usually brownish or grayish with darker sides and some irregular bands. Found in sunny areas, often basking on logs, in woodland, dunes, grasslands. Found over much of E North America as far N as DE.

WESTERN FENCE LIZARD *Sceloporus occidentalis* Total length 9¼in
Variable, rough-skinned. Usually brownish or grayish above with irregular bars across the back, and bluish on the sides. Male has blue throat, which he bobs when displaying. Diurnal and easily seen. Found in forests and many other habitats; often seen on fence posts, rocky walls, and derelict buildings, up to 9,000ft. Confined to W US from WA to CA, and E to UT.

SHORT HORNED LIZARD *Phrynosoma douglasii* Total length 6in
A typical horned lizard, with a flat body, short tapering tail, and "horns" on the back of the head. Coloring is variable, but generally sandy, grayish, or brownish, with darker markings. The female gives birth to live young. Found in a wide range of habitats. The most widespread of the horned lizards, being found from Canada to Mexico, up to 9,000ft.

WESTERN WHIPTAIL *Cnemidophorus tigris* Total length 12in
Variable in coloring and markings, but generally fairly unremarkable mottled brown. Tail twice as long as the body; in young is usually bright blue. The most widely distributed of the western species of whiptails. Found from OR and ID, E UT and S to TX and Mexico.

REPTILES

TEXAS BLIND SNAKE *Leptotyphlops dulcis*   Total length up to 8in
Small, shiny, slender and wormlike, with no obvious neck, and only vestigial eyes. Brownish or tinged purple, or silvery pink, blunt tail. Feeds almost exclusively on termites, ants, insect larvae, and other small invertebrates. Has teeth only in the lower jaw. Lives almost entirely underground in desert and semi-arid habitats with sandy soils, emerging after dusk to feed. Confined from SW Kansas to SE Arizona and Mexico.

RUBBER BOA *Charina bottae*   Total length 2ft 9in
One of two species of boa found in the US. Uniform brownish coloring, and rubbery appearance. Generally nocturnal, spending the day hidden in leaf-litter, in rotten logs, or under rocks, and emerging in the early evening. It is a constrictor and feeds on lizards, birds, and rodents. When captured it rolls into a ball. Found mostly in damp habitats, including woodland, forests, meadows, and close to streams, at altitudes of up to 9,200ft. Has a wide range over much of W US, N to S Canada.

EASTERN RIBBON SNAKE *Thamnophis sauritus*   Total length 3ft 3in
A slender, streamlined garter snake, with a long tail. Usually has three bright, well-defined stripes contrasting sharply with dark back and sides. Stripes range from reddish brown, yellow, green-tinged, orange to blue; velvety black or dark brown back. Feeds on amphibians, leeches and fish. Very aquatic. Found E of the Mississippi River to ME, and S to FL.

PLAINS GARTER SNAKE *Thamnophis radix*   Total length 4ft
Characterized by a bright yellow or orange back stripe, yellow side stripes, and a double row of squarish black spots between side and back stripes. Feeds on amphibians and small rodents. Up to 60 or more live young are born in summer. Usually found in wet meadows, prairies along margins of lakes, streams, and marshes, as well as urban areas. Common through much of its range. Found from IN through the Great Plains to the Rockies, with numerous scattered, isolated populations.

COMMON GARTER SNAKE *Thamnophis sirtalis*   Total length 4ft
Highly variable coloring, but back and side stripes are usually well defined, and red blotches or a double row of alternating black spots are often present between stripes. Feeds on amphibians and earthworms, and occasionally small fish and mice. It is bad-tempered when captured, biting or expelling musk. Gives birth to up to 85 live young. The most widely distributed snake in North America. Found from Atlantic to Pacific coasts, except in the desert regions of the SW, usually near water.

ROUGH EARTH SNAKE *Virginia striatula*   Total length 12in
Uniform reddish brown, brown or gray, paler on the belly, with a pointed snout. The young often have a pale band on the back of the head, which disappears as they grow. Feeds on invertebrates and amphibians. Mostly nocturnal. Very secretive and rarely seen, hiding in leaf litter or under logs, and preyed on by other snakes and even shrews. Up to 13 young are born late June to mid-September. Found from VA to northern FL, and W to TX in dry coastal plains, woodland, as well as forests.

PLAIN-BELLIED WATER SNAKE *Nerodia erythrogaster*   Total length 5ft
Reddish brown, brown, greenish, or gray, lighter on the sides. Young have vivid dark blotches on the back, alternating with dark crossbars on sides. Belly red, orange, or yellow. It is found close to water, fresh, brackish, and salt, in lakes, ponds, cypress and mangrove swamps, marshes, where it feeds on fish, frogs, and tadpoles. Found from DE to northern FL, and W to TX and NM. Scattered populations in MI, OH, and IA.

BROWN SNAKE *Storeria dekayi*   Total length 20in
Small, usually gray, yellowish brown, brown, or reddish brown. Paler belly with small black spots along the sides. Young have a yellowish collar. Feeds mostly on earthworms, slugs, and snails. Found in moist woodland, marshes; margins of swamps, bogs, and ponds; vacant lots, as well as gardens, parks, cemeteries, and golf courses. Widespread from S Canada S to the Florida Keys, through TX and Mexico to Honduras.

NORTHERN WATER SNAKE *Nerodia sipedon*   Total length 4ft 6in

Usually reddish, brown, or gray to brownish black, with dark crossbands on neck region, and alternating dark blotches on back and sides. It darkens with age, becoming black. The young are more vivid. Frequently seen basking on rocks or logs. Can produce up to about 100 young, but normally fewer than 30. Found in most aquatic habitats, where it feeds on small fish and amphibians. Range from ME, GA, AL, and W to CO and NE to ON and QC.

RINGNECK SNAKE *Diadophis punctatus*   Total length 2ft 6in

A small, slender snake, gray, olive, brownish, or black; with a bright yellow, orange, or red belly, frequently marked with black spots. The characteristic yellow, cream, or orange neck ring may be obscure.The female lays a clutch of up to 10 elongate, white or yellow-ish eggs, in communal nesting sites. Found in damp habitats including forest, grassland, as well as rocky hillsides, chaparral, and upland desert. Found from NS to the Florida Keys, W to the Pacific coast, and S to Mexico.

WORM SNAKE *Carphophis amoenus*

Tiny, glossy, with a cylindrical body and a short tail tapering to a sharp point. Plain brown, gray, or black, with a bright reddish pink belly.Very secretive; most likely to be seen in spring while its habitat is still moist. Up to 8 elongate, thin-shelled eggs are laid in June or July. Lives in damp woodlands, grassy hillsides, and farmland bordering woodlands, and feeds mostly on earthworms. Found from S New England to GA, W to NE, and S to NE TX.

EASTERN HOGNOSE SNAKE *Heterodon platyrhinos*   Total length 4ft 9in

Stout-bodied, with a pointed, slightly upturned snout and a wide neck. Coloring variable, but usually yellowish, tan, brown, gray, or reddish, with rectangular dark blotches on the back interspersed with round dark blotches. All-black individuals are known. Feeds mostly on amphibians. The female lays up to 60 thin-shelled eggs. It is most common on open, sandy soils, on thinly wooded upland hillsides, in cultivated fields, and meadows. Wide distribution: MN to southern NH, S to FL, W to TX and KS.

WESTERN SHOVELNOSE SNAKE *Chionactis occipitalis*   Total length 18in

Secretive, with head modified for digging in loose, sandy desert soil. Although it can be aggressive, it has only tiny teeth, and feeds mostly on insects, centipedes, and scorpions. Generally nocturnal, it is rarely seen, but may be encountered as it crosses roads at night. The female lays up to 4 eggs. Confined to S CA and adjacent states, and Mexico.

SCARLET SNAKE *Cemophora coccinea*   Total length up to 2ft 6in

Superficially similar to a coral snake, but the black-bordered yellow bands separating the scarlet are narrower, and do not completely encircle the body. Rarely seen, as it is largely nocturnal, burrowing in loose soil, or under logs during the day. Its principal food is eggs of other reptiles. It produces up to 8 eggs; the young are about 6in long when they hatch. Found in SE US from NJ to E TX, and S to FL, where it occurs in open wooded areas.

COMMON KINGSNAKE *Lampropeltis getulus*   Total length up to 7ft

Large, chocolate brown to black with a very variable pattern. Light-centered scales may form distinct patterns on the back. Belly can be plain white, heavily blotched, or black. The female lays up to 24 creamy white eggs. Found in a wide variety of habitats including pine barrens, swamps, dry rocky hillsides, and coastal marshes, as well as prairies, desert, and chaparral. Found from NJ to FL, and W to the Pacific from OR to Baja CA and Mexico.

MILK SNAKE *Lampropeltis triangulum*   Total length 3ft

Extremely variable, with several well defined subspecies. The eastern form is generally grayish with black-edged brown blotches. Other populations, notably the "scarlet king-snakes" from FL and SE US, are banded red, yellow, and black, closely mimicking coral snakes. Feeds on lizards, snakes, rodents, and birds. The female lays up to 17 eggs, under a log or in leaf litter. Found over most of E US, from the Rockies to TX, and N to ME and S Canada, in a wide range of habitats.

CORN SNAKE *Elaphe guttata*   Total length 6ft
Long, slender, usually orange or brownish yellow to light gray, with large black-edged red, brown, olive-brown, or dark gray blotches down the middle of the back and two rows of smaller blotches on the sides. Characteristic large rectangular black marks on belly. Feeds on mice, rats, birds, and bats. The female lays a clutch of up to 20 eggs. Found in a very wide range of habitats: rocky hillsides, meadows, farms and derelict houses. Found from NJ south through FL to TX, Mexico, and W to CO and UT.

RAT SNAKE *Elaphe obsoleta*   Total length up to 8ft
Long, powerful constrictor that is found in three main color phases: plain, striped, and blotched. Plain is generally blackish with white showing between the scales. Striped is red, orange, yellow, brown, or gray with four dark stripes. Blotched is light gray, yellow, or brown with dark blotches down back. The young are vividly blotched. Lives in forests, wooded canyons, swamps, rocky areas, farmland, old fields, barnyards. Found from MI, ON and VT S to Florida Keys, and W TX and Mexico

BULLSNAKE *Pituophis melanoleucas*   Total length 4–8ft, occasionally more
Heavily built, light brown with dark patches on the back and sides. Normally active by day, often nocturnal during the hotter months. Feeds mostly on rodents. When disturbed it sometimes mimics rattlers, hissing, flattening the head, and vibrating the tail, as well as lunging. Generally found in dry woodlands, as well as fields and prairies, desert and other arid habitats. It is found in two main areas: FL and adjacent states, and in the W, but extending to the Great Lakes in the N.

ROUGH GREEN SNAKE *Opheodrys aestivus*   Total length up to 3ft 10in
Distinctive, plain green, paler on the head with a pale belly. It is a good climber, and is frequently found above the ground, where it feeds on caterpillars, grasshoppers, crickets, and spiders. It is only normally active by day, sleeping in bushes and trees at night. A clutch consisting of up to 14 elongate eggs with thin, leathery shells is laid in summer. Most frequently found in damp habitats near water. Ranges from NJ through FL, W to KS, and S to TX and Mexico.

INDIGO SNAKE *Drymarchon corais*   Total length up to 8ft, occasionally longer
The largest non-poisonous North American snake. Heavy-bodied, lustrous blue-black or brownish and black with chin, throat, and sides of head suffused with cream. Feeds on frogs, small mammals and birds, other snakes, lizards, and young turtles. Found in pine and oak woods, dry grassland, and palmetto stands near water, orange groves, and tropical hammocks, often hiding in burrows. Confined to the SE US, S to Mexico. It is protected in the US.

RACER *Coluber constrictor*   Total length 6ft
Large, slender, agile, and fast-moving. Usually black, blue, brown, or greenish above, and white, yellow, or dark gray below. Young are gray, marked with dark spots on sides and dark gray, brown, or reddish brown blotches down the back. Feeds on large insects, frogs, lizards, snakes, small rodents, and birds. Occurs in a wide range of habitats, including overgrown fields, grassland, prairies, woodland, meadows, and rocky wooded hillsides. Found from S BC and ON through the US to Guatemala.

REPTILES

EASTERN CORAL SNAKE *Micrurus fulvius* Total length 4ft
Distinctive, with bright "warning" coloration. Red and black rings separated by narrow yellow rings; usually some black spotting on the red rings. Feeds almost exclusively on other snakes and lizards. Not normally aggressive, but the venom is extremely toxic and can cause respiratory failure. Occurs in densely vegetated hammocks near ponds or streams, forests, pinewoods, rocky hillsides, and canyons. Found in SE US as far N as NC.

COPPERHEAD *Agkistrodon contortrix* Total length 4ft 3in
Stout-bodied, with a facial pit on each side of a triangular head. Usually copper, orange, or pink-tinged, with reddish brown cross-bands on the back. Feeds on small rodents, lizards, frogs, and large insects and larvae. Basks during the day in spring and fall, becomes nocturnal in summer. It is found on rocky hillsides near streams or ponds, edges of swamps and seasonally flooded areas, and also dense canebrakes. Found from MA W to NE and S to FL and TX.

COTTONMOUTH *Agkistrodon piscivorus* Total length 6ft
Dark, heavy-bodied water snake, with a broad head, wider than the neck, and a facial pit on the side of the head. Usually uniform olive, brown, or black above, sometimes with dark cross-bands. Young are strongly patterned and have yellow-tipped tails. Unlike other water snakes, it swims with head well out of the water. Feeds on fish, sirens, frogs, snakes, and birds. Lives close to water in swamps, lakes, rivers, ditches, canals, and rice fields. Found from VA to the upper Florida Keys, W to IL and TX.

MASSASAUGA *Sistrurus catenatus* Total length 4ft
Head more oval than that of other species of rattlesnake. Has a short tail with a moderately developed rattle. Well-defined, rounded dark blotches on back and sides. It feeds on lizards, small rodents, and frogs. Found in bogs, swamps, marshland, and flood plains (in the E) as well as dry woodland, rocky hillsides, sagebrush prairie, and desert grassland (in the W). It has a wide, though patchy, range from ON and PA, S to Mexico.

PYGMY RATTLESNAKE *Sistrurus miliarius* Total length 2ft 6in
Small, with a tiny buzzing rattle. Usually gray to reddish, with brown to black blotches along the middle of the back; and up to three rows of spots on the sides. It feeds mostly on lizards, small snakes, mice, and insects. The female gives birth to up to 32 (usually fewer than 10) live young. Occurs in a variety of habitats, including prairie, palmetto, pinewoods, sandhills, mixed forest, and close to lakes and marshes. Found from NC to Florida Keys, and W to OK and TX.

EASTERN DIAMOND-BACKED RATTLESNAKE *Crotalus adamanteus* Total length 8ft
The largest rattlesnake in North America. Heavy-bodied, with a large head sharply divided from the neck. Back is patterned with dark, light-centered diamonds. Loud rattle. Feeds on large rodents such as squirrels, rabbits, and birds. Very venomous. It is found in dunes, sandhills or pine and oak country, and other dry habitats, as well as abandoned farmland. Found from NC to Florida Keys, and W to MS and E of LA.

WESTERN DIAMOND-BACKED RATTLESNAKE *Crotalus viridis* Total length 5ft
Variable, usually with brownish blotches along the back which become cross-bars near the tail. It feeds on small mammals, birds, and lizards, hunting mostly at night during the summer. The female gives birth to about 20 young. It is very venomous and, like all rattlers, frequently persecuted. Wide range of habitats, including rocky mountainsides, cliffs, and canyons, and often associated with prairie dog towns. Widespread over most of the Rockies and W America at altitudes of up to 11,000ft.

NORTHERN CRICKET FROG *Acris crepitans*   Total length 1½in
Small, warty tree frog with no toe pads. Variable in coloring, usually with a dark triangle between the eyes, and an uneven dark stripe on the thighs. When disturbed it leaps away zig-zagging, up to a yard each leap. Name comes from the male's cricketlike call (also sounds like pebbles being clicked together). Found in marshes, around ponds, lakes, and streams over most of E US and S of Canada.

NORTHERN LEOPARD FROG *Rana pipiens*   Total length 5in
Distinctive, with long legs, a pointed snout, pale stripes running the length of the body, and characteristic black spots. The male's breeding call is a rattling snore. Often abundant, and outside breeding season may migrate up to a mile from its breeding ponds. Found in damp meadows, pasture, marshes, bogs, prairie potholes, and close to rivers and streams. Range extends from S Canada and New England, W to the Rockies.

PICKEREL FROG *Rana palustris*   Total length 3in
Similar to Northern Leopard Frog, but generally smaller, with larger spots, and rarely found far from water. When it is disturbed, it leaps into the water and dives and hides in mud. It has a poisonous skin secretion that deters many predators. The male has a low snoring breeding call. Found from S Canada, S to TX, and E to WI, generally in cool, clear mountain streams, lakes, meadows, and bogs, with dense vegetation.

BULLFROG *Rana catesbeiana*   Total length 8in
The largest frog in North America. Generally greenish or brownish, and the eardrum is very obvious. The male's breeding call is a low resonant call, usually rendered as "jug-o-rum." Voracious, eating almost any small animal it can swallow. Found around lakes, ponds, and streams. Widely distributed over most of the E of the continent, and has been extensively introduced from CA to BC.

WOOD FROG *Rana sylvatica*   Total length 3in
Medium-sized, reddish brown, with a dark brown "mask". The male's breeding call is a series of short ducklike quacks. In the US it is found in damp woodlands, but in the N it is found in tundra habitats, and it often breeds before the ice has disappeared. Widely distributed in the N of the continent, and the only frog found N of the Arctic Circle. Range also extends S in E US, to SC.

GREEN FROG *Rana clamitans*   Total length 4in
Medium-sized, very variable coloring. Although usually green, can also be bronze or brownish. Extremely prominent eardrum, and ridges down its sides. The male's call is like the twang of the lowest string on a banjo when it breaks. Found in shallow water around ponds and lakes, in swamps and other shallow water. The range extends over most of E North America from NS to TX.

SPRING PEEPER *Hyla crucifer*   Total length 1½in
Small, with characteristic large toe pads, and a distinctive "X" mark on its back. Its noisy chorus, which sounds like jingling bells, is one of the best known sounds of spring. The male usually calls from inside or close to the breeding ponds, and the individual call is a birdlike "peep-peep." Found in ponds and swamps, usually in well-wooded areas. Abundant, and found over most of E North America.

GREEN TREE FROG *Hyla cinerea*   Total length 2½in
Small, bright green, often with a pale yellow or white stripe down the side, and large toe pads. Nocturnal, hiding among vegetation during the day, and hunting at night. The male's call is a "quonk-quonk," which from a distance sounds like cow-bells. Confined to E US, and found close to ponds, lakes, and swamps, usually surrounded by thick vegetation.

PACIFIC TREE FROG *Hyla regilla* Total length 2in

Lives close to water, often hiding among rocks, in rodent burrows, or thick vegetation. The male's call is a high-pitched "kreck-kek," and because the species is common in southern CA, is often heard as the background sound in movies filmed in this area. Confined to W North America from S BC to Baja CA, at altitudes of over 11,000ft in the S of its range.

COMMON (GRAY) TREE FROG *Hyla versicolor* Total length 2½in

There are actually two species of Gray Tree Frog: *H. versicolor* and *H. chrysoscelis* (Cope's Gray Tree Frog), which are almost identical in appearance. Skin of both is warty; usually gray, it can be greenish, pale brown, and have dark blotches. Both have high-pitched trills, but that of *H. versicolor* is slower. Found in trees, coming to ground level only to breed. Their ranges overlap extensively over most of E North America from S Canada to TX.

NORTHERN CHORUS FROG *Pseudacris triseriata* Total length 1¼in

A small tree frog without toe pads that is extremely difficult to see, although its chorus is a familiar sound. The call is like a fingernail clicking the teeth of a comb. Markings distinctive, with dark stripes on a pale background. There is always a stripe through the eye, but other stripes and blotches are variable. It has an extensive range over much of North America, extending N into the Northwest Territories of Canada, and S through the Great Plains to TX, and E to NJ.

GREAT PLAINS TOAD *Bufo cognatus* Total length 3½in

Easily distinguished from all other American toads by its pattern of paired, pale-edged dark blotches. The male has a high-pitched metallic call lasting up to 50 seconds. After heavy rain in spring or summer huge numbers often gather to breed in ditches, ponds, and even flooded fields. Found from extreme S of Canada to Mexico.

SOUTHERN TOAD *Bufo terrestris* Total length 3in

A relatively large, plump toad, variable in color but usually brown, reddish, or dark brown, with dark spotting, and sometimes a pale stripe down the back. The breeding call of the male is a loud, high-pitched trill. Breeds throughout the warmer months, often in temporary pools of water after rains. It is found in sandy areas, often excavating burrows. It also comes to suburban gardens to feed on insects attracted by porch and garden lights. Found in coastal E US from VA to FL and LA.

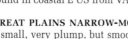

GREAT PLAINS NARROW-MOUTHED TOAD *Gastrophryne olivacea* Total length 1½in

A small, very plump, but smooth-skinned toad with a pointed snout, and a fold of skin across the back of its head. Rarely seen outside the breeding season, spending the day in burrows. It breeds soon after heavy rain during the summer months and the male's call is a faint, high-pitched buzz of up to 2½ seconds followed by a squeak. Found in deserts, grasslands, and woodland from NE S to Mexico.

EASTERN SPADEFOOT *Scaphiopus holbrooki* Total length 2¼in

Like other spadefoots, has a characteristic vertical pupil, giving it a catlike eye. Male's breeding call is a sharp, often repeated "quonk." The only spadefoot of E North America; four others found in W US. It is found in sandy habitats and floodplains from New England to TX. Range is in two distinct populations separated by the Mississippi floodplain.

AMERICAN TOAD *Bufo americanus* Total length 4½in

Warty skin with large paratoid glands behind the eye and over the eardrum. Nocturnal, emerging in the twilight, and often found in suburban gardens and parks as well as marshes and forests. The breeding call of the male is a long trill lasting up to ½ minute. One of the commonest toads of E North America.

WOODHOUSE'S TOAD *Bufo woodhousei* Total length 4in

Differs from the American Toad in having a pale stripe down the center of its back. The male's call is rather like a bleating sheep. Found in many habitats, including suburban gardens, woodland and desert arroyos, and close to beaches. Familiar species, often seen hunting insects attracted to porch lights. Range extends from N US to TX and Mexico.

LONG-TAILED SALAMANDER *Eurycea longicauda* Total length 7½in
Slender, tail longer than body. Coloring variable, ranging from bright orange or yellowish, with numerous blackish spots, stripes or barring. The female lays about 90 eggs in rock crevices close to water. Found in streams, springs, caves, and often in woodlands. Widespread over much of the E but absent from most of FL.

 TWO-LINED SALAMANDER *Eurycea bislineata* Total length 4½in
Slender, buff-brown with a broad yellowish stripe down the back bordered by a dark line from the eye to the tail. The female guards the cluster of eggs, which are laid under a stone in running water. Found alongside streams and swamps. It spends the day hiding under stones, bark, and logs, in or close to the water's edge. Common in E.

NORTHERN DUSKY SALAMANDER *Desmognathus fuscus* Total length 5½in
Yellowish brown with some dark spotting, and usually a darker line or spots extending down either side and along the tail. Has a characteristic pale line from the eye to the jaw. Nocturnal. The female lays a cluster of eggs under or on a log or stone, close to the water's edge. Common in its range, which extends from QC and NB S to LA. Absent from FL and most of GA and the Carolinas.

 TIGER SALAMANDER *Ambystoma tigrinum* Total length 13in
The world's largest land-dwelling salamander. Heavily built, with a smooth damp skin, blackish with pale spots, blotches, or bars. It is found close to ponds in woodlands, but also in pine savanna and sagebrush. Widespread from S Canada to Mexico, but absent from the W, and the NE, where it is replaced by related species.

 SPOTTED SALAMANDER *Ambystoma maculatum* Total length up to 10in
Similar to the Tiger Salamander, it is usually soft-skinned, blackish with yellow or orange-yellow spots. Breeds in winter in the S of its range and spring in the N, migrating to traditional breeding ponds that do not contain fish, which prey on salamanders. Found in deciduous forests and woodland. Distribution more north-easterly, found as far N as NS.

 BLUE-SPOTTED SALAMANDER *Ambystoma laterale* Total length 5in
Smooth, damp-skinned, with coloring reminiscent of the blue-gray flecking of old enamel pots. Breeds in ponds and ditches. Closely related to parthenogenetic species of mole salamander. One of the most northerly salamanders, found from the N shore of the Gulf of St Lawrence S to New England, with isolated populations as far S as Long Island.

 SLIMY SALAMANDER *Plethodon glutinosus* Total length 8in
Shiny black with whitish spots. The female lays her eggs in a burrow or under a log, and the fully metamorphosed young hatch in late summer to fall. Nocturnal. Active all the year round in the S of its range, but hibernates in the N. One of a group of at least 25 species confined to North America. Widespread over much of E US, N to New England.

ENSATINA SALAMANDER *Ensatina eschscholtzii* Total length 5½in
Easily distinguished from other salamanders by the narrow constriction at the base of its tail, which snaps if grasped by a predator, enabling it to escape. Pattern and coloring extremely variable, uniform brown, spotted, or barred. When disturbed it goes rigid and arches its tail. Found in forests at altitudes of 4,000–10,000ft along the W coast from BC to Baja CA.

RED-BACKED SALAMANDER *Plethodon cinereus* Total length 5in
Slender salamander. It is found in two color phases: the more widespread has a broad red-brown or yellow-brown stripe down the back, the other is uniform dark gray-black. Abundant, found in cool humid woodlands and forests from NS and ON, S to MO and SC. In W it is replaced by *P. vehiculum*.

RED SALAMANDER *Pseudotritin ruber* Total length 6in
Bright orange-red, with small black spots. Coloring mimics the poisonous terrestrial form of the Eastern Newt. Breeds in cold streams and springs. Found in damp woodlands and meadows at altitudes of up to 5,000ft. Range extends from NY to LA.

ROUGH-SKINNED NEWT *Taricha granulosa* Total length 8in
Black or dark brown above, with a yellow, orange, or red underside. When attacked, it curls the head backwards and the tail over the body, exposing the bright colors as a warning to predators that it is poisonous, with highly toxic skin secretions. The female lays eggs singly attached to vegetation under water. The most aquatic of the newts, found in or close to water, often near rainforests or wet meadows. The most widespread of the western newts, being found from southern AK, along the Pacific coast to central CA, at altitudes of up to 9,000ft.

EASTERN NEWT *Notophthalmus viridescens* Total length 3¼in
Unusual, starting life as an aquatic larva, then spending 2–3 years on land as an eft, before returning to water to breed, remaining in the water afterwards. The terrestrial eft is bright orange-red, with black-edged red spots which persist in the adult when the rest of the skin turns greenish or brownish. The coloring is a warning to potential predators that it has toxins in the skin. Range extends over most of the US E of the Rockies, and N to S Canada. In the SE of its range neotenous forms are common (in which the larval characters are retained), and the terrestrial stage does not occur.

MUDPUPPY *Necturus maculosus* Total length up to 18in or more
A large aquatic salamander with external gills (which the Hellbender lacks) and hind feet (which the sirens lack). Five external-gilled species are found in North America, and the Mudpuppy is the most widespread, being found over much of E US, but absent from the SE and most of the coastal plain. The female guards up to 180 eggs, laid under logs or stones, until they hatch.

HELLBENDER *Cryptobranchus alleganiensis* Total length usually less than 18in
One of the world's largest salamanders (its record length is reported to be 2ft 5in), related to the giant salamanders of Asia. Also known as the Water Dog or Allegheny Alligator, it is entirely aquatic, with a very flattened head and body. Brownish or olive with some blotches or mottling, and paler on the underside. Feeds on crayfish, mollusks, and other invertebrates, and the female lays up to 200 eggs in a mass of long strings, in a nest cavity under logs or stones, which the male guards. Found from southern NY to GA and AL, with some isolated populations.

DWARF SIREN *Pseudobranchus striatus* Total length 10in, usually less
The smallest of the sirens, it is thoroughly aquatic and retains external gills throughout its life. It has a long eel-like body, brownish with pale stripes, tiny forelegs with 3 toes, and no hind legs. The eggs are laid singly on water plants. It lives in ditches, swamps, and overgrown ponds; it is often abundant in waters that have been colonized by water hyacinth. Confined to SE US from SC to FL.

GREATER SIREN *Siren lacertina* Total length 3ft, usually less
A large eel-like salamander, completely aquatic, with external gills, and tiny forelegs with four toes. It is usually grayish or brownish, with yellowish markings on the back and sides, but can be almost black. Like other sirens it is mostly nocturnal, hiding by day, and emerging at night to feed on invertebrates, fish, and plants. It is found in shallow slow-moving rivers, muddy-bottomed lakes and ponds, and weed-choked ditches. When the ponds dry up it burrows into the mud and aestivates in a cocoon secreted by the skin glands. It is found in the coastal plain of E US from VA south to FL,

TENNESSEE CAVE SALAMANDER *Gyrinophilus palleucus* Total length up to 8½in
A neotenous species that retains its bright pink feathery gills as an adult. It is found in underground rivers and lakes in south TN and adjacent states. The limits of its range are poorly known and it is possible more than one species is involved.

PHOEBUS PARNASSIAN *Parnassius phoebus*   Wingspan 3in
A moderately large, attractive, white butterfly with two large white-centered red spots on each hindwing, and red and black markings on the forewing. The caterpillars feed on stonecrops, and overwinter to complete development the following year. It is found near mountain tops in the Rockies, and N through Canada to the Alaskan tundra.

GREAT SOUTHERN WHITE *Ascia monuste*   Wingspan 3in
A large white butterfly, with black tips to the forewings; female is grayer than male. It is found in coastal habitats from FL to TX, migrating N in summer, up the E coast and up the Mississippi Valley.

CLOUDED SULFUR *Colias philodice*   Wingspan 2in
Clear pale yellow with black edges to the wings; a small black spot on the forewing, and small orange spot on the hindwing. It is widespread over most of North America, in open grassy habitats. The caterpillars feed on white clover and other related species.

CLOUDLESS SULFUR *Phoebis sennae*   Wingspan 2in
The male has almost pure yellow wings; the female is yellow or white with some black spots around the edges and a black spot in the middle of the forewing. The caterpillars are yellow or pale green with narrow black bands, and feed on clovers and their relatives. Widespread over the US, particularly in the S.

ORANGE SULFUR *Colias eurytheme*   Wingspan 2in
A deep yellow with dark borders to the wings, an orange spot on the hindwing, and a black spot on the forewing. The caterpillar is dark green with white stripes on the sides, and feeds on alfalfa and clover, sometimes becoming a pest. It is widespread over North America, but rare in the N.

QUESTIONMARK *Polygonia interrogationis*   Wingspan 3in
Takes its name from a silvery comma and dot forming a question mark on the underside of the wing (some imagination is needed). The upperside is orange with black markings and with some violet on the edges. The caterpillars are striped with branched spines and they feed on elm, and hops. Widespread over SE Canada and E US, except S FL.

EASTERN COMMA *Polygonia comma*   Wingspan 2¼in
The commalike marking is on the underside of the wing. The caterpillars feed on nettles and hops, often rolling the leaves to help protect them. They can be a pest on hops. A widespread and often abundant butterfly in North America E of the Rockies.

GREAT SPANGLED FRITILLARY *Speyeria cybele*   Wingspan 3½in
A fast-flying butterfly of open meadows and woodlands. The adult feeds on nectar of thistles and milkweed. The caterpillars feed on violets, and are blackish with orange at the base of the spines. Found over much of the US and S Canada.

PEARL CRESCENT *Phyciodes tharos*   Wingspan 1in
The caterpillars are dark brown with yellow bands and brown tubercles; they feed on asters, stripping the leaves and leaving a skeleton. Often seen on disturbed ground, farmland, and meadows. A common butterfly over most of North America.

MONARCH *Danaus plexippus*   Wingspan 4in
A very large butterfly. The caterpillars are banded black, yellow, and white, and are poisonous to most birds and other predators. Widespread, found wherever milkweed grows. Successive broods migrate N during the summer, and in winter they migrate to S US and Mexico to hibernate in huge agglomerations, numbering millions.

AMERICAN COPPER *Lycaena phlaeas*   Wingspan 1in
A small butterfly with bright orange on the wings. The caterpillar, which is short-bodied and bright green, feeds on sheep sorrel, usually hiding on the underside of the leaves. Most common in and around disturbed habitats, including farmland. Found over much of E US.

VICEROY *Limenitis archippus*   Wingspan 3in
A large butterfly which mimics the Monarch, but has thicker black veins. The caterpillar mimics a bird-dropping on a leaf, and feeds on willows and their relatives. The male's flight is slow, with gliding interspersed with wing flaps. Widespread over most of North America from NT to Mexico.

QUEEN *Danaus gilippus*   Wingspan 3½in
Superficially similar to the Monarch. It has white spots and no obvious black veins on the wings from above. Caterpillars and adults feed on poisonous milkweeds, and are poisonous to most predators. Has a more southerly distribution than the Monarch but is not migratory, though it does move N during summer.

PAINTED LADY *Vanessa cardui*   Wingspan 2in
The caterpillars have a greenish yellow body and generally feed on thistles, but also burdock and knapweeds. Although widespread over North America, the species may be a recent colonist which arrived with the Europeans.

AMERICAN PAINTED LADY *Vanessa virginiensis*   Wingspan 2in
An orange-brown butterfly with brown markings, and two blue spots on the rear wings.The black caterpillars are banded with yellow and have black spines. They feed on cudweed and related plants. Widespread over much of North America.

PURPLISH COPPER *Lycaena helloides*   Wingspan 1in
A small orange-brown butterfly; the male has a purple sheen and bright orange markings on the hindwing. The caterpillar is green with yellow strips and feeds on docks. Widespread in North America, but absent from the S and E US.

AMERICAN SNOUT *Libytheana carinenta*   Wingspan 2in
Has a distinctive long snout, and the forewings appear to be cut off. The adult often feeds on rotting fruit. It is found in E US, usually close to hackberry trees, which are the food of the dark green, yellow-striped caterpillars.

MORMON METALMARK *Apodemia mormo*   Wingspan 1in
A small butterfly speckled with bright orange, white, and dark brown. The caterpillars, which are purplish, feed on buckwheat. Found mostly in the Rockies, in arid habitats.

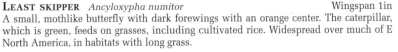

LEAST SKIPPER *Ancyloxypha numitor* Wingspan 1in
A small, mothlike butterfly with dark forewings with an orange center. The caterpillar, which is green, feeds on grasses, including cultivated rice. Widespread over much of E North America, in habitats with long grass.

LONG-TAILED SKIPPER *Urbanus proteus* Wingspan 2in
The body is green, contrasting with brown wings and forked "tail," which trails. The underside is gray-brown. The caterpillar feeds on beans and their relatives and is sometimes a pest of agriculture (known as the Bean Leaf Roller). It is common in the southern US, rarer in the N.

CORAL HAIRSTREAK *Satyrium titus* Wingspan 1in
A dark butterfly with orange spots along the edge of the hindwing. The male attacks other males. The caterpillars feed on wild cherries and plums and are tended by ants. They are widespread but nowhere common.

BROWN ELFIN *Callophrys augustinus* Wingspan 1in
A small brown butterfly. Caterpillars feed on blueberries and azaleas, eating both vegetation and fruits. Found in woodlands and pine barrens. Widespread over North America from AK to TX, absent from the Great Plains.

LITTLE WOOD-SATYR *Megisto cymela* Wingspan 2in
A round-winged sandy-brown butterfly, with two white-edged black spots on each wing; similar on the underside. The caterpillar has a white forked tail and feeds on grasses. Confined to E US, and extreme SE Canada.

COMMON WOOD-NYMPH *Cercyonis pegala* Wingspan 3in
Grayish brown with sandy-brown patches on the forewing and prominent white-centered black wing spots. The caterpillar is greenish with short yellow hairs and has a reddish forked tail; it feeds on grasses. Widespread over most of Canada and US except parts of S and S FL.

COMMON BUCKEYE *Junonia coenia* Wingspan 2in
Inconspicuous with closed wings, but when they open, the eyed appearance is startling. There are two broods; the second, which overwinters, is larger and dull red on the underwing. The caterpillars feed on foxgloves, plantains, toadflax, and other plants. Resident in the southern states of the US, migrating N in summer.

RED ADMIRAL *Vanessa atalanta* Wingspan 2in
An easily identified butterfly, dark with bright red bands and white spots. The caterpillars live in groups, and curl the leaves of their food plants, which include nettles and hops. Summer migrant over most of US and Canada. Resident in SE from TX to Vancouver.

RED-SPOTTED ADMIRAL *Limenitis arthemis*   Wingspan 3in
A large, dark butterfly with broad white bands on the wings. The caterpillar is hump-backed with spines, and feeds on willows and birches. Confined to E North America, usually around woodlands.

ZEBRA *Eurytides marcellus*   Wingspan 3in
A large, attractive butterfly with contrasting black and white stripes, and long "tails." Its flight is fast and swooping. The adults often gather around puddles or stream edges to drink. Confined to the SE of the US, close to pawpaw plants on which the large green caterpillars feed.

ZEBRA HELICONIAN *Heliconius charitonius*   Wingspan 3in
An elegant, large butterfly with unmistakable wide wings, black with yellow bands. Caterpillars are white with long black spines. Caterpillars feed on poisonous passion flowers, and retain the poisons to protect them from predators. Found in the S US.

BLACK SWALLOWTAIL *Papilio polyxenes*   Wingspan 3in
A large, dark swallowtail, with two rows of creamy yellow spots, as well as blue and red spots. The caterpillars are green with yellow-spotted blackish bands; they feed on carrots, parsnips, and their relatives, and can be a pest. Widespread and often common in SE US, less common to the N.

SPICEBUSH SWALLOWTAIL *Papilio trolius*   Wingspan 4in
A large, dark swallowtail. Like other swallowtails, the adults are fast-flying. The caterpillar is green with an enlarged front end, with two eye spots. It is nocturnal, feeding on sassafras and spice bushes. Found in E US.

EASTERN TIGER SWALLOWTAIL *Papilio glaucus*   Wingspan 5in
A spectacular large butterfly. Although normally yellow with black markings, and red spots on the edge of the hindwing, some females, particularly in the SE of their range, are bluish black. The caterpillars feed on tree leaves, such as cherry and willow, and are often found in city parks. Common in the E of US and Canada, rarer elsewhere.

ICARIOIDES BLUE *Icaricia icarioides*   Wingspan 1¼in
A small, lilac blue dark bordered butterfly (male). The female is normally browner. They feed on lupine species and are tended by ants. Found in forest clearings, dunes, praries and fields. Widespread in W N America but some localised sub-species critically endangered.

MELISSA BLUE *Lycaeides melissa*   Wingspan 1in
The male is pale blue, the female more like copper, with orange-edged brown wings. The caterpillars feed mainly on lupins and their relatives, and are tended by ants. Found mostly in W North America in dry grassy areas, and threatened in many parts of the eastern limits of the range.

EASTERN TAILED-BLUE *Everes comyntas*   Wingspan 1in
A small blue butterfly with short, thin "tails" on the hindwings; the female is grayer. The caterpillars feed on clovers and their relatives. They often gather in groups around puddles. Found in a wide range of habitats over most of the US and SE Canada.

GRAY HAIRSTREAK *Strymon melinus*   Wingspan 1in
A delicate, pale gray butterfly, with red markings and short "tails" on the hindwings. The caterpillar feeds on flowers and fruits of a wide range of plants including beans and cotton. Often found along roadsides and other disturbed habitats, and widely distributed throughout North America.

LUNA MOTH *Actias luna*   Wingspan 3¾in
The Luna Moth is one of the large nocturnal moths called Saturnids. There are yellow eyespots on the fore- and hindwings; large, dark featherlike antennae; long "tails" on the hindwings and a dark brown leading edge to the forewing. Widely distributed in E North America.

POLYPHEMUS MOTH *Antheraea polyphemus*   Wingspan 6in
Like the Luna this large nocturnal moth does not feed as an adult. Has large yellow eyespots on the fore- and hind wings, the hindwing spot incased in black on yellow-brown wings; has large, dark feathery antennae. Found throughout North America.

REGAL MOTH *Citheronia regalis*   Wingspan 5in
The Regal Moth is the largest of the royal moths. It is a spectacularly beautiful moth with reddish wings with yellow spots, and a large red and yellow body; small antennae. Adults feed on the leaves of nut trees. Spines on the caterpillars can irritate the skin. It is found in E North America.

WHITE-LINED SPHINX *Cilerio lineata*   Wingspan 3½in
Sphinx moths have a characteristic birdlike shape with long, narrow wings and a large body. The long proboscis is used to suck nectar from flowers. Sometimes mistaken for hummingbirds, sphinx moths are abundant and broadly distributed throughout S Canada and North America, with more than 100 species.

CABBAGE LOOPER *Trichoplusia ni*   Wingspan 1¼in
The Cabbage Looper is one of a very large family of moths found throughout S Canada and North America. They are generally small and brown or gray in color. The larvae move like inchworms. The larvae of some species are major commercial pests and gardeners are familiar with these as cutworms.

EASTERN TENT CATERPILLAR *Malacosoma americanum*   Total length ⅝in
Tent caterpillars are familiar to most everyone from S Canada and throughout the US. Adults lay their eggs in large, silken tents created by many adults to act as communal nurseries. Caterpillars feed at night and retreat to the safety of the tent during the day. Although there are relatively few species (about 35) in the family, they are common and well distributed.

GYPSY MOTH *Porthetria dispar*   Wingspan 1½–1¾in
The Gypsy Moth was accidentally introduced into North America in MA and has since spread to become a major pest on ornamental trees throughout NE North America. At the peak of its abundance cycle, the caterpillars are everywhere: on cars, on screens, in gutters and driveways. In the forest you can actually hear them feeding as a rain of detritus falls to the forest floor. The eggs are covered with a brown, silken cocoon to overwinter.

TUSSOCK MOTH *Hemerocampa plagiata*   Wingspan 1in
Like gypsy moths, these moths can do serious damage to commercial forests and ornamental trees. Tussock moths are named because of hairlike protrusions on the back of the caterpillar that can be irritating to the skin when handled. The moths are generally medium-sized to small with mottled gray, brown and black coloration. Widely distributed in S Canada and the US.

EBONY JEWELWING *Calopteryx maculata* — Total length up to 2in
One of the easiest damselflies to identify, with its iridescent bright green body and black wings. Has fluttery flight compared to darters. Found over small streams and brooks; prefers moving water. One of five species of blackwing damsels in North America. Common from S Canada to FL and W to TX.

CIVIL BLUET *Enallagma civile* — Total length up to 1¼in
Head, thorax and abdomen blue with black on top. Wings clear. Slender species. Lives along sandy shores of clear lakes and ponds. One of a large family of damsels and one of the most widespread and common of the North American species.

NORTHERN BLUET *Enallagma cyathigerum* — Total length up to 1¼in
Wings clear. More robust than Civil Bluet, but similarly colored bright blue with black on the top, increasing to the rear. Flies low and well; prefers still waters of ponds, swamps and bogs. Often abundant in the spring. Widely distributed throughout North America from AK south.

COMMON GREEN DARTER *Axas junius* — Total length up to 3¼in
One of the most vibrant and largest of the easily seen dragonflies. Abdomen bright blue with black on top, including the tail tip. Thorax and head bright green; wings clear. Common on shorelines of ponds and lakes with significant vegetation. Strong flyer and active mosquito predator. Larvae are aquatic, themselves voracious predators. Found throughout North America from AK to Mexico.

COMMON WHITETAIL *Libellula lydia* — Total length 1¾in
This easily identified dragonfly is unmistakable with a bright, white abdomen, brown head and thorax and wings with large dark bands ⅔ of the way out on fore- and hindwings. Wanders widely and can be encountered in almost any habitat; strongly territorial and chases off other species. Common over ponds, rivers, and streams throughout the US from Canada to Mexico.

WESTERN WIDOW *Libellula forensis* — Total length 1¾in
The western counterpart of the Whitetail, but the abdomen is more of a blue-white. Fore- and hindwings have large black bands with black at the bases. Highly territorial and aggressive, this species defends its ponds and still-water habitats against other dragonflies of the same and other species. Found from W Canada, S to Mexico.

BIDDIE *Cordulegaster dorsalis* — Total length 1¾in
This brightly colored western species is one of the most easily identifiable inland. Both fore- and hindwings are clear, thorax and abdomen are black with bright yellow spots on top. Flies slowly and wanders, rather than flying in a straight line. Prefers stream habitats where it patrols territory and hunts for insects. Common in the US from AK to CA.

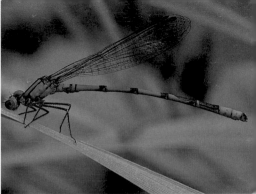
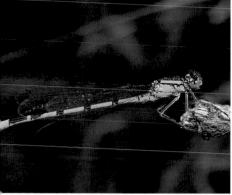

INSECTS • BEETLES

NUTTALL BLISTER BEETLE *Lytta nuttalli* Total length ¾in
Blister beetles have a rectangular head from above (i.e. wider than the neck or pronotum), and a long and slender abdomen. There are more than 300 species. Generally they are dark, but this species is an iridescent blue-green. When caught, these beetles can exude a liquid toxin that can cause the skin to blister. Sometimes a commercial pest, from Canada to Mexico.

AMERICAN STAG BEETLE *Lucanus elephus* Total length 2in
A spectacular scarab beetle; black with enormous jaws. Adult male is over 2in long; female is smaller and without the characteristic large jaws. The head shape is distinct, with the neck and prothorax forming a hood over the head. Found in SE of US, this remarkable animal is always a great find.

DINGY GROUND BEETLE *Harpalus* sp. Total length to 1in
Uniform black or dark in color. Has threadlike antennae and lines that seem to be sculpted into the upper wing covers. Generally oval in shape, can grow to be 1in long. Nocturnal and attracted to lights. Common and widely distributed.

EYED CLICK BEETLE *Alaus oculatus* Total length 1½in
This spectacular beetle has two large black spots surrounded by yellow on its pronotum, and has speckled gray upper wing covers. Click beetles are so named because adults can arch their back and snap themselves up into the air when they are placed or fall on their backs, a performance that is often accompanied by a loud, snapping sound. This is the largest North American species, and is found in E North America.

TENLINED JUNE BEETLE *Polyphylla decemlineata* Total length 1¼in
There are more than 1500 species of scarab beetle in North America, of which around 500 are in the June beetle group. They are identified by their large, clubbed antennae, large size (up to 1½in), and stripes on the elytra. Larvae live in the ground and feed on roots and tubers. Commonly seen at night on screen doors and around lights. Formerly more abundant; adversely affected by pesticides. It is now found in central and SW US.

TIGER BEETLE *Megacephala carolina* Total length ¾in
Tiger beetles are solitary, fast-moving, aggressive, and aware beetles that hunt other insects. Many species are spectacularly iridescent blue or green, with or without spots. They pounce on prey, can move rapidly, and are very difficult to catch. They are found in open, sandy areas on the ground where they run and hunt by day. They have a characteristic habit of facing danger, in particular, beetle collectors. They are found throughout North America.

JAPANESE BEETLE *Popilla japonica* Total length ½in
Generally oval in shape, and an iridescent green or brown in color, with very strong hooks on its legs. This may be one of the most familiar garden insect pests in North America. It feeds on a wide variety of plants, eating leaves, flowers, and fruit. It is particularly damaging to roses, but also attacks grape arbors and other commercially valuable species. It can become super-abundant, so that shaking a rose bush can set hundreds of the beetles into flight. It is trapped in gardens in bags set with female pheromones. It is found throughout North America.

CALIFORNIA LADY BEETLE *Coccinella californica*   Total length ¼in
The ladybird beetles are small, round to oval in shape, and often red in color with black spots. They eat aphids and are considered to be one of the most beneficial groups of abundant beetles throughout North America. The California Lady Beetle is unspotted, with a black head and red elytra. The beetles often hibernate in groups and can be found in the corners of door frames, window sashes, and any other protected places. It is found in W US.

TWO-SPOTTED LADY BEETLE *Adalia bipunctata*   Total length ¼in
Like the California Lady Beetle but slightly smaller and with one large black spot on each elytra. Some species in this group are black with red spots, reversing the common pattern. Feeds on aphids and scale insects; beneficial and welcomed in gardens. Can be abundant, and is found throughout North America.

SOUTHERN PINE SAWYER *Monochamus titillator*   Total length 1in
Gray in color with mottling; antennae longer than body length; spectacular looking and always a great find. However, the Southern Pine Sawyer is a major pest of coniferous pine plantations. Larvae bore into the bark and mine through heartwood, affecting the marketability and strength of the lumber. Pine sawyers can propagate with incredible speed to take advantage of natural disasters affecting forests. Adults feed on needles and other growing parts of the trees. It is found in SE US.

BOLL WEEVIL *Anthonomus grandis*   Total length ¼in
The Boll Weevil is perhaps the best known small snout weevil in North America and is a notorious pest of cotton crops. Attacking the flowers, the weevils prevent the formation of seeds and thus of cotton. Arriving in the US just under 100 years ago, the Boll Weevil spread throughout TX and the American South with the introduction of cotton farming. Many other weevil species are pests of fruit and nut trees.

FLAT-HEADED BORER *Buprestis gibbsi*   Total length ¾in
The wood-boring beetles are large, colorful, flattened beetles that live under the bark of many commercially important trees. The Flat-headed Borer is a large species that attacks oaks. Iridescent and much sought by beetle collectors, this borer is yellow and black. The elytra have a sculptured appearance with deep lines running toward the back. It is found in SE US.

LIGHTNING BUG *Photuris pennsylvanica*   Total length ¾in
The Lightening Bug (also called Firefly) is one of the most delightful and familiar insects of suburbs and countryside. It is easily distinguished in the hand by the pronotum, which is shaped as a large half circle and covers the head and mouthparts when viewed from above. The elytra and abdomen are soft compared with most beetles. Light is produced by a chemical process; these light flashes are important for courtship and sex recognition. The Lightning Bug is neither a bug nor a fly, but a beetle, and is found mostly in E US.

BLOODSUCKING CONENOSE *Triatoma sanguisuga*   Total length 1in
The Bloodsucking Conenose is a species of assassin bug. While most species are black or dark green, the Bloodsucking Conenose has orange on the abdomen. Assassin bugs are distinguished by thick front legs and a protruding head; the abdomen extends sideways and is not fully covered by the wings. They are, as the name implies, significant predators on other insects. Widespread in North America. Found in SE of US, W to TX.

SOUTHERN GREEN STINK BUG *Nazara viridula*   Total length 1in
Stink bugs are shield-shaped with the elytra only partially covering the underwings. A triangular, central piece of carapace, the scutellum, points backward. Usually uniformly colored green or brown, stink bugs also have bright colors. They produce a musky liquid when handled. Often seen sitting on leaves raised up on their front legs; wary and alert. Widely distributed throughout North America.

FORK-TAILED BUSH KATYDID *Scudderia furcata* Total length up to 2in
Bush katydids have well-developed, transparent wings which are twice as long as the abdomen. They are usually green and large. Antennae are as long as the wings, as are the hind legs which, when stretched out, go well beyond the tip of the wings. Songs are loud and important for sex recognition at breeding. Common in trees, bushes, and weed patches throughout North America.

HORSE LUBBER *Taeniopoda eques* Total length 2¼in
A heavy-bodied grasshopper, striking black with yellow markings on the face and body. The forewings are black edged in yellow and the hindwings red with black borders. A short-horned grasshopper, with antennae that are not much longer than the length of its head. A spectacular species found in dry areas of the SW. A similar species is found in the American SE.

DIFFERENTIAL GRASSHOPPER *Melanoplus differentialis* Total length 1½in
Brown to green, with short antennae no more than one-third of the body length, and strong jumping legs with black bands. A capable singer, it uses its wings and legs for sound. Can be a major pest species, eating more than ten times its weight each day. May be the most abundant and widely known grasshopper in North America, and is found throughout the continent.

MEADOW GRASSHOPPER *Conacephalus brevipennis* Total length 1in
Meadow grasshoppers, like bush katydids, are characterized by very long antennae, but have very short wings that do not extend beyond the abdomen. They are generally small and green with very long rear legs. The song is high-pitched and buzzy. The Meadow Grasshopper, as the name implies, prefers wet meadows and damp, marshy grasses. It is a common and widely distributed species.

CALIFORNIA MANTIS *Stagmomantis californica* Total length 1½in
Green in color and absolutely distinctive. Often called Praying Mantis because the well-developed front legs are held like arms in prayer. With them, the mantis catches and holds its prey, which it eats immediately. Praying mantis are ambush feeders and very effective at killing and eating grasshoppers and other garden pests; they are for sale commercially through some garden outlets. Their natural habitat is low vegetation, and gardens are ideal places to find this. They are found from S Canada to Mexico.

NORTHERN MOLE CRICKET *Gryllotalpa hexadactyla* Total length 1½in
The Mole Cricket is unmistakable with its large, bulbous head, heavy body, spadelike front legs, and many body hairs. As the name implies, it is subterranean, burrowing into moist earth and feeding on plant and animal material. Seldom seen, it is nonetheless widely distributed and common in places.

SNOWY TREE CRICKET *Oecanthus fultoni* Total length ¾in
A small, brown cricket with a strong characteristic song that reveals its presence even though it is somewhat reclusive and hides in bushes from its numerous predators. Usually dark brown with long antennae, longer than its body length, including the extended ovipositors. It is found in S Canada and throughout the US.

FIELD CRICKET *Gryllus assimilis* Total length 1in
The Field Cricket is distinguished from other crickets by having a light-colored head with dark markings. Wings clear except for a rectangular spot on fore- and hindwings. One of the most vocal species, singing any time of day, particularly from dark areas. The most common and widely distributed cricket that is found closely associated with people, often coming into houses and basements.

AMERICAN COCKROACH *Periplaneta americana*   Total length 2in
The American Cockroach is twice as big as the Oriental Cockroach. Antennae are half again the body length, and sensitive. Light brown in color. Native to the American South. Cockroaches are abundant in wild habitat throughout the S. Only a few species enter homes, where they become pests.

WALKING STICK *Diapheromera femorata*   Total length 4in or more
The Walking Stick is very large, and flightless throughout its life. Shaped like a long tube, it resembles a twig, and is found on bushes and trees where it feeds on plants. Some tropical species are a foot long, and camouflaged gray or brown. Difficult to see, but can be quite common. Attracted to nightlights placed in the forest. Found in S US.

EUROPEAN MANTIS *Mantis religiosa*   Total length 3½in
Introduced from Europe, this predator is green or brown, like other mantis, and has highly modified front legs for catching and holding prey. An ambush hunter with excellent vision, and a strong flyer whose wing spread is 4–5in. The most abundant mantis throughout the N US, and the one seen most commonly in gardens.

EUROPEAN EARWIG *Forficula auricularia*   Total length ¾in
The large, spinelike protrusions from its abdomen and the lack of wings make this species easily recognizable. Although it has wings, it is functionally flightless and lives under rocks in cracks and in damp soil. Nocturnal, and feeds on a wide variety of plants. Sometimes it is a pest in flower gardens. Cosmopolitan in distribution and probably introduced into the US early in the last century.

ANT LION *Brachynemurus ferox*   Total length 1½in
The Ant Lion is a weak-flying, damselflylike adult with flimsy, transparent wings. As a larva it is a large-jawed, highly predacious killer of ants and other insects that fall down the cone-shaped depression that it makes. Larvae feed on the body fluids of victims. Although seldom seen, larvae can be dug out. Found throughout Canada to Mexico wherever soil conditions allow pit formation.

GREEN LACEWING *Chrysopa carnea*   Total length ¾in
The Green Lacewing is related to the Ant Lion, but the adult lacewing is a far better flyer and a highly attractive species. The wings are transparent and the veins obvious. Wings are folded over the abdomen. Abundant, and attracted to lights in open areas throughout North America.

PREDACIOUS DIVING BEETLE *Dytiscus harrisi*   Total length 1¼in
Generally black with some brown, predacious diving beetles are large aquatic predators that eat a variety of aquatic insects and invertebrates. The largest species can take even small fish. Predacious diving beetles are generally found in permanent water bodies, where they overwinter. Adults are attracted to lights at night and this is where they are most readily seen. Broadly distributed across the continent.

WHIRLIGIG BEETLE *Gyrinus limbatus*   Total length ¼in
Seen on permanent water, where it swims rapidly in circles, supported on the surface film. It feeds on dead plants and animals, and kills minute aquatic organisms as needed. A good flyer, readily colonizing new habitat. Compound eyes allow it to see both under and above water simultaneously. It is confined to E US.

WATER BOATMAN *Notonecta undulata*   Total length ½in
The last pair of legs is modified with long hairs to act as oars, allowing it to swim rapidly with long strokes. Feeds on aquatic invertebrates and vegetation. Common in still water or ponds, slow streams, and near weedy vegetation. Widely distributed in North America. The closely related Back Swimmer bites, and is larger.

GIANT WATER BUG *Belostoma flumineum*   Total length 2in
The largest aquatic bug. A voracious predator, it can inflict a painful bite. Like Praying Mantis, its front legs catch and hold prey including small fish. It can fly, and is attracted to lights at night, where it is most readily seen. Relatively common in permanent ponds or pools.

SEVENTEEN-YEAR CICADA *Magicicada* sp.   Total length 1¼in
Spends 13–17 years as a larva underground before climbing a tree, truck, or bush and changing into adult. Wings are strong and clear. Red legs, eyes, and wing veins. Male sings a very loud buzzy song familiar to anyone who has lived in the S or SE. Discarded exoskeletons of the larvae can be seen gripping tree trunks. Range primarily E US.

REDBANDED LEAFHOPPER *Graphocephala coccinea*   Total length ¼in
Basically yellow or green body with green and red bands across wings and thorax. Feeds on sap of plants and flowers. Some species are garden pests. Leafhoppers discharge through the anus a liquid containing sugar, called honeydew, which ants and other insects utilize. A small, common insect of gardens and roadsides throughout North America.

WATER STRIDER *Gerris remigis*   Total length ¾in
Brown, long and cylindrical in shape; first pair of legs small, next two long. Water striders are among the most well known aquatic insects, readily visible skating on a cushion of air under their feet across the surface of pools, ponds, and permanent water bodies. Predacious, feeds on insects. Found throughout North America.

CRANE FLY *Tipula illustris*   Total length 1in
Crane flies are large, long-legged brown flies that look like gigantic mosquitoes. Larvae are aquatic and feed on invertebrates and vegetative matter. Adults do not bite or draw blood like mosquitoes; generally poorly known. This species is found in the Pacific NW, but other species are broadly distributed from Canada to Mexico.

YELLOW JACKET *Vespuda maculifrons*   Total length ¾in
Black with yellow bands on the thorax and abdomen, this familiar wasp holds its wings along its sides rather than across the back. Can sting repeatedly without losing its stinger. They are called "paper wasps," because hives are made from chewed material; they are attached to eaves of houses and sheltered places. Broadly distributed throughout North America.

MUD-DAUBER *Sceliphron* sp.   Total length 1in
Distinguished from Yellow Jacket by short neck or pronotum, and wings that fold across the back not along the sides. Nests are of fine mud lined with either insects, pollen or nectar, depending on species, to feed young. Some nest in sand, in the ground, or in natural cavities. Major predators of insects, spiders, and invertebrates. Common throughout North America, with different species inhabiting different areas.

PAPER WASP *Popistes exclamans*   Total length 1in
Generally black with few obvious markings. A fierce stinger, and needs to be treated with caution. Six-sided paper cells are created in small open nests; each cell containing a larval wasp. Often nests are attached to porches, in light fixtures, under eaves, and in other human structures. Most common in the W, but some found throughout the country.

EUROPEAN HONEYBEE *Apus mellifera*   Total length ¾in
The honeybee was introduced from Germany as part of the introduction of many agricultural plants and animals to provide food for colonists. German bees are tractable and centuries of cultivation have made them perfect for raising honey. Care needs to be taken since they can become alarmed and sting. In TX and some parts of the SW, German honeybees are crossbreeding with African bees and becoming more aggressive. In addition, African bees seem to be invading and colonizing parts of the US.

BUMBLEBEE *Megabombus pennsylvanicus*   Total length 1in
Bumblebees are large, hairy, black and yellow bees. They nest in the ground or in a natural crevice; some species are solitary but most are colonial. Bumblebees can sting, but generally are not aggressive. They feed on pollen and its products. Commonly seen in flower gardens throughout North America.

SALTMARSH MOSQUITO *Aedes taeniorhynchus*   Total length ½in
A serious pest and a major vector of diseases. Has a painful, itching bite. Larvae are aquatic and are a major food source for other coastal aquatic insects, fish, and birds. They are found in tidal pools, brackish marshes, and saltwater ponds. Abundant and widely distributed. Controls included ditching and drainage of most of the tidal marshes of the E.

HOUSE FLY *Musca domestica*   Total length ½in
Black with blue-tinted wings; long hairs cover much of the body. Found everywhere, House Flies may act as vectors for disease with bacteria clinging to the numerous body hairs. Does not bite, but feeds on vegetative and animal matter, any debris, or exposed food. Part of a large family of flies common throughout the continent. Found in all of North America.

FIRE ANT *Solenopsis xyloni*   Total length less than ⅛in
Red in color and inflicts a painful bite. Fire ants live in enormous colonies and scavenge for plants and animals; they have become a major predator of ground-nesting birds and even small mammals. They are invasive into the US, having spread from TX and FL across most of the S. Control has been unsuccessful.

BLACK WIDOW *Latrodectus mactans*   Total length up to ⅜in
One of several poisonous cobweb weavers. Often in human habitation. Characterized by black with red markings on the abdomen. A similar species is common in BC in woods and protected places, but that species has red spots on the abdomen rather than the characteristic "hourglass" of the Black Widow. It is found throughout the US, N to Oregon and New York.

 BROWN RECLUSE *Loxosceles reclusa*   Total length over ½in
Large, heavy body. Long-lived, particularly the female; a ground-dweller in holes or among rocks. Mygalomorphs are active nocturnal predators of other insects and other invertebrates; may even take small reptiles. Rears on hind legs when threatened. It is found in E and S US.

 ARIZONA HAIRY MYGALOMORPH *Aphonopelma chalcodes*   Total length over 2½in
This large tarantula has hairy legs and a large, heavy body. Mygalomorphs are active nocturnal predators of insects, invertebrates, or even small reptiles. They rear on their hind legs when threatened. This species is long-lived, particularly the females, and is a ground dweller in holes or among rocks on rubble hillsides. It is found in the deserts of the SW US.

 AMERICAN HOUSE SPIDER *Achaearanea tepidariorum*   Total length less than ½in
Mottled yellow and brown with large, swollen abdomen. House spiders create a web of irregular threads of sticky silk to entangle insects that fly or stumble into them. They are cobweb weavers and feed on the juices of caught insects. Often in human habitations. Worldwide family.

 BLACK AND YELLOW ARGIOPE *Argiope aurantia*   Total length 1in
One of the most spectacular of all North American spiders. The abdomen is striking, black with golden blotches, and the head is silvery; legs are black and yellow. Found regularly in gardens from S Canada to Mexico. It is a lucky gardener that has this beneficial animal in his garden.

 SILVER ARGIOPE *Argiope argentata*   Total length 1in
Body mostly silver with black, brown, and white on the abdomen. Like its relatives, it holds its legs together in pairs so that it appears to have 4 legs when, in fact, there are 8. Creates spectacular large webs 2ft across. A tropical species found in FL. These spiders are part of a family called orb weavers, which is abundant worldwide.

 ARROWSHAPED MICROTHENA *Microthena sagittata*   Total length less than ½in
The Arrowshaped Microthena is also an orb weaver, but this species and its many tropical relatives are small, and look like hard colorful thorns. Microthenas make large and complicated geometric webs in tropical gardens, where these miniature predators catch and kill insects.

WOLF SPIDER *Lycosa lenta*   Total length up to 1in
Large, and generally light and dark brown in color. Wolf spiders eat other insects, pouncing and killing them within their legs. Females carry the egg sacs with them until the young are born. The young ride the mother's abdomen through at least the first molt. Common from S Canada to Mexico.

DOG TICK *Rhipicesphalus sanguineus*   Total length less than ¼in
The Dog Tick is a mottled reddish brown with black. It is not usually attracted to people (unlike its close relative the Wood Tick).Ticks are the largest relatives of mites. They are widespread in grass and brush, and may be vectors of diseases such as Rocky Mountain Spotted Fever.

DEER TICK *Ixodes damani*   Total length ⅟₁₆in
The Deer Tick is a distinctive red and dark brown, and is now recognized as a dangerous vector for Lyme's Disease. It goes through an intermediate host, usually a mouse, before reaching deer or people. Tick bites should be reported to a doctor and, in removing a tick, all mouthparts must be removed to minimize infection. The species has spread in the E and Midwest.

SWOLLEN-STINGER SCORPION *Anuroctorus phaeodactylus*   Total length to 2½in
Scorpions are among the most easily recognized of arthropods. Characterized by large pinchers for the front legs, and an abdomen that bends to the side or up and over the back, ending with a terminal stinger. Body color is sandy to black. Scorpion bites are painful but seldom life-threatening. Nocturnal, hiding by day in crevices, under rocks, or in litter. Widely distributed in the American SW.

CHIGGER (HARVEST MITE) *Trombicula* sp.   Total length ⅟₁₀₀in
Mites are parasites or blood predators usually too small to see with the naked eye. They burrow into the skin, feeding on blood and body fluids before dropping off. Bites itch, and scratching them can lead to secondary infection. Attracted to tight areas such as around the belt or the tops of socks. Found in S US.

ARIZONA CENTIPEDE *Scolopendra heros*   Total length under 2in
Centipedes are long, flat arthropods with one pair of long legs per segment. "Centipede" implies that they have 100 legs, but most species have between 30 and 50 pairs. They are fast, active predators that bite to kill prey. The bite is also painful to people. They can roll into a defensive ball, but usually run to hide in leaf litter. They are found in SW US including AZ.

AMERICAN MILLIPEDE *Narceus americanus*   Total length up to 5in
Millipedes have long, cylindrical bodies and short legs. They have over 100 pairs of legs, but not 1,000 as the name implies. They move more deliberately and slowly than centipedes, and are vegetarians rather than active predators. Found from S Canada to Mexico.

PILLBUG *Glomeris* sp.   Total length up to ½in
The Pillbug is actually a very short relative of the millipede, usually with a dozen or fewer segments and pairs of legs. Generally brown, but varies by species. It can curl into a tight ball when threatened. Pillbugs are found in damp areas such as in leaf litter or under rotting bark.

SILVERFISH *Thermobia domestica*   Total length 1¼in
A soft-bodied, wingless, primitive insect with long antennae and long tails from its abdomen. A nocturnal scavenger, feeding on a wide variety of materials including paper and glues used in book bindings. Clearly adaptable, and unchanged for millions of years. Often found in damp situations in homes and basements.

BREADCRUMB SPONGE *Halichondria panicea*   Diameter over 12in
An encrusting sponge, which forms on a hard surface such as a rock and spreads, covering the rock with an irregular shape. Usually light green or yellow, breaks apart like a slice of dry bread when handled. A large colony can cover an area of up to 2 sq. ft. Breadcrumb sponges are found from the intertidal zone to deep water on both coasts.

BORING SPONGE *Cliona celata*   Diameter up to 12in
This unique yellow sponge and its relatives secrete chemicals that dissolve shell or rock, allowing the sponge to fill the space. Bores into shells, rocks, and crevices with much of the sponge material hidden below the surface. Individual colonies may reach 1ft in diameter. Found from intertidal zone to deep water. Occurs worldwide, and found on both North American coasts.

MOON JELLYFISH *Aurelia aurita*   Diameter 9in
A medium-sized and translucent white jellyfish shaped like a flattened ball. May appear yellow or brown. Has four obvious white horseshoe-shaped gonads from above. More than 95 per cent water. Feeds by trapping organisms in short, stinging tentacles at the edge of the bell. Common in temperate seas on both coasts.

LION'S MANE JELLYFISH *Cyanea capillata*   Diameter 18in
One of the largest and most spectacular jellyfish. Rich golden brown or yellow. Bell more than 1½ft in diameter and tentacles can be over 30ft long. Catches fish and other marine life in its long, stinging tentacles. Found in surface waters; dangerous to swimmers and divers. Occurs on both coasts from Canada to FL and Baja CA.

GIANT GREEN ANEMONE *Anthopleura xanthogrammica*   Diameter 12in
Anemones are like jellyfish, attached by their heads and waving their stinging tentacles in the water to trap unwary small animals. The Giant Green Anemone is 12in wide and 6in high. Vibrant green in color from food-making algae incorporated into its body, which give the anemone some nutrition. Found on rocks below midtide on W coast from AK to CA.

FRILLED ANEMONE *Metridium senile*   Diameter 9in
This lovely large anemone, 9in in diameter and twice as high, is often white in color but can be brown or dusky red. It often grows in groups reproducing by asexual budding, and can move and change locations. It lives in quiet waters attached to rocks, pilings, or shells along the W coast.

PROLIFERATING ANEMONE *Epiactis prolifera*   Diameter 2in
This small anemone is usually red, pink, or green. Being small, it attaches to a wide variety of surfaces including kelp, and is often abundant. Young are born inside the cavity of the adult and as they mature they often stay on or close to the parent. Grows in clusters intertidally and in shallow water from AK to CA.

PACIFIC GIANT CHITON *Cryptochiton stelleri*   Total length 12in
Identified by its amazing size and its leathery, reddish-brown covering. Also called the
Gumboot Chiton, it is the largest chiton in the world. It can live over 20 years; slow grow-
ing. Grazes on red algae, keeping rocks available for other life forms to settle. Found from
AK to central CA.

LINED CHITON *Tonicella lineata*   Total length 2in
One of the most handsome common chiton species. Oval, with 8 plates visible on top;
brown or reddish-brown lines alternate with white across the plates. Margin smooth, not
hairy, and brown with white spots; grazes on algae, and is eaten by sea stars. Intertidal and
below on rocks. Found from AK to Mexico.

BLACK KATIE CHITON *Katharina tunicata*   Total length 5in
Easily recognized by shiny black color and smooth margin. Dorsal plates clearly visible
like a backbone down the middle of the chiton. These animals have enormous suction and
can cling to rocks in currents and waves. Grazes on algae covering rocks, creating habitat
for barnacles, urchins, and anemones. Found intertidally and below from AK to CA.

COMMON WEST INDIAN CHITON *Chiton tuberculatus*   Total length 3in
This medium-sized species is distinguished from other chitons in North America by its
size and color. Feeds on algae on rocks. Smaller than Pacific species. Can tolerate extreme
conditions and varied habitats. One of the most common chitons in tropical waters.
Widely distributed in FL and on the Gulf Coast.

MOSSY CHITON *Mopalia muscosa*   Total length 3½in
Distinguished by the long, dark hairs which cover the girdle around its dark brown or gray
plates. Feeds on organic materials adhering to rocks. A common intertidal species. Tolerant of brackish water and found in estuaries, and on rocky shores from AK to CA.

COMMON PERIWINKLE *Littorina littorea*   Total length 1in
Brown, with a brown to black operculum which keeps the snail from drying out on expo-
sure at low tide. Shell is heavy to prevent damage during severe storms and wave action.
Herbivorous, eats algae attached or covering rocks. The most abundant snail in the intertidal zone N of Chesapeake Bay.

MARSH PERIWINKLE *Littorina irrorata*   Total length 1in
The spiral is more sharply pointed than the Common Periwinkle and it is not as heavy-
bodied. Lighter in color, creamy or gray with interrupted black streaking. The columella
is brown. Lives on eel grass and rocks. Abundant in the right habitat. The common periwinkle of the Gulf Coast.

NORTHERN ROUGH PERIWINKLE *Littorina saxatilis*   Total length ¼in
Gray, brown, or black, with a strong shell to withstand pounding from coastal waves and
severe intertidal weather. One of the smallest of the periwinkles. Common at the highest
of the high tide lines on rocky shores. Found N of Puget Sound to AK; replaced farther S
by the Eroded Periwinkle *L. planaxis*.

ATLANTIC SLIPPER SHELL *Crepidula fornicata*   Total length 1½in
A common intertidal snail, flattened like a limpet to cling to hard surfaces with suction-like foot. Top light brown and covered by a thin skin; underside with shelf halfway down the body. Sexes are separate and males are smaller than females. Shells are almost always found along the tideline, from Canada to TX.

ROUGH KEYHOLE LIMPET *Diodora aspera*   Total length up to 3in
Gray with darker gray radiating lines. Pumps water over its gills and out of a hole at the apex. Eats a great variety of species clinging to rocks and opens areas for colonists. A commensal worm is often found associated with a live limpet. Nocturnal predator; eaten by sea stars. Found low in the intertidal zone and subtidally from AK to CA.

RED ABALONE *Haliotis rufescens*   Total length 12in
So named because its outer shell is dark red with stripes of green or gray. One of the largest abalones. Most prized for food, and its value makes it worth harvesting by divers. Long-lived; found in coastal CA and usually subtidal.

QUEEN CONCH *Strombus gigas*   Total length 12in
One of the largest and heaviest marine snails in the world. Spectacular shell with large knobs on the shoulders and a bright pink flaring operculum. Well known in the Caribbean as the basic ingredient of conch chowder. Top predator on sandy bottoms; much prized by shell collectors. In North America, only found S from the Florida Keys.

ATLANTIC DEER COWRY *Cypraea cervus*   Total length up to 4in
The largest member of this group in the N Atlantic. Shell is lustrous brown, covered with small white spots with a central line down the top. Among the most beautiful species in shallow waters. Prefers reefs or rocky bottoms, but can be found at jetties. Found from FL to the Yucatan Peninsula.

CHESTNUT COWRY *Cypraea spadicea*   Total length 1½–2in
Distinguished from other cowries by having solid brown or chestnut back and bluish-white bottom. Shell oval. Teeth flank the aperture on the underside of cowries; their color, number and size are helpful in identification. Chestnut Cowry's teeth are white. The only cowry found on the W coast.

BANDED TULIP *Fusciolaria hunteria*   Total length 3–4in
Shell is egg-white with numerous narrow brown lines starting from the first whorl; aperture is long and oval. A predator of other snails and clams. Found from Cape Hatteras to the Gulf of Mexico.

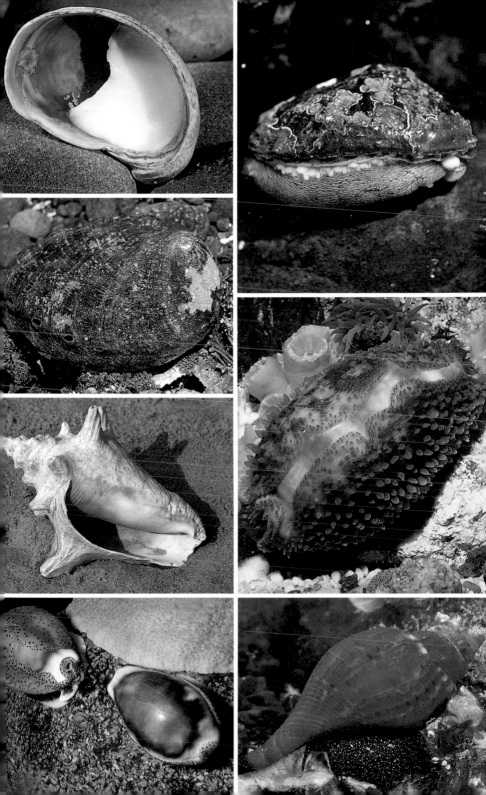

CHANNELED WHELK *Busycon canaliculata*   Total length 8in
One of the largest Atlantic coast snails. Distinguished from other whelks by a deep, channel-like groove running along the base of each whorl. Aperture brownish yellow; shell dirty white to cream. Covered with thin periostracum usually eroded away in large specimens. An active predator. Found from Cape Cod to FL on sandy bottoms.

 LIGHTNING WHELK *Busycon contrarium*   Total length 6in
Aperture is on the left side of the spire rather than the right. Smaller than the previous species with bright, lightninglike browns, reds, and oranges. More slender and delicate than other whelks. Found in shallow waters from Cape Hatteras S; most abundant in warmer water.

 CALIFORNIA CONE *Conus californicus*   Total length 1in
Conical shaped at spire; reddish-brown periostracum. Has poison gland and tooth to inject venom into its prey, which can include worms and also small fish. Found from central CA S; the only cone found on the W coast. Similar species, Alphabet Cone (*C. spurius*), is common from FL through the Gulf. 2in long with a long, straight aperture. Varies greatly in color; orange and white.

 FLORIDA CROWN CONCH *Melongena corona*   Total length 2½in
Shell has sharp spines along shoulders; brown with interspersed black and white bands. An active predator, partial to oysters and clams, but also other snails. Common species of brackish water where it frequents oyster beds, mangrove forests, and tidal shallows in FL and the Gulf Coast.

 FLORIDA HORSE CONCH *Pleuroploca gigantea*   Total length 18in
The largest snail in North America, reaching up to 1½ft in length. Brown periostracum usually worn in older specimens; 8–9 whorls. Early whorls have distinct knobs absent in older specimens. Common in eelgrass; a predator of snails and bivalves. Found from Cape Hatteras to FL.

BLUE MUSSEL *Mytilis edulis*   Total length 2in
Shell outside is dark blue to black, inside, pearly blue; no ribs. Also called the Edible Mussel, it is eaten by fish, birds, sea stars, and ducks, as well as by humans in stews, soups, and paella. Mussels form dense beds where they mat together. Found from Canada S to Cape Hatteras and introduced to Pacific coast.

CALIFORNIA MUSSEL *Mytilis californianus*   Total length 4in
Larger than Blue Mussel, and shell has obvious ribs. Forms into dense masses on pilings and rocks where it is the favorite food of sea stars, fish, and birds. Capable of concentrating toxins and causing disease; it is important to eat only mussels from a reliable source. It is found from AK to CA.

BAY SCALLOP *Aequipectin irradians*   Diameter 2–3in
Strong ribs; shell wavy at margin. Bright blue eyes. Important commercially for the edible muscle that holds the two shells together. Commercial scallops are caught in dredges. Adults are found on sandy bottoms from Canada to Cape Hatteras; they move seasonally.

VIRGINIA OYSTER *Crassostrea virginica*   Total length 3in
Chalky brown with rough, layered shell and irregular margin. Individuals modify calcium shells to fit tightly packed oyster bed. Tolerates low salinity; oyster bars often upriver. Innumerable predators. A valuable shellfish. Abundant from Cape Cod to Gulf of Mexico; widely transplanted elsewhere.

GIANT PACIFIC OYSTER *Crassostrea gigas*   Total length 6in
Purple muscle scar on white interior. The oysters live attached to hard surfaces or to each other. Edible; best raw when young and small, larger ones excellent as fried oysters or in soups and stews. Found from W Canada to CA.

GIANT EASTERN MUREX *Muricanthus fulvescens*   Total length 5–6in
Recognized by its ornate and attractive shell, which is whitish and marked with darker lines. Note the conical spire that is adorned with hollow, pointed spines. Shell aperture is whitish and lip is toothed. Favors sandy substrates and locally common in coastal seas off SE USA.

COMMON RAZOR CLAM *Ensis directus*   Total length 6in
Long, cylindrical animal with two flattened shells.Shell has a dark periostracum and white to light blue interior. Has a powerful digging foot; burrows rapidly and deeply to escape predators. Often used in stews. Lives in sand and sandy mud bottoms from N Canada to FL.

SOFT-SHELL CLAM *Mya arenaria*   Total length 3in
Shell oval to slightly rectangular with dirty brown periostracum often peeling or eroded. Internal surfaces are white. Siphon on top and muscular foot below to dig into soft mud and sand. Common on mud or sandy mud bottoms. A major commercial clam from Canada to Cape Hatteras. Widely introduced elsewhere.

NORTHERN QUAHOG *Mercenaria mercenaria*   Total length to 5in
Shell has numerous closely spaced lines and a brown periostracum; interior white and purple. A heavy-bodied clam, adapted to the surf line, or to shallow water where there is wave action. Abundant intertidally in sand from Canada to the Gulf of Mexico.

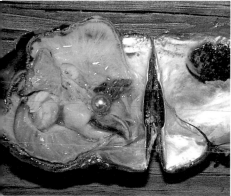

MANED NUDIBRANCH *Aeolidia papillosa*   Total length 4in
A spectacular species with two rows of papillae along its sides. Also called Plumed Sea Slug. Found in tide pools, where it feeds on anemones. Stinging cells from anemones are incorporated into its filaments for protection. Common from Arctic to Chesapeake Bay;

NOBLE DORIS *Anisodoris nobilis*   Total length 8in
A giant sea slug also called Sea Lemon for its lemon-yellow color. Red, brown or black speckles. Six branchial plumes; leaflike on the back end. Papillae are short, giving a rough texture; antennae are also short. Hermaphrodite; eats sponges. Found on rocky shores and under seaweed, but is confined to CA.

RED-GILLED NUDIBRANCH *Coryphella verrucosa*   Total length 1in
A small species, fairly slender; characterized by long, red papilla tipped in white. Body white, tapering to a point in the rear; two long-pointed antennae. Spiral egg masses found on rocks or in crevices. Feeds on hydroids. Found intertidally on seaweed and rocks on the E coast from Canada to NJ.

COMMON ATLANTIC OCTOPUS *Octopus vulgaris*   Total length 6–8ft across
A spectacular mollusk without a shell. Its eight arms have strong suckers up to 1in in diameter on the underside. Arm length may reach 3ft. Difficult to keep in captivity, amazing escape artists; very strong. Octopus are excellent swimmers, and voracious predators of crabs and other crustaceans. They can change color to match the ocean bottom. This species is found on rock or mixed rock-sand bottoms, subtidally, from Long Island Sound S to the West Indies.

PACIFIC GIANT OCTOPUS *Octopus dofleini*   Total length up to 20ft across
A giant, although larger specimens are rare; long-lived and perhaps the most intelligent of the cephalopods. Pacific octopus have been implicated in attacks on divers, and large individuals should be considered dangerous. Octopus are widely eaten wherever they are found and considered an expensive delicacy. An active predator of crabs, mollusks, and other octopus. Range from AK to CA.

MARKET SQUID *Loligo opalescens*   Total length 12in
Color variable; like octopus, can change color.Large eyes and very wary; can maneuver rapidly. An active predator that feeds on crustaceans, fishes, or other squid; catches prey with two long tentacles. Found in near-shore waters, like many squid species. Common in schools over sand and mud bottoms from AK to Mexico.

LONG-FINNED SQUID *Loligo pealei*   Total length 2ft
Medium-sized squid with 10 arms, 8 short tentacles, and 2 long, hunting tentacles. Body is long and cylindrical; has internal skeleton, often used in parrot cages for beaks. Important food for fish, marine mammals, and birds. Commercially important. Common in the Atlantic Ocean from Canada to the Caribbean.

ATLANTIC HORSESHOE CRAB *Limulus polyphemus*   Total length up to 2ft
Large, leathery-brown carapace with long, spikelike tail. Five pairs of legs, pincherlike; final pair modified for crushing clams and other prey. One of the oldest species on earth, related to spiders and mites. An intertidal predator of mud flats and sandy beaches from Canada through the Gulf of Mexico.

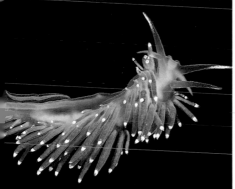 

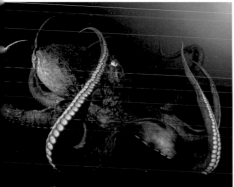 

NORTHERN ROCK BARNACLE *Balanus balanoides* — Total length 1in
A white, flattened cone about ½in high, about 1in wide. Feeds by using its legs to trap animals moving by in the water. Barnacles are among the most abundant and most visible of marine animals. They are found in groups at the water's edge, attached to rocks, pilings, or ocean debris, from Canada to Delaware Bay.

GIANT ACORN BARNACLE *Balanus nubilus* — Total length 4in
The largest barnacle in North America. Because of its size, often has other species living on its outside, and when dead, its inside provides shelter for other organisms. Spectacular and unmistakable. Often grows in colonies, forming a great mass. Common in the Pacific in shallow water on pilings and rocks up to the edge of low tide.

COMMON GOOSENECK BARNACLE *Lepas anatifera* — Total length up to 6in
Has a long black stalk topped with white shell and body mass. Hangs down, sifting the water for food with its legs. Commonly attached to floating debris, floats, moorings, and ships. Found from AK to Mexico.

LEAF BARNACLE *Pollicipes polymerus* — Total length 3in
Stalk dark gray to reddish; shell gray and red. Stalk is flexible and bends in waves. Opercula dark red. Often grows in clumps on exposed rocks washed by the waves; can be seen sticking upright like stubby fingers. Found attached to rocks from the intertidal into shallows on the W coast.

SPINY LOBSTER *Panulirus argus* — Total length 12in
Bright red and white, spectacular looking. A familiar crustacean with long antennae and without large claws. Covered with sharp spines, it darts forward in defense, driving the spines at its attacker. Commercially important. Found from NC throughout the Caribbean. Related species in CA.

NORTHERN LOBSTER *Homarus americanus* — Total length 2ft
Famous for its two large front claws, used in catching and crushing prey. Usually over 2ft long, rarely 3ft; can weigh well over 20lb. Most commercial lobsters weigh 1½–2lb and are about 1ft long. Lays many thousands of eggs, depending on size of female. Larvae planktonic after hatching. Found from Canada to DE; widely introduced elsewhere.

CLAM WORM *Nereis virens* — Total length 12in
Has over 200 body segments and may reach over 12in long, but most are smaller. Excellent burrower in sand or mud and can swim rapidly in open water. Nocturnal predator on other marine worms and invertebrates. One of the best known of the marine worms because it is used as fish bait on the E coast. Found from S Canada to Chesapeake Bay.

SERPULID TUBE WORM *Serpula vermicularis* — Total length 3–4in
This common subtidal marine worm lives in a white lime tube which it secretes, attached to algae, snails, rocks or other firm surfaces. Also called Plume Worm after the feeding filaments, which are a vivid red on a reddish-orange body. A numerous family found on all coastlines; often seen attached to debris on the shore after storms.

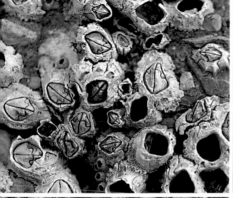

BLUE CRAB *Cancer sapidus*   Total length 9in
Green or blue-green above and white below with blue legs. Carapace oval, pointed at the sides. Eyes on stalks. A fast swimmer, darting sideways in the shallows, and an active predator and scavenger, catching and eating a variety of marine invertebrates, even ones caught in baited traps. Called "soft-shelled" crabs when molting. An important shellfish from Cape Cod into Gulf of Mexico.

SAND FIDDLER CRAB *Uca pugilator*   Total length 1¼in
Carapace 1½in wide. Male has one large claw. Feeds on algae and decaying debris. Can be found in enormous concentrations. Lives in burrows in muddy sand or mud at the edge of the tideline. Males wave to females from the mouth of their burrows. Fiddler crabs are an important food for numerous coastal birds and fish. Found from Cape Cod to the Gulf of Mexico.

DUNGENESS CRAB *Cancer magister*   Total length 6in
Large, with a carapace width to almost 10in. Gray or brown. Strong but small claws. A predator of clams and other mollusks, and a scavenger. Molts and changes its exoskeleton to accommodate growth. Important commercially and prized by seafood lovers. Common in quiet waters. Found from AK to CA.

PURPLE SHORE CRAB *Hemigrapsus nudus*   Total length 2in
Carapace 2in in diameter, slightly wider than it is deep. Pinchers are distinctive with dark purple spots; general body color dark purple, although it varies. Feeds on detritus, algae, and other organic material; a scavenger. Common intertidally where it hides in crevices and under rocks. Found on the entire Pacific coast to Mexico.

CALIFORNIA SEA CUCUMBER *Stichopus californicus*   Total length 12in
Cucumber-shaped, 2in in diameter. Rows of feet on underside for locomotion. Usually quite colorful: reds, greens, blues, and gray. Occasionally has long projections coming from the body. Often not recognized as an animal when first found along the shore. Ingests mud and debris to extract organic material; can process large volumes. Sea cucumbers are a large and varied group found on sand or mud bottoms subtidally on both coasts.

COMMON SAND DOLLAR *Echinarachinius parma*   Diameter 3in
A flattened, short-spined relative of the sea urchin, ¼in deep. Shaped like a small pancake, with a flowerlike pattern with 5 petals on the upper surface. Brown to purple; found in sand from low tide down. White skeleton often found after storms. Abundant. Found from Canada to Chesapeake Bay.

ECCENTRIC SAND DOLLAR *Dendraster excentricus*   Total length 3in
Thicker and heavier than the previous species, with short purple to brown spines. A filter feeder. Commonly seen alive along sandy beaches after storms; its gray and white skeleton with the characteristic 5-petal pattern is often found on the tideline. These are sometimes called "sea cookies." Found on the W coast from AK to CA

SOLITARY SEA SQUIRT *Pyura haustor*   Total length 2in
Variable in color and globular; large in-current and ex-current siphon. A filter feeder, taking in water through red siphons and straining it for food. Often has internal commensals such as worms, crabs, or amphipods. Found attached to rocks and debris. Occurs from NK through NW.

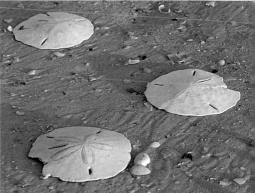

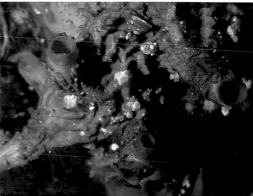

BAT STAR *Asterina miniata*   Total length 8in
Outline is the classic star any child would draw. Often bright red, but variable to green or brown. Arms are short. Lacks spines; smoother than other sea stars. Feeds on algae and small invertebrates. Common on rocky coasts, around pilings, and on sandy bottoms from intertidal to deep water. Found on W coast from AK to CA.

OCHRE SEA STAR *Pisaster ochraceus*   Diameter 12in
Often orange; surface rough with numerous white spines. Uses sticky feet radiating from inside the grooves in the arms to cling tenaciously to rocks in surf, and uses this suction to pull apart clams and mussels to eat. Extrudes stomach to dissolve the victim in place before ingestion. An important predator. Common intertidally from AK to CA.

SUNFLOWER STAR *Pycnopodia helianthoides*   Diameter 3ft or more
Red, orange, or purple in color; color changes with food availability. The most spectacular of the W coast sea stars, also the largest sea star in the world and a major predator of sea urchins. As it grows, new legs are added so a large adult can have over 20 legs. Found from AK to S CA.

FORBES' SEA STAR *Asterias forbesi*   Diameter 9–10in
Usually five arms; short blunt spines; color highly variable, orange, brown, green, or purple. A major predator of snails, clams, and particularly oysters in southern waters. Fast-moving over rocks in pursuit of prey. Found from New England to the Gulf of Mexico, this is the common intertidal sea star.

DAISY BRITTLE STAR *Ophiopholis aculeata*   Total length 5in
Central disc is small with 5–6 radiating 3in arms; color variable, disc often red and arms banded red and white. A scavenger and nocturnal predator. One of the most common, easily seen brittle stars in low tide pools and subtidally. Often found after storms. Range from the Arctic to NJ on E coast and from AK to CA on the W coast.

GREEN SEA URCHIN *Strongylocentrotus droebachiensis*   Total length 3in
Short green spines ¼in long; body 3½in in diameter. Sticky tube feet on underside keep it firmly attached in currents and waves. Grazes, scouring surface of rocks for algae. A favorite food of sea stars. Numerous on rocky bottoms and in tide pools. Found on both Atlantic and Pacific coasts in cold waters.

PURPLE SEA URCHIN *Strongylocentrotus purpuratus*   Total length 3in
Like the Green Sea Urchin in size, but the spines are longer and the base color is dark purple for body and light purple for spines. Difficult to dislodge when wedged into a crevice. A grazer, feeding on algae and bacterial scum on rocks. The preferred food of many marine predators. Found from AK to CA in tide pools to subtidally.

AMERICAN SHAD *Alosa sapidissima*   Total length 2ft 6in
Dark blue above, silvery below, sides compressed with dark spots. Feeds on small invertebrates. An important game fish. Found on E coast from Canada to FL; introduced to entire W coast. Ascends coastal rivers in spring and summer to spawn.

ATLANTIC SALMON *Salmo salar*   Total length 5ft
Silvery with black spots on the sides, single dorsal fin midway and a small, fleshy fin just before the tail. Fast, active hunter; eats other coastal fish. One of the best known game fish in North America. Formerly abundant, now endangered by coastal development, pollution, and overfishing. Ascends rivers to spawn over gravel. Many landlocked populations. Found from Greenland to ME.

COHO SALMON *Oncorhynchus kisutch*   Total length 3ft
Blue above and silvery below with black spot on back and tail. Changes color for spawning run to green, red, and black, then dies. Ascends rivers from AK to Mexico to spawn on gravelly streams. Introduced to Great Lakes. One of North America's most important game fish.

SOCKEYE SALMON *Oncorhynchus nerka*   Total length 2ft 6in
Also called Red Salmon, the male has a bright red body, green head and white lower jaw when the fish return to freshwater streams to breed. Formerly an abundant species, now much reduced in number. Breeds from AK to CA, but eliminated from many southern streams by dams and poor water quality. Some landlocked populations exist.

CHINOOK SALMON *Oncorhynchus tsahwytscha*   Total length 5ft
Also called King Salmon, this is the largest salmon, weighing up to over 100lb. Silvery gray, becoming darker with age. Despite its loss from many areas, it is still one of the most important food and game fishes in North America. All spawning salmon are a critical food source for bears, eagles and other predators. Found on the entire Pacific coast to Mexico, rarer in the S. Goes far inland to spawn in large rivers and streams.

BROWN TROUT *Salmo trutta*   Total length 3ft 4in
Brown, with red and black spots encircled in white. Larger and more wary than native Rainbow or Brook Trout; can grow to more than 30lb. Feeds on insects, aquatic invertebrates, and fishes. Introduced from Europe; now a widely distributed and often common game fish in cold-water lakes and streams of the N states and Canada.

BROOK TROUT *Salvelinus fontinalis*   Total length 2ft
One of the most colorful species, with pale blue haloes around red or pink spots along the sides. Ventral fins with a white leading edge against a black line. A top predator in cold, clear streams and small rivers. Not pollution tolerant. Found from E Canada S through the Appalachians, this popular game fish has been introduced widely elsewhere in North America and around the world.

RAINBOW TROUT *Salmo gairdneri*   Total length 3ft 9in
Sea-going Rainbow, called Steelhead, is silvery with black spots. Freshwater populations variable in color, but usually with broad, red or pink band on side and black spots. Sea-going adult usually survives after spawning in coastal streams. Important, common game fish of the NW, widely introduced throughout North America and elsewhere.

DOLLY VARDEN TROUT *Salvelinus malma*   Total length 2ft
Breeding male is red to orange below, otherwise the color is highly variable from dark to bright with numerous pale spots. Usually anadromous, but some landlocked populations. Found in clear, cool lakes and streams with deep pools and runs. Widely distributed on the N Pacific coasts in North America from AK to CA.

CHAIN PICKEREL *Esox niger*   Total length 2ft
A long fish, round in cross section, with dorsal fin far back in front of the tail; black bar straight below the eye, green with darker chain pattern down length of sides. Feeds on other fishes, frogs, and aquatic invertebrates. Aggressive, important predator. Introduced widely. Found in E in clear, shallow rivers, ponds, and lakes with vegetated borders.

GRASS PICKEREL *Esox americanus*   Total length 15in
A long species with dorsal fin far back in front of the tail, black line down from the eye, angled backward; green with darker side bars. Smaller than Chain Pickerel, but they do not coexist. Active predator. Found in clear, slow-moving and quiet streams, ponds and lakes with vegetation. Widely distributed in E except in the Appalachians; introduced elsewhere.

NORTHERN PIKE *Esox lucius*   Total length 4ft 4in
Green with yellow-green spots, light belly; black spots on fins. Top predator of fish, water birds, small aquatic mammals; eats most anything. Important sport fish. Found in cold, clear lakes and rivers with vegetation. A fish of AK, Canada, and the N states of the Midwest and NE.

ROCK BASS *Amblophites rupestris*   Total length 18in
This common bass prefers hiding under roots or ledges in small, clear streams or lakes with vegetated borders. Deep-bodied and dark above with a large mouth and rows of dark spots on the sides and belly. Feeds on fish, crayfish, and insects. Native to the Midwest Great Lakes and S Canada.

SMALLMOUTH BASS *Micropterus dolomieu*   Total length 2ft
Large game fish identified by having corner of the mouth ending before the eye; black tail, dark olive-green or brown fading to white on the belly, double dorsal fin with front fin spiny and rear soft-rayed. Nests in depression in mud or sand; guarded by male. Active, aggressive predator, which has been introduced throughout the US.

LARGEMOUTH BASS *Micropterus salmoides*   Total length 3ft
Largest freshwater bass identified by having corner of the mouth ending directly below or beyond the eye. Common in wide variety of clear waters, lakes, ponds, rivers, streams, and reservoirs. A favorite of anglers. Native to E and central US and Canada, now introduced widely in W.

YELLOW PERCH *Perca flavescens*   Total length over 12in
Yellow with broad, brown vertical bars and a double dorsal fin. Feeds on aquatic invertebrates and small fish. Prefers clear, cool lakes and ponds, hiding in vegetation from predators. One of the most abundant and best-known fish of the NE US and S Canada.

BLACK CRAPPIE *Pomoxis nigromaculatus*   Total length 12in
A small, black bass speckled with light spots enlarging toward belly; fins and tail black with white spots; female lighter overall. Male builds a scrape nest in gravel in shallows. Popular as a food and game fish. Prefers clear, cool streams, ponds, and reservoirs. Found from SE Canada to Gulf of Mexico.

GRASS CARP *Ctenopharyngodon idella*   Total length over 3ft
Large vegetarian fish which reaches 100lb. Identified by single dorsal fin, light color, large scales, and large size. Numerous eggs are free-floating and distributed widely, hastening its spread. It is introduced in most states for weed control, but this is controversial since it can destroy much valuable habitat for native species, so it is prohibited in some states.

REDEAR SUNFISH *Lepomis microlophus* Total length 15in
A large blue-gray fish with dark, irregular vertical bars, black earflap with red edge, yellow-orange chin and breast. Cracks and eats snails as main food source. Found in warm, shallow ponds and quiet streams, by fallen logs, rocks, and debris, in SE states, FL to TX.

BLUEGILL *Lepomis macrochirus* Total length 9in
A large sunfish with uncolored fins, black earflap, blue throat, and dark, vertical bars on sides. Adaptable. Feeds on small crustaceans, insects, worms, and other aquatic species. Popular as important food and game fish. Voracious eater, easily caught. Native to E, now stocked continent-wide in ponds, lakes, and creeks.

YELLOW BULLHEAD *Ictalurus natalis* Total length 16in
A fish with white whiskers (barbels) above and below mouth. Skin without scales; yellow-brown. Feeds on aquatic insects and other invertebrates. Prefers slow, quiet waters, oxbows, natural and manmade ponds, over mud or soft sediments. Native to E US, barely into Canada; widely introduced elsewhere.

BROWN BULLHEAD *Ictalurus nebulosus* Total length 18in
Called Hornpout from spines in pectoral fins used in defense. Brown back grading to yellow with speckled sides and dark barbels. Found in quiet waters of ponds and slow streams over mud, from E coast, W to Dakotas and TX in suitable habitats. Widely introduced elsewhere. Common over range.

PUMPKINSEED *Lepomis gibbosus* Total length 9in
A pretty sunfish with yellow belly, orange and ochre spots, blue lines on face, and otherwise brown. Nests in shallow water of vegetated ponds, lakes, or streams in summer. Male builds nest and defends area. Schools in deep water in winter. Originally eastern, now introduced widely including Pacific NW.

CHANNEL CATFISH *Ictalurus punctatus* Total length 4ft
Like Blue Catfish (*Ictalurus furcatus*) but with rounded, not straight-edged anal fin, blue-black fading to white below; white barbels. Young green with black spots. Feeds on invertebrates and fish. The most widespread and abundant large catfish in rivers and reservoirs with deep pools. Found in E and central states from S Canada to Gulf of Mexico.

WALKING CATFISH *Clarias batrachus* Total length 16in
Brownish above, white below, rear flecked with white, large head tapering to small tail. Found over mud in weedy ditches, canals, swamps, and ponds. On wet nights, can walk overland to new habitat using spines in pectoral fins for support. Introduced to FL by aquarium trade; now common and spreading N to adjacent states.

GOLDEN SHINER *Notemigonus crysoleucus*   Total length 12in
Gold or silver in color with small head and compressed body; large scales. Feeds on aquatic insects and other invertebrates. Sticky eggs laid on aquatic vegetation. Found in shallows of lakes and ponds. Widespread over most of US, S Canada, absent Pacific NW.

COMMON SHINER *Notropis cornutus*   Total length 6in
Olive to blue above, silver below, faint side stripes, fins orange-red in breeding. Males dig shallow nest in gravel into which eggs are laid in late spring or summer. Found in cool, clear streams, rivers, or ponds over gravel or rocks, in S Canada, and N central and E states.

MOSQUITOFISH *Gambusia affinis*   Total length 2in
Small head, rounded tail, single dorsal fin; last third of body constricted and belly looks swollen. Female larger by half, with black spots. Feeds on insect larvae and other invertebrates. Gives birth to live young. Widespread and abundant in shallow, vegetated pools, ditches, canals, and ponds throughout the SE but widely introduced elsewhere.

CARP *Cyprinus carpio*   Total length 4ft
Green body with white belly; two fleshy barbels hang from upper lip; large scales. Grows to over 70lb and can live more than 40 years. Feeds on vegetation, often destroying native habitat. Lays over a million eggs. An abundant Eurasian species introduced to US over 100 years ago; now found throughout S Canada and US except FL.

RAINBOW DARTER *Etheostoma caeruleum*   Total length 2in
A colorful fish: breeding male is dark red with dark, vertical blue bars; colors fade in nonbreeding. Male defends nesting territory. Eggs laid and fertilized in gravel where they develop. Feeds on insects and other invertebrates. Lives in clear, cold streams with gravel bottoms, in the central states S to LA.

MOZAMBIQUE TILAPIA *Tilapia mossambica*   Total length 15in
Black to olive above, blue upper lip, white chin, single dorsal fin elongated toward the tail. Feeds on aquatic vegetation and invertebrates. Common in warm, shallow waters, ditches, canals, ponds, and in the Salton Sea of CA. A valued food fish, widely introduced to North America from Africa.

THREE-SPINE STICKLEBACK *Gasterosteus aculeatus*   Total length 4in
Has three dorsal spines (two long, one short), numerous bony plates on sides, big eye. Brown or green above, lighter below; fins red or pink in breeding. Nest of cemented small twigs and debris, built on or near bottom. Found in ponds, small streams, and tidemarsh pools. A common native of W and E coasts from Hudson Bay to Chesapeake Bay and inland to Lake Ontario.

ALLIGATOR GAR *Lepisosteus platostomus*   Total length 9ft
The biggest gar (over 200lb), and one of North America's largest freshwater fish. Dark, olive body, lighter below with a short, wide snout. Spots on tail and fins, dorsal fin far back by tail. Eats almost anything: fish, birds, mammals, and reptiles. Found in quiet waters, bayous, and swamps of the lower Mississippi drainage, coastal TX and E to FL Panhandle.

PADDLEFISH *Polydon spathula*   Total length 7ft
An amazing fish with oar-shaped snout and a large spotted and pointed ear flap. Feeds on plankton, with mouth open like Basking Shark. A sport fish, growing to over 150lb. Prefers quiet, slow waters. Found in the Mississippi River basin and E and W along the Gulf. Formerly in the Great Lakes drainage.

GOLDFISH *Carassius auratus*   Total length 16in
Familiar to many as a household pet. Darkens with age. Pollution tolerant. Feeds on algae and other aquatic vegetation. Readily interbreeds with the introduced and related Common Carp. Introduced to North America from Asia, now found in slow or still warm waters from Canada throughout the US.

BLUE SHARK *Prionace glauca*   Total length over 12ft
An elegant, long predator with long, thin pectoral fins. Cobalt blue with white belly. Feeds on fish and even seabirds, resting on water. Dangerous to people in the water at sea. Fast swimmer. Gives birth to several dozen live young per litter. Common worldwide in temperate and tropical seas, often close to shore.

NURSE SHARK *Ginglymostoma cirratum*   Total length 12ft
Recognized by barbels hanging from nostrils, long upper lobe of tail, and two dorsal fins placed far down the back. Brown above, white below. Feeds on invertebrates such as crabs, lobsters, urchins, and squid. Non-aggressive, but bites if harassed. Often seen on reefs by divers and snorkelers. Bottom dweller in shallow, warm water in the E.

BULL SHARK *Carcharhinus leucas*   Total length 10ft
Recognized by large dorsal and pectoral fins, short snout, and blunt head, gray above and white below. Eats fish, garbage (at river mouths), rays, and other sharks. Aggressive; attacks bathers and divers. Coastal, and enters estuaries and bays. Found in warm waters from NC S through Gulf.

TIGER SHARK *Galeocerdo cuvieri*   Total length 20ft
One of the largest sharks. Young sharks have bars on the sides which fade with age. Adults grayish brown, broad snout. Will eat anything that gets its attention, including debris. Dangerous, often in shallow waters, bays and river mouths. Found worldwide in warm to temperate water. Seems to be migrating in the Pacific, with set routes coinciding with food availability.

SAND TIGER SHARK *Odontaspis taurus*   Total length 10ft
This large species is one of the most common sharks of coastal waters. Dark brownish gray above, fading to light belly; long dorsal fins. An active predator of other fishes; teeth distinct, symmetrical, long and pointed. Not usually considered dangerous in North America, but close relatives elsewhere attack humans. Found in the Atlantic from Canada to Argentina.

GREAT WHITE SHARK *Carcharodon carcharias*   Total length 25ft
Dark gray to black above, with characteristic white below; deep-bodied, with a large triangular dorsal fin; very large triangular teeth. Popularized as the most dangerous shark because of its method of attack, using one massive initial bite. It is in fact a rare species, possibly endangered, which feeds on marine mammals, sea otters, seals, porpoises and whales as well as other sharks and fishes. Found in N Atlantic and Pacific Oceans.

GREAT BARRACUDA *Sphyraena barracuda* Total length 6ft
Body shape is similar to that of the freshwater Northern Pike; long and slender, silvery sides and belly, with partial bands and a few black blotches on the sides. A fast predator of fish near shore and on reefs. Curious; investigates swimmers and disturbances. Human attacks rare but documented. Found in warm waters of Atlantic and Gulf.

GREEN MORAY *Gymnothorax funebris* Total length 7ft
This crevice- and reef-dwelling fish holds its mouth open with long, thin teeth, presenting a fearsome appearance to divers or snorkelers from its hiding hole. Uniform green to brown color. Dorsal fin long from neck to tail tip; no pectoral fins. Feeds on fish and invertebrates. Found in warm water of E coast.

CALIFORNIA MORAY *Gymnothorax mordax* Total length 5ft
Brown or green in color with some mottling on the sides. No pectoral or pelvic fins. A nocturnal hunter of fish, octopus, and other invertebrates. Will bite severely when threatened. Found in shallow waters in rocks or crevices. The W coast equivalent of the Green Moray.

ATLANTIC COD *Gadus morhua* Total length 6ft
Green or brown with strong, light lateral line, three dorsal fins, many black spots on sides, and long chin barbel. An omnivorous bottom feeder, found in schools. One of the world's best-known and most important fish. A staple of early colonists, often salted and dried. Found in cold Atlantic waters from Canada to Cape Hatteras.

GARDEN EEL *Heteroconger halis* Total length 20in
Slender; brown to gray, with a light spot behind the large eye. Lives in mucous tubes in the sand near coral reefs. It feeds on plankton which is picked from the water without the fish leaving its home. A colony of feeding eels seems to wave in synchronization like flowers in the wind, hence its common name. A colonial species of S FL and the Caribbean

SPOTTED MORAY *Gymnothorax moringa* Total length 3ft 6in
This beautiful nocturnal eel is yellow or white in color with numerous black or brown spots. Morays have no pectoral or pelvic fins but the dorsal fin is continuous with the tail and anal fins to form one long fin. Teeth are long, sharp and cylindrical. Not aggressive unless provoked, but can give a painful bite which often becomes infected. Hides in coral and rock crevices during the day. Ranges from Carolinas through Caribbean.

GAFFTOPSAIL CATFISH *Bagre marinus* Total length 2ft
Blue-gray above and silvery white below. Named for the long barbels extending back from the mouth and the long filaments on the dorsal and pectoral fins. Often caught by coastal fishermen. Found from Cape Cod S, but most common in the shallow waters of the Gulf of Mexico.

CALIFORNIA GRUNION *Leuresthes tenuis* Total length 7in
Long and silvery with two small dorsal fins. Spawns on sand beaches of CA and Mexico each spring and summer. Female digs into the sand, tail first, to lay, and male fertilizes eggs through the sand. Egg laying coincides with high tides after full and new moons; hatching occurs 2 weeks later on next series of high tides.

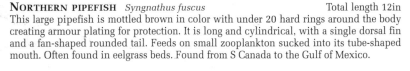

NORTHERN PIPEFISH *Syngnathus fuscus*   Total length 12in
This large pipefish is mottled brown in color with under 20 hard rings around the body
creating armour plating for protection. It is long and cylindrical, with a single dorsal fin
and a fan-shaped rounded tail. Feeds on small zooplankton sucked into its tube-shaped
mouth. Often found in eelgrass beds. Found from S Canada to the Gulf of Mexico.

LINED SEAHORSE *Hippocampus erectus*   Total length 5in
Related to pipefish but with a prehensile tail and fan-shaped tail fin; body armored. Color
changes with vegetation background, making it inconspicuous and hard to find. Feeds by
filtering plankton. Male broods and protects young. Locally common in coastal grasses
and seaweed from Canada to Mexico.

DOLPHIN *Coryphaena hippurus*   Total length 6ft
Brilliantly colored blue-green above, flashing golden-green on the sides, numerous tiny,
dark spots. High forehead with continuous dorsal fin. Feeds on fish and squid. A fast
swimmer. Called mahi mahi in Hawaii. Found in oceans worldwide.

BLUEFIN TUNA *Thunnus thynnus*   Total length over 10ft
Enormous: known to exceed 1,500lb. Blue-black above, blue sides with white belly; short
pectoral fins. A voracious feeder on anything available. Much sought on both coasts and
worldwide as a sport fish. Moves N in summer until fall; some are known to cross Atlantic
to Europe.

SWORDFISH *Xiphias gladius*   Total length 15ft
Few have seen this gigantic oceanic fish. It has a large, flattened bill, with no scales or pectoral fins, and is brown to gray-black, dirty-white on belly. A deep water species, rising at
night to feed on fish and squid. Found worldwide in temperate and tropical seas. Threatened by over-fishing by long-liners in some areas.

CHINA ROCKFISH *Sebastes nebulosus*   Total length 15in
A handsome species; black with a broad yellow band from the dorsal fin along the side
with much yellow spotting. Territorial under rocky ledges and crevices. Unwary, but not
much sought by anglers. A common solitary species in AK, diminishing in abundance S
to N CA.

ATLANTIC WOLFFISH *Anarchichas lupus*   Total length 5ft
Olive to blue-gray with prominent dark bars on the sides. Front teeth are conical and protruding, but rear teeth are molarlike for cracking starfish, shellfish and urchins. Often
caught by bottom fishermen seeking cod and haddock. A common fish on rocky bottoms
from Canada to Long Island.

BONEFISH *Albula vulpes*   Total length 3ft
Long and slender, silvery with blue or green back; single dorsal fin, deeply forked tail.
Feeds on snails, worms, shrimps, and other invertebrates. Avidly sought by anglers in
sand-covered shallows. A primitive fish of an ancient family found worldwide in tropical
waters. Found on both coasts; Cape Hatteras S in E, and San Francisco S in W.

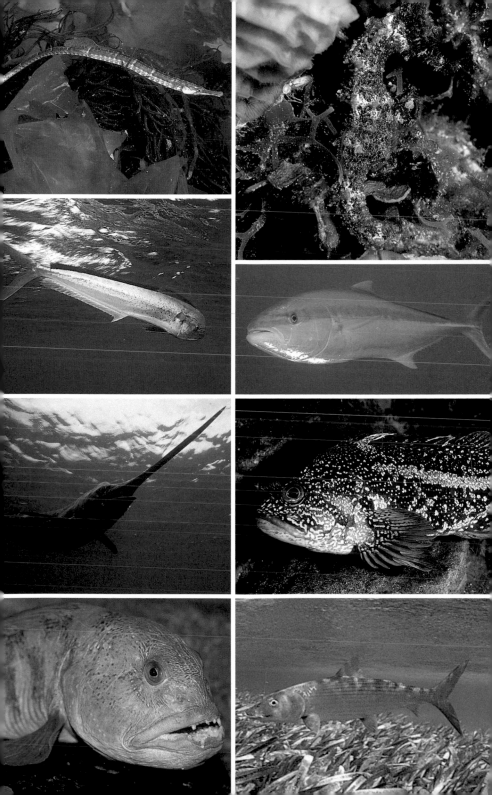

SNOOK *Centropomus undecimalis*   Total length 4ft
Dark to light brown with prominent black lateral line, two dorsal fins, protruding lower jaw. Feeds on fish and crustaceans. Primarily marine, but penetrates estuaries, streams, ponds, and lakes connected to the sea. Found in tropical waters of both coasts, Snook are important game fish.

GRAYSBY *Epinephelus cruentatus*   Total length 12in
Orange-brown spots cover the body over a pale reddish or gray base. Distinguished by 3–5 black spots at the base of the single, long dorsal fin and a round caudal fin. Solitary and generally unwary of divers. One of the most common groupers seen by divers and snorkelers on Atlantic coral reefs around FL and the Gulf of Mexico.

WEAKFISH *Cyoscion regalis*   Total length 3ft
This long food fish is greenish olive above and pale below with numerous rows of small, dark spots above the lateral line. The common name comes from the tendency of hooks to rip out of its fleshy mouth. Found over shallow, soft bottoms in coastal waters. Found from Canada through N FL in the Atlantic.

QUEEN ANGELFISH *Holocanthus ciliaris*   Total length 10in
One of the most spectacular of the reef angelfishes. Dark blue with yellow pectoral, pelvic and tail fins and extensive yellow in the face. Yellow edges to the body scales. Diurnal; feeds on sponges and other invertebrates. Found in FL and the Gulf of Mexico. Not abundant, but often seen by snorkelers and divers.

SERGEANT MAJOR *Abudefduf saxatilis*   Total length 6in
Abundant tropical damselfish. Yellow back grades to silvery gray below with 5 black, vertical bars. Small mouth; feeds on plankton and algae, in Sargassum. Found in large schools in tropical areas worldwide, but diminishing in number in cooler waters as far N as Long Island in the Atlantic. A common marine aquarium species.

STOPLIGHT PARROTFISH *Sparisoma viride*   Total length 2ft
A common, deep green reef species. Adult male has a bright yellow spot above the pectoral fin and two bands of yellow on the tail. Young males and females are mottled white on reddish brown with red on fins and tail. One of a spectacular group which have strong teeth for eating coral or algae on coral. Spits unwanted debris in a cloud. Found in S FL and Gulf of Mexico.

BLUE TANG *Acanthurus coeruleus*   Total length 12in
Disc-shaped surgeonfish, deep blue in color with a whitish spine at the base of the tail. Sub-adults blue with yellow tail; juveniles are all yellow. Diurnal and feeds on algae. Often seen schooling over reefs and isolated coral heads. Common to abundant; found on Atlantic coral reefs, but also N over rocks to Long Island.

PORCUPINEFISH *Diodon hystrix*   Total length 3ft
Brown to olive back with white belly; very large, dark eyes; body covered with short spines. Can inflate body by swallowing water or air to erect the spines for defense. Feeds on mollusks, particularly snails, with beaklike, fused teeth. Can change color. Found in a wide variety of coastal waters from river mouths to coral reefs as well as in plankton in open water, from Cape Cod through the Gulf of Mexico.

TREES AND SHRUBS

GINKGO (MAIDENHAIR-TREE) *Ginkgo biloba* Height up to 70ft
Elegant and distinctive tree. Spreading habit with age but retains pyramidal-shaped crown. Leaves lobed, fan-shaped; light green turning yellow in autumn. Originally from Asia, now planted widely, mainly in E and W coastal districts.

CALIFORNIA TORREYA *Torreya californica* Height up to 70ft
Broadly conical evergreen. Unpleasantly aromatic. Leaves narrow, pointed-tipped; paired and borne in 2 rows. Seeds resemble nutmegs hence alternative name California-nutmeg. Favours wooded mountain slopes in N CA.

TAMARACK (EASTERN LARCH) *Larix laricina* Height up to 80ft
Deciduous conifer with spreading horizontal branches. Needles narrow, 3-angled and in clusters; blue-green, yellow in autumn. Cones ovoid with rounded scales. Damp, peaty soils. Widespread northern North America.

WESTERN LARCH *Larix occidentalis* Height up to 150ft
Impressive narrowly conical deciduous conifer. Needles up to 1½in long, borne in clusters; light green, yellow in autumn. Cones ovoid, upright, and brown, with rounded scales and pointed bracts. Free-draining slopes in northwest.

CALIFORNIA RED FIR *Abies magnifica* Height up to 120ft
Attractive evergreen conifer with tapering conical outline and rounded tip. Needles 4-sided, curved, and blue-green with white lines; in 2 upward-pointing rows. Cones upright, purple-brown, and cylindrical. Mountains of CA and SW Nevada.

GRAND FIR *Abies grandis* Height up to 200ft
Towering narrowly conical evergreen conifer. Needles curved, up to 2in long, dark green above, and silvery below; in 2 rows. Cones cylindrical, upright, and green or brown. Pacific NW mountains (mainly BC, WA, and OR) and Rocky Mountains.

NOBLE FIR (RED FIR) *Abies procera* Height up to 150ft
Tall evergreen conifer; conical outline but domed crown. Needles flat, often notched, and blue-green; in 2 rows. Cones upright, cylindrical; green ripening purplish brown. High altitudes in Coastal Ranges and Cascades, mainly OR and WA.

PACIFIC SILVER FIR *Abies amabilis* Height up to 150ft
Tall narrowly conical evergreen conifer; downcurved branches. Needles curved, 1–2in long, dark green above, and silvery below; in 2 rows. Cones 4–6in long, cylindrical, and purplish. Pacific coastal belt and mountains from S AK to OR.

WHITE FIR *Abies concolor* Height up to 160ft
Impressive evergreen conifer. Tapering conical outline with pointed crown. Needles 1–3in long, flat, and bluish with white lines; in 2 rows. Cones 4–7in long, cylindrical, and purplish green. Widespread in mountains of SW US.

BALSAM FIR *Abies balsamea* Height up to 60ft
Aromatic evergreen conifer. Broadly conical outline and pointed crown. Needles up to 1in long and flat, dark green above with pale bands below. Cones upright, conical, and dark purple. Widespread E Canada, W to AB; limited range in NE US.

BLACK SPRUCE (BOG SPRUCE) *Picea mariana* Height up to 60ft
Evergreen conifer. Lower branches often dead or fallen, crown irregularly conical. Needles ½in long, 4-angled, bluish, and pointed. Cones ovoid, pendant on short stalks. Widespread across most of Canada; limited range in NE US.

BLUE SPRUCE *Picea pungens* Height up to 100ft
Tall evergreen conifer. Irregularly cylindrical shape with conical crown. Needles 1in long, bluish with white lines, pointed, and 4-angled. Cones 3–4in long, cylindrical, and brown. Mountain valleys; central W US, mainly UT, CO, and NM.

TREES AND SHRUBS

WHITE SPRUCE *Picea glauca*   Height up to 100ft
Tall evergreen conifer with tapering, irregular conical outline. Needles ¾in long, bluish green with pale lines, 4-angled, and pointed. Cones up to 1–3in long, cylindrical, and brown. Widespread across northern North America, mainly AK and Canada.

SITKA SPRUCE *Picea sitchensis*   Height up to 160ft
Massive evergreen conifer with broadly conical outline. Needles up to 1in long, dark green, flat, and pointed. Cones 2–4in long, cylindrical, reddish brown, and pendant. Native to foggy coastal areas of Pacific northwest.

RED SPRUCE *Picea rubens*   Height up to 80ft
Evergreen conifer with a distinctly conical outline. Needles up to 2in long, dark green with white lines, 4-angled, and pointed. Cones up to 1½in long, cylindrical, brown, and pendant. Mountains of NE, NS S to Appalachians.

BRISTLECONE PINE *Pinus aristata*   Height up to 40ft
Irregularly conical evergreen in maturity; ancient specimens (1,000s of years old) gnarled and distorted. Needles up to 1½in long, dark green with white lines; in groups of 5. High altitudes in mountains of SW, mainly CA, NV, UT, and CO.

PONDEROSA PINE *Pinus ponderosa*   Height up to 130ft
Impressive evergreen conifer with tapering conical outline. Needles 5–8in long and dark green; in groups of 2 or 3. Cones 3–6in long, reddish brown, and ovoid to conical. Widespread in mountains of W, from NM to MT westwards, N to BC.

LODGEPOLE PINE *Pinus contorta*   Height up to 80ft
Narrowly conical evergreen conifer; older specimens lose many lower branches. Needles 1–3in long, green, and often twisted; in pairs. Cones 1–2in long, ovoid, and pale brown. Mountains in W half of North America, mainly BC and AK, S to CO.

SUGAR PINE *Pinus lambertiana*   Height up to 160ft
Immense evergreen conifer; in maturity lower trunk bare and foliage forms irregularly conical outline. Needles 3–4in long, twisted, blue-green with pale lines; in 5s. Cones 1–2ft long, cylindrical, pendant. Mountains of OR and CA.

EASTERN WHITE PINE *Pinus strobus*   Height up to 100ft
Evergreen conifer; lower trunk bare, foliage irregularly cylindrical in outline in maturity. Needles 3–4in long and bluish; in 5s. Cones 4–8in long, cylindrical, and brown. Widespread on sandy soils in E, mainly MN to NS, S to Appalachians.

LONGLEAF PINE *Pinus palustris*   Height up to 100ft
Tall evergreen conifer. In maturity lower trunk bare, crown open and irregular. Needles 1ft long and dark green; in 3s. Cones up to 10in long, cylindrical to conical, and brown. Lowland sandy soils, E coastal states from TX to VA.

JACK PINE *Pinus banksiana*   Height up to 70ft
Evergreen conifer with irregular domed outline. Needles 1–2in long, green, and twisted; in pairs. Cones 1½–2in long, yellowish, and curved upwards. Sandy soils. Widespread across S half of Canada, W to SK. In US, mainly MI, WI, and MN.

PITCH PINE *Pinus rigida*   Height up to 60ft
Evergreen conifer with irregularly domed outline. Needles 3–5in long, yellowish, and usually twisted; in 3s. Cones 1–3in long, ovoid, and yellowish brown. Favors free-draining soils. Widespread from MA S to Appalachians.

SLASH PINE *Pinus elliotii*   Height up to 100ft
Tall evergreen conifer. In maturity, lower trunk bare, crown open and domed. Needles 7–10in long, green, and stiff; in pairs or 3s. Cones 3–6in long, ovoid, and dark brown. Coastal SE US, mainly FL, GA, AL, and MS.

202

DOUGLAS-FIR *Pseudotsuga menziesii*   Height up to 200ft
Huge evergreen conifer. In maturity, lower trunk is bare, crown narrowly conical. Needles 1in long, dark green, and flat; in 2 rows. Cones 2–3in long, ovoid, and brown. Widespread in W of North America, from BC to CA and W to CO and NM.

COAST REDWOOD *Sequoia sempervirens*   Height up to 300ft
Immense evergreen conifer; world's tallest tree. Lower trunk bare, crown narrowly conical. Leaves either narrow, ½–1in long, flat, and pointed or small and scalelike. Cones ½–1in long, elliptical. Coastal S OR, S to central CA.

GIANT SEQUOIA *Sequoiadendron giganteum*   Height up to 250ft
Massive evergreen conifer. Trunk huge and reddish; lower half bare. Crown open and irregular in maturity. Leaves ½in long, narrow, scalelike, bluish green with 2 white lines. Cones 2–3in long, ovoid, and pendant. CA only (Sierra Nevada).

EASTERN HEMLOCK *Tsuga canadensis*   Height up to 70ft
Evergreen conifer; conical outline almost ground level; leader often droops. Needles ½in long, flat, green above, and 2 white lines below; in 2 rows. Cones ½–¾in long, ovoid, and brown. Temperate NE, mainly NS to WI, S to Appalachians.

WESTERN HEMLOCK *Tsuga heterophylla*   Height up to 150ft
Evergreen conifer, narrowly conical in outline. Needles ½in long, flat, dark green above, with 2 white lines below; in 2 rows. Cones 1in long, ovoid, and brown. Damp, acid soils. Coastal Pacific northwest and Rocky Mountains.

ATLANTIC WHITE-CEDAR *Chamaecyparis thyoides*   Height up to 90ft
Aromatic evergreen conifer; in maturity lower trunk bare, crown a domed cone. Leaves short, bluish, and scalelike; opposite, forming fan-shaped sprays. Damp, acid soils in coastal lowlands. E coast states, MS N to ME.

ALASKA-CEDAR *Chamaecyparis nootkaensis*   Height up to 100ft
Tall evergreen conifer. In maturity, lower trunk bare, crown narrowly conical. Leaves small, scalelike, and yellow-green; in 4 rows. Cones ½in across and spherical. Damp mountain slopes. Pacific northwest, mainly BC, WA, and OR.

NORTHERN WHITE-CEDAR *Thuja occidentalis*   Height up to 70ft
Evergreen conifer; resinous and aromatic. Leaves small, scalelike, yellow-green above, bluish below; in 4 rows. Cones ½in long, ovoid, and brown. Neutral to calcareous soils. Widespread central E of North America, from ON and MN, E to NS.

WESTERN RED-CEDAR *Thuja plicata*   Height up to 175ft
Evergreen conifer; broad-based trunk and tapering conical outline. Leaves small, scalelike, dark green above, whitish below; in 4 rows. Cones ½in long, ovoid, and brown. Damp, acid soils. Pacific northwest and Rocky Mountains.

BALD CYPRESS *Taxodium distichum*   Height up to 120ft
Domed and spreading deciduous conifer. Buttressed trunk and submerged roots. Needles ½in long, pale green above, whitish below; in 2 rows. Cones 1in across, spherical, and gray. Saturated soils. E coast states, mainly NC to TX.

COMMON JUNIPER *Juniperus communis*   Height up to 4ft
Spreading, evergreen shrub. Leaves ½in long, narrow, and pointed, white above and yellowish below; in 3s. Cones ½in across, berrylike, and bluish white when ripe. Upland slopes. Widespread Canada and AK; mountains only elsewhere in US.

WESTERN JUNIPER *Juniperus occidentalis*   Height up to 30ft
Evergreen shrub or small tree. Domed, conical outline. Leaves small, scalelike, and grayish green. Cones ½in across, berrylike, bluish-black when ripe. Rocky ground and mountains at high altitudes. Mainly WA to central CA.

BALSAM POPLAR *Populus balsamifera*   Height up to 80ft
Deciduous tree; sticky, balsam-smelling buds. Leaves 3–5in long, ovate with wavy margin and pointed tip. Flowers 2–3in long catkins in pendant sprays. Fruits ovoid and ¼in long. Widespread Canada; US, mainly NE states around Great Lakes.

EASTERN COTTONWOOD *Populus deltoides*   Height up to 100ft
Open, spreading deciduous tree. Leaves triangular to heart-shaped with toothed margin; green, yellow in autumn. Flowers 2–3in long catkins; in pendant sprays. Damp soils. Widespread in E half of US, W to TX and MT. Also Canadian Rockies.

BLACK COTTONWOOD *Populus trichocarpa*   Height up to 120ft
Deciduous tree. Sticky, balsam-smelling buds. Leaves 3–6in across, ovate, and toothed; green, yellow in autumn. Flowers 2–3in long catkins in pendant sprays. Cottony seeds. Damp soils. Widespread within range: BC to WY to CA.

QUAKING ASPEN *Populus tremuloides*   Height up to 70ft
Narrow deciduous tree. Leaves 2–3in across, rounded to heart-shaped, and toothed; rustle in the breeze. Flowers 1–3in long catkins in pendant sprays. Cottony seeds. Free-draining soils. Widespread Canada and AK. Uplands elsewhere in US.

FELTLEAF WILLOW *Salix alaxensis*   Height up to 25ft
Hardy deciduous shrub or small tree. Leaves 2–4in long, elliptical; green and smooth above, felty white below. Flowers 2–3in long catkins. Fruits woolly. Damp soils and tundra valleys. Widespread in AK and NW Canada.

BLACK WILLOW *Salix nigra*   Height up to 100ft
Deciduous, often multi-trunked tree. Leaves 3–5in long, lanceolate, pointed, and toothed. Flowers 1–3in long catkins. Margins of rivers and other saturated ground. Widespread and locally common throughout E half of US, except FL.

PUSSY WILLOW *Salix discolor*   Height up to 20ft
Deciduous multi-stemmed shrub or small tree. Leaves 2–4in long, ovate to lanceolate, toothed. Flowers 1–3in long catkins with long, silky hairs. Damp soils. Widespread Canada in zone from BC to NS; in US, mainly NE states.

NETLEAF WILLOW *Salix reticulata*   Prostrate
Spreading deciduous shrub. Leaves 1–2in long, rounded-ovate, shiny dark green with conspicuous netted veins. Flowers 2–3in long reddish catkins; upright on stalks. Tundra and mountains. Widespread Arctic and upland Canada and AK.

BITTERNUT HICKORY *Carya cordiformis*   Height up to 80ft
Domed deciduous tree. Leaves pinnately divided; 7–9 narrow ovate leaflets, each 2–6in long, green, yellow in autumn. Flowers small, yellowish, pendant; sexes separate. Fruits 1in across and spherical, husk in 4 parts. Widespread in E US.

TREES AND SHRUBS

SHAGBARK HICKORY *Carya ovata*   Height up to 100ft
Broad deciduous tree with shaggy bark. Leaves pinnate, with 5 ovate leaflets, each
4–7in long; yellowish, golden in autumn. Flowers small and greenish; sexes separate.
Fruits 1½–2½in spherical, green then brown. Widespread across E US.

WATER HICKORY *Carya aquatica*   Height up to 100ft
Deciduous narrowly domed tree. Leaves pinnate, with 9–13 leaflets, each 2–5in long.
Flowers small and greenish; sexes separate. Fruits 1–2in long, ovoid, and brown, husk in
4 parts. Damp lowlands. Mainly E seaboard and Gulf states of US.

PECAN *Carya illinoensis*   Height up to 100ft
Domed, spreading deciduous tree. Leaves pinnate, with 11–17 ovate to lanceolate leaflets,
each 2–7in long. Flowers small and greenish; sexes separate. Fruits 1½–2in long, ovoid,
and ridged; edible seed. Native to E US but planted widely.

BLACK WALNUT *Juglans nigra*   Height up to 90ft
Deciduous, open-crowned tree. Leaves pinnate, with 9–21 leaflets, each 3–5in long. Flowers small and greenish; sexes separate. Fruit 1–3in long, ovoid, and greenish brown; edible seed. Widespread but generally uncommon in E US.

BUTTERNUT *Juglans cinerea*   Height up to 70ft
Domed and open-crowned deciduous tree. Leaves pinnate with 11–17 ovate leaflets, each
2–4in long. Flowers small and greenish; sexes separate. Damp soils. Widespread in E US
as far S as MO to NC.

HAZEL ALDER *Alnus serrulata*   Height up to 20ft
Multi-trunked deciduous shrub. Leaves 2–4in long, ovate, often rounded at tip. Male flowers in pendant catkins, females in cones. Seed-bearing cones ½in long, brown. Widespread
from Great Lakes E, S to Appalachians, N to NS.

SPECKLED ALDER *Alnus rugosa*   Height up to 20ft
Multi-stemmed deciduous shrub. Leaves 1–1½in long, ovate, toothed. Male flowers pendant in catkins, females in reddish cones. Seed-bearing cones ½in long and dark. Widespread in sub-Arctic Canada; also locally NE border states of US.

MOUNTAIN ALDER *Alnus tenuifolia*   Height up to 30ft
Deciduous tree with domed, open crown. Leaves ovate, toothed, and lobed. Male flowers
in yellow catkins, females in brown catkins. Seed-bearing cones ½in long, ovoid, and dark.
Damp ground. AK and BC, S through mountains to CA and NM.

DWARF BIRCH *Betula nana*   Height up to 1½ft
Low-growing deciduous shrub. Leaves ½in across, rounded, and toothed; turn orange in
autumn. Male flowers in pendant catkins, females in greenish upright catkins. Seed-bearing cones ½in long. Tundra and mountains in N.

WATER BIRCH *Betula occidentalis*   Height up to 25ft
Narrowly domed deciduous tree; lower branches droop. Leaves 1–2in long, ovate, toothed.
Males flowers in pendant catkins, females in short, erect catkins. Cones 1in long, cylin-
drical, brown. Widespread but local. Mountains, W US.

RIVER BIRCH *Betula nigra*   Height up to 80ft
Domed, spreading deciduous tree; open crown. Leaves 2–3in long, ovate, toothed; green
above, downy white below. Male flowers in pendant catkins, females in small, erect
catkins. Cones 1in long, brown, cylindrical. Widespread E US.

PAPER BIRCH *Betula papyrifera*   Height up to 70ft
Elegant deciduous tree with domed crown. Leaves 2–4in long, ovate, and toothed. Male
flowers in pendant catkins, females in short, erect catkins. Cones 2in long, cylindrical, and
brown. Widespread across Canada, also uplands in N US.

208

EUROPEAN WHITE BIRCH *Betula pendula*   Height up to 80ft
Open-crowned tree. Branches pendulous towards tips. Leaves 1–2in long, oval to triangular, toothed; turn yellow in autumn. Male flowers in pendant catkins, females in small upright catkins. Damp soils. Planted widely throughout North America.

YELLOW BIRCH *Betula alleghaniensis*   Height up to 100ft
Tall, domed evergreen tree. Leaves 3–5in long, ovate to elliptical, and toothed; dark green above, yellowish below. Male flowers in pendant catkins, females in small erect catkins. Seed-bearing cones 1in long and oblong. Widespread NE US.

AMERICAN HORNBEAM *Carpinus caroliniana*   Height up to 30ft
Domed, spreading deciduous tree. Leaves 2–4in long, elliptical, double-toothed. Male flowers in 1in long pendant catkins, female in shorter reddish catkins. Fruits paired, ovoid with green scale; in 3in long clusters. E of North America.

GIANT CHINKAPIN *Castanopsis chrysophylla*   Height up to 80ft
Domed, evergreen tree. Leaves 2–5in long, lanceolate; dark green above, yellowish below. Flowers small and white, in 2in long catkins. Fruits 1½in across, spherical, very spiny; 1–2 ovoid edible nuts. Pacific coast, WA and CA.

AMERICAN BEECH *Fagus grandifolia*   Height up to 80ft
Domed and spreading deciduous tree. Leaves 3–5in long, ovate, dark green above, yellowish below; golden in autumn. Flowers small; males yellowish, females reddish. Fruits ½in long, ovoid, and prickly; 2 edible nuts. Widespread E US.

EUROPEAN BEECH *Fagus sylvatica*   Height up to 70ft
Domed, deciduous tree. Leaves 2–3in long, ovate, toothed, and parallel-veined; dark green above, paler below, golden in autumn. Flowers inconspicuous, greenish. Fruits 1in long, ovoid, prickly; 2 brown nuts. Non-native but planted widely.

COAST LIVE OAK *Quercus agrifolia*   Height up to 80ft
Domed, spreading evergreen with broad-based trunk. Leaves ovate to elliptical, toothed, dark green above, downy yellowish below. Acorns up to 1½in long, narrow-ovoid with scaly cup; stalkless. Valley slopes, coastal CA.

CANYON LIVE OAK *Quercus chrysolepis*   Height up to 100ft
Spreading evergreen. Leaves 1–2in long, ovate to elliptical, shiny green above, often downy yellow below. Acorns 1–2in long, ovoid with scaly and hairy cup. Free-draining canyon slopes. Pacific coasts of CA and S OR; also mountains AR.

INTERIOR LIVE OAK *Quercus wislezenii*   Height up to 70ft
Tall, rounded-crowned evergreen. Leaves 1–2in long, lanceolate, and toothed; dark green above, yellowish below. Acorns 1–1½in long, ovoid with a deep scaly cup. Lower mountain slopes. CA only.

PIN OAK *Quercus palustris*   Height up to 90ft
Tall, narrowly domed deciduous tree. Has pinlike twigs. Leaves 4–5in long, elliptical, and lobed; dark green above, paler and downy below, red in autumn. Acorns ½in long with shallow cup. Damp soils. Central E US, mainly MO to VI.

SOUTHERN RED OAK *Quercus falcata*   Height up to 80ft
Domed, open-crowned deciduous tree. Leaves 4–8in long, elliptical, and lobed; shiny green above, downy below, brown in autumn. Acorns ½in long, rounded with a conical cup. Widespread in SE US, TX to NJ, W to MO

TREES AND SHRUBS

LIVE OAK *Quercus virginiana*   Height up to 50ft
Broadly spreading evergreen. Leaves 2–4in long, elliptical, and lobed; shiny green above, yellowish below. Acorns ½–1in long, narrow-ovoid, and pointed; cup scaly and stalked. Sandy soils in coastal districts. E coast states, TX to VI.

NORTHERN RED OAK *Quercus rubra*   Height up to 90ft
Deciduous tree with rounded crown and lower trunk bare in maturity. Leaves 4–8in long, lobed, and toothed; dark green above, paler and hairy below. Acorns 1in long, ovoid with scaly cup. Widespread in E, Great Lakes to NS, S to AR and GA.

SCARLET OAK *Quercus coccinea*   Height up to 80ft
Domed, open deciduous tree. Leaves 3–7in long, deeply divided into 7 pointed lobes; green above, yellow below, scarlet in autumn. Acorns ½–1in long, ovoid with deep, bowl-shaped cup. Uplands in E, mainly ME to GA, W to TN.

SWAMP WHITE OAK *Quercus bicolor*   Height up to 70ft
Upright, irregular, and open deciduous tree. Leaves ovate and lobed: shiny green above, downy white below, reddish in autumn. Acorns 1in long, ovoid with a scaly cup. Damp lowlands. E of North America, mainly MO and IA, E to ME and NC.

TURKEY OAK *Quercus laevis*   Height up to 40ft
Elongate, open deciduous tree. Leaves 4–8in long with 3–5 narrow lobes; shaped like a bird's foot. Acorns up to 1in long, ovoid with hairy and scaly cup. Free-draining soils. SE coastal states of US, from NC to MS.

WATER OAK *Quercus nigra*   Height up to 100ft
Open-crowned deciduous tree. Leaves ovate to oblong and 3-lobed; bluish above, pale green below, yellowish in autumn. Acorns ½in long, rounded with shallow cup. Damp soils, mainly lowlands. SE states, mainly NC to TX.

WHITE OAK *Quercus alba*   Height up to 100ft
Domed deciduous tree. Leaves 4–8in long, broadly ovate with 5–9 rounded lobes; green above, pale below, reddish in autumn. Acorns ½–1in long, ovoid with shallow cup. Free-draining soils. E of North America, mainly WI to ME, S to TX and FL.

ARIZONA WHITE OAK *Quercus arizonica*   Height up to 60ft
Evergreen with rounded crown and lower trunk bare. Leaves 1–3in long, ovate to oblong with shallow-toothed lobes. Acorns up to 1in long and ovoid; cup with hairy scales. Uplands and canyons. SW US, mainly AZ and NM.

HACKBERRY *Celtis occidentalis*   Height up to 90ft
Domed, open-crowned deciduous tree. Leaves 2–5in long, ovate, and pointed; green above, whitish below, yellow in autumn. Flowers small, green. Fruits ¼in across reddish drupes on long stalks. Damp ground. Central E US, MN to OK eastwards.

AMERICAN ELM *Ulmus americana*   Height up to 100ft
Elegant and spreading deciduous tree. Leaves 3–6in long, elliptical, and toothed, sides unequal at base. Flowers small and green. Fruits ½in long, reddish, and winged. Widespread in E half of North America. Range reduced by Dutch Elm disease.

TREES AND SHRUBS

WINGED ELM *Ulmus alata*　　　　　　　　　　　　Height up to 80ft
Open-crowned deciduous tree. Leaves 1½–2½in long, elliptical, toothed, hairless above, downy below; green, yellow in autumn. Flowers small and green. Fruit ½in long, reddish, elliptical, and winged. SE US, mainly TX to MO, E to FL and NC.

RED MULBERRY *Morus rubra*　　　　　　　　　　Height up to 60ft
Rounded deciduous tree. Leaves 4–7in long, ovate, toothed, and in 2 rows; dark green, turn yellow in autumn. Flowers small and greenish. Fruits small, spherical, and reddish; in cylindrical, edible mulberries. Widespread across E US.

YELLOW-POPLAR (TULIPTREE) *Liriodendron tulipifera*　　Height up to 120ft
Tall and rather slender deciduous tree. Leaves 3–6in long, roughly square with 4 pointed lobes; fresh green, yellow in autumn. Flowers 2in across, 6 greenish petals. Fruits 3in long, conelike. Damp soils. E US; planted on W coast.

BIGLEAF MAGNOLIA *Magnolia macrophylla*　　　Height up to 40ft
Rounded deciduous tree. Leaves 20–30in long, oblong to ovate with 2 basal lobes. Flowers 12in across, bowl-shaped, fragrant with 6 white petals. Fruits 3in long and conelike. Damp soils. Native to SE US; planted elsewhere.

SOUTHERN MAGNOLIA *Magnolia grandiflora*　　Height up to 80ft
Broadly conical evergreen. Leaves 6–8in long, narrow-ovate, shiny green above, downy-rusty below. Flowers 6–8in across, bowl-shaped, fragrant; 3 white sepals and 6+ petals. Fruits 4in long, conelike. Native coastal SE states of US.

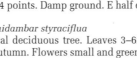

SASSAFRAS *Sassafras albidum*　　　　　　　　Height up to 60ft
Open-crowned deciduous tree; aromatic roots. Leaves 3–5in long, elliptical with basal lobes; shiny green above, downy below. Flowers ½in long and yellowish. Fruits ½in long blackish berries on red stalks. Damp ground. E half of North America.

WITCH-HAZEL *Hamamelis virginiana*　　　　　　Height up to 30ft
Multi-stemmed spreading deciduous shrub or small tree. Leaves 4–5in long, ovate to rounded with wavy margin. Flowers 1in across with 4 yellow, thin petals. Fruits ½in across, ovoid with 4 points. Damp ground. E half of North America.

SWEETGUM *Liquidambar styraciflua*　　　　　　Height up to 100ft
Open, rather conical deciduous tree. Leaves 3–6in long, divided into 5 pointed lobes; green, reddish in autumn. Flowers small and greenish. Fruiting heads 1in across, stalked, prickly balls of numerous fruits. SE of line from TX to VI.

SYCAMORE *Platanus occidentalis*　　　　　　　Height up to 100ft
Elegant deciduous tree with a domed, open crown. Leaves 4–8 in long, with 3 or 5 toothed and pointed lobes. Flowers small and greenish. Fruiting heads 1in across, stalked, brown; comprise many seeds. Widespread across E half of US.

WESTERN SERVICEBERRY *Amelanchier alnifolia*　Height up to 30ft
Multi-trunked deciduous shrub or small tree. Flowers 1in across, 5 white petals; in terminal clusters. Fruits ½in across, blackish, edible; in stalked clusters. Widespread temperate and sub-Arctic W half of North America, S to NE and OR.

BLACK HAWTHORN *Crataegus douglasii*　　　　Height up to 30ft
Rounded deciduous shrub or small tree. Leaves 1–3in long, ovate, toothed, and lobed. Flowers ½in across, 5 white petals; in clusters in spring. Fruits ½in across, stalked, and black; in pendant clusters. Pacific NW and N Rocky Mountains.

BEAKED HAZELNUT *Corylus cornuta*   Height up to 20ft
Much-branched deciduous shrub. Leaves 2–4in long, elliptical, and toothed. Male flowers in pendant catkins; female flowers small and spiky. Fruits 1in long, hard-shelled nuts. Forest understorey species. Widespread C and E half of North America.

SOUTHERN CRAB-APPLE *Malus angustifolia*   Height up to 30ft
Open-crowned deciduous tree. Leaves 1–3in long, elliptical, and toothed. Flowers 1–2in across with five pinkish white, rounded petals; stalked and in clusters. Fruits 1in across, yellow-green, stalked apples. SE states of US.

WESTERN CRAB-APPLE (OREGON CRAB-APPLE) *Malus fusca*   Height up to 30ft
Multi-trunked deciduous shrub or small tree. Leaves 1–3in long, ovate, and toothed. Flowers 1in across with five pinkish rounded petals; stalked and in clusters. Fruits ¾in long reddish apples. Pacific coast, mainly BC, WA and OR.

AMERICAN PLUM *Prunus americana*   Height up to 30ft
Open deciduous shrub or small tree. Leaves 3–4in long, elliptical, and toothed. Flowers 1in across with 5 white rounded petals; stalked and in clusters. Fruits 1in across reddish plums. Mainly E half US, S to CO in W and Appalachians in E.

BEACH PLUM *Prunus maritima*   Height up to 3ft
Low-growing, spreading deciduous shrub. Leaves ½–2in long, elliptical, and toothed. Flowers up to 1in across, whitish with 5 rounded petals; stalked. Fruits ½in across reddish purple plums. Swales or interdune swales. Atlantic coasts.

BLACK CHERRY *Prunus serotina*   Height up to 80ft
Open-crowned, aromatic deciduous tree. Leaves 2–5in long, elliptical, and toothed. Flowers ½in across with 5 white, rounded petals; in frothy spikes. Fruits ½in across, blackish cherries. Widespread across E half of US.

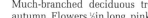

EASTERN CHOKECHERRY (COMMON CHOKECHERRY) *Prunus virginiana*   Height up to 20ft
Branching, often multi-trunked shrub or small tree. Leaves 2–3in long, elliptical, and toothed. Flowers ½in across with 5 white petals; in spikelike clusters. Fruits ½in across blackish chokecherries. Across N US and S Canada.

AMERICAN MOUNTAIN-ASH *Sorbus americana*   Height up to 30ft
Much-branched, spreading shrub or small tree. Leaves 6–8in long, lanceolate, and toothed. Flowers ¼in across with 5 white petals; in clusters. Fruits ¼in across, spherical, and red. Damp ground. Widespread temperate NE of North America.

YELLOW PALOVERDE *Cercidium microphyllum*   Height up to 25ft
Open, much-branched tree. Greenish yellow bark. Leafless in most months; leaves with rows of tiny rounded leaflets appear briefly in spring. Flowers ½in across with 5 yellow petals. Fruits 3in long pods. Sonoran desert, mainly AZ.

EASTERN REDBUD *Cercis canadensis*   Height up to 40ft
Much-branched deciduous tree. Leaves 3–4in long, heart-shaped; green, yellow in autumn. Flowers ½in long, pink, pealike; in spring before leaves. Fruits 3in long, flat pods; beanlike seeds. Native to E US, N to IN; planted elsewhere.

HONEYLOCUST *Gleditsia triacanthos*   Height up to 80ft
Spreading deciduous tree. Leaves 4–8in long, pinnately or bipinnately divided with paired, ovate leaflets. Flowers ½in across, yellowish, bell-shaped with 5 petals. Fruits 10–15in long, flat pods. C US states; planted elsewhere.

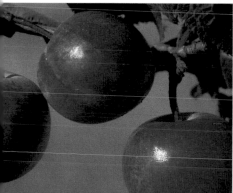

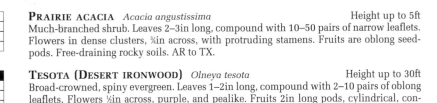

PRAIRIE ACACIA *Acacia angustissima*   Height up to 5ft
Much-branched shrub. Leaves 2–3in long, compound with 10–50 pairs of narrow leaflets.
Flowers in dense clusters, ¾in across, with protruding stamens. Fruits are oblong seed-
pods. Free-draining rocky soils. AR to TX.

TESOTA (DESERT IRONWOOD) *Olneya tesota*   Height up to 30ft
Broad-crowned, spiny evergreen. Leaves 1–2in long, compound with 2–10 pairs of oblong
leaflets. Flowers ½in across, purple, and pealike. Fruits 2in long pods, cylindrical, constricted between seeds. Deserts. S AR and S CA.

SCREWBEAN MESQUITE *Prosopis pubescens*   Height up to 20ft
Much-branched, spiny deciduous shrub or small tree. Leaves 2–3in long, compound with
5–8 pairs of oblong leaflets. Flowers ¼in long, yellow, in clusters. Fruits 1–2in long spiral
pods. Desert washes. Mainly S CA; locally AR and NM.

BOXELDER *Acer negundo*   Height up to 60ft
Domed and spreading deciduous tree. Leaves 6in long, pinnate with 3–7 ovate leaflets.
Flowers ¼in long, yellowish, 5-lobed; in clusters. Fruits 1–2in long, paired, winged; in
clusters. Widespread in E half of US and central S Canada.

SUGAR SUMAC *Rhus ovata*   Height up to 15ft
Compact evergreen shrub or small tree. Leaves 1–2in long, ovate, and leathery. Flowers
¼in across with 5 white petals; in clusters. Fruits ¼in across and red; in clusters. Free-
draining soils of valley slopes. S CA and AZ.

SMOOTH SUMAC *Rhus glabra*   Height up to 20ft
Distinctive, open-crowned shrub or small tree. Leaves 12in long, compound with 11–31
leaflets; green, red in autumn. Flowers small with 5 white petals; in 8in-long clusters.
Fruits small, reddish; in clusters. Widespread, mainly E US.

STAGSHORN SUMAC *Rhus typhina*   Height up to 30ft
Deciduous shrub or small tree with open crown and bare lower trunk. Leaves 1–2ft long,
compound with 11–31 lanceolate leaflets. Flowers small; in 8in long reddish clusters.
Fruits red and beadlike; in clusters. NE US and SE Canada.

AMERICAN HOLLY *Ilex opaca*   Height up to 70ft
Broadly conical, compact evergreen. Leaves 2–4in long, elliptical, and spiny. Flowers ¼in
across, 4 white petals; in clusters. Separate sex trees. Fruits (female trees only) ¼in across,
red, berrylike. E coast US states, N to VI.

ROCKY MOUNTAIN ELDER *Acer glabrum*   Height up to 30ft
Deciduous shrub or small tree. Leaves 2–4in long with 3 or 5 broad and pointed lobes.
Flowers small, greenish, and in clusters. Fruits 1in long, paired, winged, and forked keys.
Damp ground. Mountains and valleys in W, mainly from CA to BC.

RED MAPLE *Acer rubrum*   Height up to 80ft
Much-branched deciduous tree. Leaves 3–4in long with 3 broad, pointed, and toothed
lobes. Flowers small, greenish, and in clusters. Fruits 1in long, paired, winged, and forked
keys; in clusters. Damp ground. E half of US and locally SE Canada.

SILVER MAPLE *Acer saccharinum*   Height up to 80ft
Much-branched deciduous tree. Leaves 4–6in long with 5 broad, pointed, and toothed
lobes. Flowers small, greenish, and in clusters. Fruits 2in long, paired, winged, and forked
keys. Damp ground. E half of US, except far south; locally SE Canada.

STRIPED MAPLE *Acer pensylvanicum*   Height up to 30ft
Deciduous tree, much-branched from near base. Leaves 5–7in long with 3-pointed and
toothed lobes. Flowers small, yellow, and in clusters. Fruits 1in long, paired, winged, and
forked keys. Damp ground. Uplands of NE US and SE Canada.

SUGAR MAPLE *Acer saccharum*   Height up to 100ft
Domed, much-branched deciduous tree. Leaves 4–5in long with 5 pointed and toothed
lobes; green, turning red and golden in fall. Flowers small, yellowish, and in clusters.
Fruits 1in long, paired, winged, and shallow-forked. NE US and SE Canada.

HORSECHESTNUT *Aesculus hippocastanum*   Height up to 70ft
Spreading deciduous tree. Leaves 3–7in long, palmate with 7 obovate leaflets. Flowers 1in
long with 5 white petals, red-spotted at base; in clusters. Fruits 2in across spiny capsules
with 2 shiny brown seeds. Non-native but planted widely.

CALIFORNIA BUCKEYE *Aesculus californica*   Height up to 25ft
Broadly domed deciduous tree. Leaves 4–7 in long, palmate with usually 5 ovate leaflets.
Flowers 1in long with 5 pink petals and long stamens; in clusters. Fruits 2–3in long
smooth, splitting capsules; 1 shiny brown seed. Native to CA.

YELLOW BUCKEYE *Aesculus octandra*   Height up to 90ft
Much-branched deciduous tree. Leaves 5–9in long, palmate, with 5–7 obovate, toothed
leaflets. Flowers 1in long, 4 yellow petals; in clusters. Fruits 2–3in across smooth, splitting capsules; 1–3 shiny brown seeds. Mainly Appalachians.

BLUEBLOSSOM *Ceanothus thyrsiflorus*   Height up to 20ft
Compact evergreen; domed crown. Leaves 1–2in long, elliptical, finely toothed. Flowers
¼in across with 5 blue petals; in frothy clusters. Fruits ¼in across, blackish, stalked, berrylike. Native to coastal N CA and S OR; also planted.

AMERICAN BASSWOOD *Tilia americana*   Height up to 100ft
Much-branched deciduous tree. Leaves 4–6in long, ovate to heart-shaped, and toothed.
Flowers ¼in across, 5 yellowish petals; stalked, in pendant clusters with leafy bract. Fruits
¼in across, rounded, and hard. NE US and SE Canada.

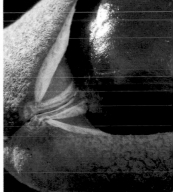

FLOWERING DOGWOOD *Cornus florida* Height up to 30ft
Spreading deciduous tree. Leaves 1–2in long, elliptical with wavy margin. Flowers tiny and tightly packed but surrounded by 4 white petal-like bracts, each 2in long. Fruits ¼in long, red, and berrylike. Widespread E US; also SE Canada.

 RED-OSIER DOGWOOD *Cornus stolonifera* Height up to 10ft
Multi-stemmed deciduous shrub; young twigs reddish. Leaves 1–3in long, elliptical; green above, downy white below. Flowers small, 4 white petals; in 2in wide flat clusters. Fruits ¼in across, whitish. Sub-Arctic Canada and N US.

 PACIFIC DOGWOOD *Cornus nuttallii* Height up to 45ft
Domed deciduous tree. Leaves 3–4in long, elliptical with wavy margins. Flowers small, greenish, tightly packed; surrounded by 4 white bracts, each 2in long. Fruits ½in long, red, berrylike; in compact heads. Pacific coast, BC to CA.

 WAVYLEAF SILKTASSEL *Garrya elliptica* Height up to 20ft
Compact, evergreen. Leaves 2–3in long, elliptical, and opposite with wavy margins; shiny green above, downy below. Flowers tiny and green; in 3–5in long catkinlike tassels. Fruits ¼in across and blackish; in clusters. Pacific Coast, CA and OR.

 PACIFIC MADRONE *Arbutus menziesii* Height up to 70ft
Domed evergreen. Leaves 1–3in long, elliptical; shiny green above, pale below. Flowers ¼in long, white, vase-shaped; pendant, stalked, in clusters. Fruits ¼in long, orange, and berrylike; stalked and in clusters. Pacific Coast, CA to BC.

 WATER TUPELO *Nyssa aquatica* Height up to 100ft
Deciduous tree; bare, broad-based lower trunk and domed crown. Leaves 2–4in long, ovate. Flowers small and green; clustered males and solitary females on separate trees. Fruits 1in long, purple, and berrylike. Seasonally flooding sites, SE US.

 BLACK TUPELO (BLACKGUM) *Nyssa sylvatica* Height up to 100ft
Deciduous tree with conical outline. Leaves 2–5in long, elliptical; shiny green above, downy below. Flowers small, green; clustered males and solitary females on separate trees. Fruits ½in long, berrylike, and black. Damp ground. Mainly E US.

PACIFIC RHODODENDRON *Rhododendron macrophyllum* Height up to 10ft
Dense, evergreen shrub; can form extensive patches. Leaves 2–3in long, elliptical, and shiny green. Attractive flowers 1–2in across, 5-lobed, and pink. Damp slopes. Pacific Coast, from BC to CA.

WHITE RHODODENDRON *Rhododendron albiflorum* Height up to 10ft
Dense, evergreen shrub. Leaves 2–4 in long, narrow-ovate, shiny green. Attractive flowers ¾in across, 5-lobed, bell-shaped, and white; in clusters. Favours damp ground. Upland areas of BC, WA, OR, and MT.

LAPLAND ROSEBAY *Rhododendron lapponicum* Prostrate
Creeping, mat-forming evergreen. Leaves ¼in long, elliptical, and leathery. Flowers ¼in across, 5-lobed, bell-shaped, pink; in clusters. Arctic and sub-Arctic North America; also bare mountain summits SE Canada, NE US.

MOUNTAIN-LAUREL *Kalmia latifolia*   Height up to 20ft
Multi-stemmed, spreading deciduous shrub. Leaves 3–4in long, narrow-ovate, dark green above, paler below. Flowers 1in across, bowl-shaped with 5 white lobes; in clusters. Fruits ¼in across, stalked, black. Appalachians, S to AL, N to NY.

COMMON PERSIMMON *Diospyros virginiana*   Height up to 60ft
Narrow deciduous tree. Leaves 3–6in long, ovate, shiny dark green above, paler and downy below. Fragrant flowers ½in long, bell-shaped with 4 white lobes. Fruits 1–2in across, brownish orange berry. Damp ground. Native to SE US.

GREEN ASH *Fraxinus pennsylvanica*   Height up to 60ft
Deciduous tree; dense, domed crown. Leaves 6–10in long, pinnate, usually with 7 lanceolate leaflets. Flowers small and greenish; in clusters. Fruits 2in long, narrow, winged keys; in clusters. Damp ground. E US and S central to SE Canada.

WHITE ASH *Fraxinus americana*   Height up to 80ft
Domed, much-branched deciduous tree. Leaves 8–12in long, pinnate, usually with 7 ovate leaflets. Flowers small and reddish; in clusters. Fruits 1–2in long, narrow, winged, and brown keys; in clusters. Widespread E US and SE Canada.

OREGON ASH *Fraxinus latifolia*   Height up to 80ft
Much-branched deciduous tree with tapering outline. Leaves 6–12in long, pinnate, usually with 5 or 7 elliptical leaflets. Flowers small, greenish, and clustered; separate sex trees. Damp ground. Coastal WA, OR, and N CA; also C CA.

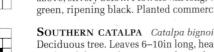

OLIVE *Olea europaea*   Height up to 20ft
Dense and irregularly domed evergreen. Leaves 1–3in long, lanceolate, grayish green above, silvery below. Flowers ¼in long, whitish, and 4-lobed. Fruits 1in long, ovoid olives; green, ripening black. Planted commercially in SW US.

SOUTHERN CATALPA *Catalpa bignoides*   Height up to 50ft
Deciduous tree. Leaves 6–10in long, heart-shaped, in 3s. Flowers 1–2in long, bell-shaped, 5 white lobes with orange and purple marks. Fruits 6–12in long, cylindrical, podlike. Damp ground. Native SE US; planted widely and cultivated.

DESERT-WILLOW *Chilopsis linearis*   Height up to 20ft
Multi-stemmed, open deciduous shrub. Leaves 3–6in long, narrow, willowlike, and curved. Flowers 1in across, bell-shaped with 5 pinkish white lobes; in clusters. Fruits 4–8in long, slender, and cylindrical. Deserts. S CA to S NM.

BLACK-MANGROVE *Avicennnia germinans*   Height up to 40ft
Evergreen shrub with a dense, domed crown. Leaves 1in long, lanceolate, shiny above, downy below. Flowers ½in across with 4 white lobes. Fruits 1in long flattened ovoid capsules. Marine and brackish silt. Sub-tropical SE US.

BUTTONBUSH *Cephalanthus occidentalis*   Height up to 20ft
Multi-stemmed, spreading deciduous tree. Leaves 3–6in long, ovate, shiny green above, paler below. Flowers tubular and white; in clustered balls, 1–2in across. Fruits 1in across brown balls. Damp ground. Native E US; planted elsewhere.

AMERICAN ELDER *Sambucus canadensis*   Height up to 15ft
Spreading deciduous shrub. Leaves 6–9in long, pinnate with 3–7 elliptical and toothed leaflets. Flowers ¼in across with 4 or 5 white lobes; in flat clusters. Fruits ¼in across blackish berries; in clusters. E US and SE Canada.

TAMARIND *Tamarindus indica*   Height up to 80ft
Domed and dense-crowned evergreen tree. Leaves 5–8in long, pinnate with 10–15 pairs
of elliptical leaflets. Flowers small with 5 yellow petals; in spikelike clusters. Fruits 5–8in
long brownish edible pods. S US; planted widely.

NANNYBERRY *Viburnum lentago*   Height up to 20ft
Much-branched deciduous shrub. Leaves 3–4in long, elliptical and toothed with obvious
veins. Flowers ¼in across with 5 white lobes; in clusters. Fruits ½in long, blackish, and
ovoid; in clusters. Damp ground. E half of N US and SE Canada.

ARROWWOOD *Viburnum dentatum*   Height up to 10ft
Multi-stemmed, branching deciduous shrub. Leaves 2–4in long, ovate, and toothed with
obvious veins. Flowers ¼in across with 5 white lobes; in clusters. Fruits ¼in across,
rounded, and blackish; in clusters. Damp ground. E US.

BLACK HUCKLEBERRY *Gaylussacia baccata*   Height up to 3ft
Dense and much-branched deciduous shrub. Leaves 1–2in long, ovate, and sticky; dark
green, reddish in fall. Flowers ¼in across, reddish, and urn-shaped; in clusters. Berries ¼in
across, spherical, and blackish. NE US and SE Canada.

APACHE PLUME *Fallugia paradoxa*   Height up to 5ft
Dense and compact evergreen shrub. Leaves ¼–½in long, hairy, and deeply divided, usually into 5 lobes. Flowers 1in across with 5 white petals. Fruits comprise small seeds and
long feathery plumes. Arid rocky slopes. SW US.

CREOSOTE BUSH *Larrea tridentata*   Height up to 5ft
Much-branched, partly deciduous shrub. Leaves ¼-½in long, resinous, 2-lobed, and wing-
like. Flowers ¼-½in across, with 5 yellow petals; extremely attractive to insects. Fruits ¼in
long, ovoid, and hairy. Arid soils. S US, from CA to TX.

BRITTLEBUSH *Encelia farinosa*   Height up to 3ft
Much-branched, compact, and often domed shrub. Stems whitish and leaves ½in long, tri-
angular, and lobed; bluish green after rain but dead, withered whitish in dry months.
Flowers ½in across, yellow, and daisylike. Deserts of SW US.

JOJOBA *Simmondsia chinensis*   Height up to 10ft
Compact evergreen shrub. Leaves 1–2in long, rounded-ovate, opposite, leathery, and yellow-green. Flowers small and reddish green; clustered males on separate plants from solitary females. Fruits 1in-long acornlike nuts. Arid land. CA and AZ.

CANARY ISLAND DATE *Phoenix canariensis*   Height up to 50ft
Evergreen with scaly trunk due to leaf-stalk scars. Leaves 15–20ft long with numerous narrow leaflets; leaf stalks spiny. Flowers small, whitish, and clustered. Fruits ¾in-long edible dates; in clusters. Planted widely in S US.

CALIFORNIA WASHINGTONIA *Washingtonia filifera*   Height up to 60ft
Evergreen with huge trunk. Leaves 4–5ft long with narrow leaflets; dead leaves remain hanging. Flowers ½in long, white; in clusters. Fruits ½in long, black, berrylike, clustered. Native to SW US (stream courses); planted elsewhere in S.

CABBAGE PALMETTO *Sabal palmetto*   Height up to 40ft
Evergreen with broad trunk. Leaves 5–7ft long, broad, and fan-shaped with long narrow leaflets. Flowers small and whitish; in clusters. Fruits ¼in across, black berries; in clusters. Native to S and coastal FL; also coastal GA and SC.

JOSHUA-TREE *Yucca brevifolia*   Height up to 30ft
Distinctive evergreen with open, branched appearance. Leaves 10–14in long, narrow, toothed, and bluish. Flowers 1½in long, bell-shaped, and creamy; in clusters. Fruits 3–4in long, brown, and clustered. Mojave Desert, SW US.

PACIFIC YUCCA (BLUE YUCCA) *Yucca baccata*   Height up to 5ft
Robust evergreen. Leaves up to 3ft long, narrow, and stiff. Flowers 3–4in long, creamy white, and bell-shaped; in clustered spikes. Fruits 3–10in long cylindrical pods. Arid ground. Widespread across SW US, CA to W TX, N to S CO.

SOAPTREE YUCCA *Yucca elata*   Height up to 15ft
Evergreen shrub; usually unbranched. Leaves 1–2ft long, narrow, and spine-tipped. Flowers 2in long, white, and bell-shaped; in clustered spikes. Fruits 2–3in long podlike capsule. Deserts and arid ground. W TX, NM, and AZ.

AGAVE *Agave* sp.   Height up to 12ft
Impressive evergreen. Leaves 1–2ft long, broad lanceolate, blue-gray, and fleshy, with spine at tip and along margins; form a basal rosette. Flowers ¾in long and yellowish; in clusters at top of tall stalk, once in plant's life. SW US. Several species are found in North America.

SAGUARO *Cereus giganteus*   Height up to 40ft
Immense cactus with ribbed, spiny stem. Young specimens columnar, unbranched. Older ones have armlike branches arising roughly ½ way up plant. Flowers 3in across, creamy, and short-lived (May–Jun). Fruits 3in long, ovoid. Mainly SE AZ.

ORGAN PIPE CACTUS *Stenocereus thurberi*   Height up to 20ft
In maturity has numerous spiny, ridged, pipelike branches; these arise from central point and curve at base. Flowers 1–2in across, whitish, and terminal (May–Jun). Fruits 2in long and spiny. Found only in Organ Pipe Cactus National Monument, AZ.

SENITA *Lophocereus schottii*   Height up to 20ft
In maturity, has upright branches arising from central point, curved at base; these have a few prominent ribs armed with clusters of spines. Flowers ½–1in across and pink (Jun). Fruits ½in long and red. Found only in Organ Pipe Cactus National Monument, AZ.

OCATILLO *Fouquieria splendens*   Height up to 25ft
Cactuslike desert plant comprising long, slender, and spiny branches that radiate out from base forming a funnel shape. Leaves 2in long, ovate, and clustered. Flowers 1in long, 5-lobed, red, clustered (Mar–Jun). S US from S CA to TX.

JUMPING CHOLLA (CHAINFRUIT CHOLLA) *Opuntia fulgida*   Height up to 15ft
Extremely spiny cactus. Mature specimens comprise a tall dark trunk supporting a much-divided network of branches. Spines are silvery-sheathed. Flowers ½–1in across and purple (Mar–Apr). Fruits ovoid, green, and in chains. Deserts of S AZ.

TEDDY BEAR CHOLLA *Opuntia bigelovii*   Height up to 10ft
Densely divided and extremely spiny cactus. Stems are blackish and branches are relatively short with golden-sheathed spines. Flowers 1in across and greenish (Mar–Apr). Fruits ¾in long and yellowish. Rocky slopes, S CA to S AZ.

BUCKHORN CHOLLA *Opuntia acanthocarpa*   Height up to 10ft
Much-branched cactus. Branches slender and long. Spines with only short sheaths. Flowers 1in across; colour variable but usually orange-red or yellowish (Mar–Apr). Fruits ¾in across and greenish. Deserts of CA, AZ, S NV, and S UT.

PEYOTE *Lophophora williamsii*   Width up to 3in
Curious cactus resembling a flattened dome or button; surface is spineless and blue-gray. In maturity several buttons often grow in abutting clusters. Flowers 1in across and pink (May–Sep). Fruits ½in long and red. Deserts of S TX.

BEAVERTAIL CACTUS *Opuntia basilaris*   Height up to 10ft
A prickly pear-type cactus with jointed, flattened, and spineless gray-green stems. Mature specimens are much-branched. Flowers 2–3in across and reddish pink (Mar–Jun). Fruits 1in long, ovoid, and brown. Deserts of S CA, S NV, S UT, and W TX.

ENGELMANN'S PRICKLY PEAR *Opuntia engelmannii*   Height up to 5ft
Much-branched and spreading cactus with jointed, flattened, and spiny gray-green stems; stem segments are up to 1ft long. Flowers 2in across and yellow (Mar–Jun). Fruits 1in long, ovoid, and reddish purple. Deserts of S CA, S AZ, S NM, and W TX.

STAGHORN CHOLLA *Opuntia versicolor*   Height up to 15ft
Impressive and much-branched treelike cactus with short spines; branches are long and slender. Flowers 1in across; colour variable but often reddish or yellow (Mar–Jun). Fruits 1in long, greenish, and spineless. Deserts around Tucson, AZ.

BARREL CACTUS *Ferocactus acanthodes*   Height up to 10ft
Extremely spiny cactus, barrel-shaped when young, becoming taller and columnar with age. Spines reddish or yellow and clustered along ribs. Flowers 2in across and reddish yellow (Apr–May). Fruits 1in long and yellow. Deserts of S CA and S AZ.

FISHHOOK BARREL CACTUS *Ferocactus wislizenii*   Height up to 6ft
Impressive barrel-shaped cactus. Ribs are coated with clusters of spines; central spine in each cluster is hooked-tipped. Flowers 1–2in across and reddish yellow (Aug–Sep). Fruits 1in long and yellow. Deserts of S AZ and SW NM.

CUSHION CACTUS *Coryphantha vivipara*   Height up to 5in
Spherical cactus. Surface concealed by numerous whitish radial spines flattened against stem; longer outward-pointing spines develop with age. Flowers 1in across, usually pinkish or yellow (Apr–May). Arid ground SW Canada to CA and TX.

FISHHOOK CACTUS *Mammilaria microcarpa*   Height up to 6in
Spherical to cylindrical cactus. Spines arranged in radiating clusters; central spine is hooked-tipped. Flowers 1in across and pinkish (Apr–May). Fruits 1in long and reddish. Deserts and dry grassland. S CA to W TX.

STRAWBERRY CACTUS *Echinocereus triglochidiatus*   Height up to 10ft
Large cylindrical cactus. Spines arranged in clusters on ribs. Flowers 2in across and bright red (Apr–May). Fruits 2in long, rounded, and red. Deserts and dry slopes. S CA to TX, N to CO and S UT.

SPANISH MOSS *Tillandsia usneoides*   Epiphytic
Forms dense mosslike masses of scaly stems attached to, and cascading from, tree branches. Flowers ½in long, yellow, and 3-petalled (Apr–Jun). Leaves 2in long and slender. Coastal woodland of SW US, from VA to TX.

DUTCHMAN'S PIPE *Aristolochia durior*   Climbing
Scrambling climber with long twining stems. Leaves 6–12in long and heart-shaped. Flowers 2in long, curved, and pipe-shaped; 3 maroon to brown petallike sepal lobes at mouth (Apr–Jun). Humid woodlands, mainly S Appalachians.

WILD GINGER *Asarum canadense*   Height up to 1ft
Long-stalked leaves arise from ground level and are 4–6in across, heart- or kidney-shaped, and hairy. Flowers 1½in across with three maroon pointed lobes; on short stalk from ground level (Apr–May). Temperate woods in NW of North America.

MISTLETOE *Phoradendron serotinum*   Up to 1ft across
Semi-parasitic plant; forms clumps on branches of deciduous trees. Leaves 1–5in long and lanceolate. Flowers small, yellowish, and 3-lobed (Sep–Oct); separate sex plants. Fruits small, white, and berrylike. Temperate areas of E US.

STINGING NETTLE *Urtica dioica*   Height up to 3ft
Stinging herbaceous plant. Leaves 2–4in long, oval, toothed, and pointed-tipped; borne in opposite pairs and covered with sharp hairs. Flowers in pendulous catkins (Jun–Oct); separate sex plants. Disturbed areas throughout North America.

RUSSIAN TUMBLEWEED (PRICKLY SALTWORT) *Salsola kali*   Height up to 4ft
Much-branched, forming dense rounded clumps; when detached from ground these are blown by wind. Leaves short, narrow, bractlike, and spine-tipped. Flowers insignificant; seeds resemble pinkish flowers. Arid open ground, W US.

MARIJUANA *Cannabis sativa*   Height up to 8ft
Branching upright plant with narcotic properties. Leaves palmate, with 5–7 narrow, toothed leaflets. Flowers small, green, and clustered (Jun–Oct); separate sex plants. Non-native but widely naturalized on waste and disturbed areas.

SWAMP SMARTWEED *Polygonum coccineum*   Height up to 3ft
Variable herbaceous plant. Leaves 8in long and lanceolate when growing on land; shorter, narrower with heart-shaped base, and floating when aquatic. Flowers small and pink; in 2–6in long spikelike clusters (Jul–Sep). Wetlands, E of North America.

WATER SMARTWEED *Polygonum amphibium*   Height up to 1½ft
Amphibious perennial growing at margins of ponds and on dry land. Has floating stems and oval leaves 2–4in long when aquatic; leaves shorter in terrestrial forms. Flowers small and pink; in cylindrical spikes (Jun–Sep). Throughout North America.

WESTERN BISTORT *Polygonum bistortoides*   Height up to 2ft
Elegant herbaceous plant. Leaves 4–8in long and lanceolate. Flowers small and whitish with 5 segments; in 2in long rounded terminal clusters on long reddish stems (May–Aug). Damp upland meadows. Mountains of Pacific states and provinces.

LADY'S-THUMB *Persicaria maculosa (Polygonum persicaria)*   Height up to 2ft
Upright or sprawling annual; much-branched reddish stems. Leaves 2–6in long, narrow-oval, and typically with dark central mark. Flowers small and pink; borne in cylindrical, terminal spikes (Jun–Oct). Damp, disturbed areas throughout North America.

BITTERROOT *Lewisia rediviva*   Height up to 2ft
Low-growing plant. Leaves 1–2in long, narrow, and fleshy, forming a rosette. Flowers 2in across with 12–18 pinkish red petals; borne on short stalks from center or rosette (May–Jul). Open rocky ground. BC and Pacific states, E to MT.

MOUNTAIN SORREL *Oxyria digyna* Height up to 10in
Low-growing perennial. Leaves kidney-shaped and fleshy. Flowers small and reddish or yellowish; in spikes (Jun–Sep). Fruits reddish and similar to flowers. Rocky places. Tundra and mountains of Canada and AK; mountains of Pacific states.

SHEEP'S SORREL *Rumex acetosella* Height up to 1ft
Short, upright perennial. Leaves arrow-shaped but with basal lobes pointing forwards. Flowers small and reddish; in spikes (May–Aug). Fruits reddish; similar to flowers. Bare ground, especially on acid soils. Throughout North America.

CURLY DOCK *Rumex crispus* Height up to 3ft
Robust perennial. Leaves narrow, up to 1ft long, with wavy margins. Flowers oval, flattened, and greenish; in leafless spikes (Jun–Oct). Fruits similar to flowers. Waste and disturbed areas throughout North America.

LAMB'S QUARTERS *Chenopodium album* Height up to 3ft
Upright annual weed. Leaves green but look matt and whitish due to mealy coating; leaf shape varies from oval to diamond-shape. Flowers small and whitish; in spikes (Jun–Oct). Disturbed and cultivated soils. Non-native; widespread throughout North America.

SEA-BLITE *Suaeda maritima* Height up to 1½ft
Much-branched and clump-forming annual. Leaves usually swollen and cylindrical. Leaves and stem vary in colour from yellow-green to reddish. Flowers tiny and yellowish (Aug–Oct). Salt marshes. Atlantic coasts of US and Canada.

SLENDER GLASSWORT *Salicornia europaea* Height up to 1ft
Fleshy leafless annual; recalls a miniature cactus. Usually much-branched, segmented, and yellowish green. Flowers minute and green; at leaf junctions (Aug–Oct). Atlantic coast salt marshes; also locally inland on saline soil.

SEABEACH SANDWORT *Honckenya peploides* Prostrate
Distinctive perennial. Often forms large mats that comprise creeping stems bearing opposite pairs of fleshy, oval leaves. Flowers greenish white and ½in across (May–Aug). Stable sands and shingle. Atlantic coasts of US and Canada.

PIGWEED *Amaranthus retroflexus* Height up to 4ft
Hairy annual weed. Leaves 4–6in long, oval, alternate, and toothed. Flowers small, greenish; in 3in-long dense and clustered spikes (Aug–Oct). Favors disturbed and cultivated soils. Widespread throughout North America.

WATER HYACINTH *Eichhornia crassipes* Floating
Aquatic plant. Leaves 2–5in across, shiny green, rounded to kidney-shaped; swollen bases are air-filled floats. Flowers 2in across, 6-lobed, funnel-shaped, purple; in spikes (all year). Wetlands. Non-native; common in SE states.

PICKERELWEED *Pontederia cordata* Height up to 2ft
Creeping aquatic plant. Leaves 5–10in across, heart-shaped, and tapering. Flowers ½in across, funnel-shaped, and purple; in cylindrical spikes (Jun–Nov). Marshes and wetlands. From ON to FL eastwards.

HOTTENTOT FIG *Carpobrotus edulis (Mesembryanthemum edule)* Creeping
Mat-forming plant with trailing and rooting stems. Leaves 1–2in long, 3-sided, curved, and fleshy. Flowers 2–3in across, yellow with numerous petals; open fully only in sun (Apr–Aug). Non-native but naturalized CA; often coastal.

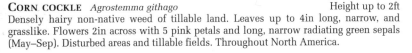

CORN COCKLE *Agrostemma githago*　　　　　　Height up to 2ft
Densely hairy non-native weed of tillable land. Leaves up to 4in long, narrow, and grasslike. Flowers 2in across with 5 pink petals and long, narrow radiating green sepals (May–Sep). Disturbed areas and tillable fields. Throughout North America.

MOUSE-EAR CHICKWEED *Cerastium fontanum (vulgatum)*　　　Height up to 1ft
Much-branched annual non-native. Often prostrate and spreading. Leaves ½in long, oval, fresh green, in opposite pairs, unstalked. Flowers ¼in across with 5 white, deeply divided petals (Apr–Oct). Disturbed areas throughout North America.

FIELD CHICKWEED *Cerastium arvense*　　　　　Height up to 1½ft
Downy perennial, often prostrate and spreading. Leaves 1in long, narrow, and lanceolate. Flowers 1in across with 5 white, notched petals (Apr–Sep). Favours free-draining grassy places, often on lime. Widespread at temperate latitudes.

WHITE CAMPION (EVENING LYCHNIS) *Silene latifolia (alba)*　　Height up to 3ft
Hairy non-native perennial. Leaves 2–4in long and oval; in opposite pairs. Flowers 1in across with 5 white deeply notched petals (Jun–Oct). Favours grassy places including roadsides. Widespread, especially in E and SW of North America.

RAGGED ROBIN *Lychnis flox-cuculi*　　　　　Height up to 2ft
Distinctive non-native perennial. Leaves 2–3in long, narrow, grasslike, and rough; upper ones in opposite pairs. Flowers ½in across with 5 pink petals, each divided into 4 lobes (May–Jul). Naturalized in damp grassland, NE US.

BOUNCING BET *Saponaria officinalis*　　　　Height up to 2ft
Hairless, straggly non-native perennial. Leaves 2–3in long, lanceolate to oval with striking veins. Flowers 1in across with 5 pale pink petals, inrolled at tip (Jul–Sep). Disturbed areas and roadsides. Locally common throughout North America.

CHICKWEED *Stellaria media*　　　　　　Height up to 8in
Much-branched non-native annual; often prostrate and spreading. Leaves ½–1in long, oval, fresh green, and in opposite pairs; upper leaves unstalked. Flowers ¼in across, 5 deeply divided white petals (all year). Disturbed areas throughout North America.

KNAWEL *Scleranthus annuus*　　　　　　Height up to 6in
Yellowish green non-native annual; often prostrate and spreading. Leaves up to ½in long, narrow, and pointed; in opposite pairs along stems. Flowers small, with green, pointed sepals, and no petals (May–Aug). Dry, bare soil. Widespread in W.

MOSS CAMPION *Silene acaulis*　　　　　Up to 9in across
Compact, cushion-forming perennial. Leaves ½in long, narrow, densely packed, and overlapping. Flowers ½in across with 5 pink petals (Jun–Aug). Widespread in Arctic and alpine zones of mountains of Canada and US, S to NH in E, AZ in W.

STARRY CAMPION *Silene stellata*　　　　　Height up to 3ft
Upright perennial. Leaves 2–4in long, narrow, and hairless; usually in whorls of 4. Flowers ¾in across with 5 deeply divided white petals; in clusters (Jun–Sep). Favours open woodland. Widespread in E half of US.

AMERICAN LOTUS *Nelumbo lutea*　　　　　Aquatic
Distinctive water plant. Leaves 1–2ft across and rounded; raised on stalks above water level. Flowers 7–10in across with numerous yellow petals; on stalks above water (July–Sep). Still or slow-moving waters. E half of US and S ON.

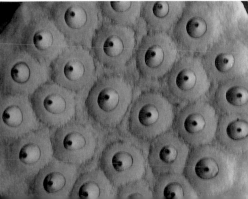

COMMON SPATTERDOCK *Nuphar advena*   Aquatic
Floating water plant. Leaves 5–12in across and heart-shaped to rounded; often raised on
stalks above water level. Flowers 2in across with numerous showy yellow sepals and
smaller petals (May–Aug). Ponds and lakes. E half of US.

YELLOW POND LILY *Nuphar variegatum*   Aquatic
Distinctive water plant. Leaves 5–10in across and heart-shaped to rounded; floating on
water. Flowers 2in across with 6 yellow sepals and many smaller petals; borne on stalks
(May–Sep). Ponds and backwaters. E half of North America.

FRAGRANT WATER LILY *Nymphaea odorata*   Aquatic
Aquatic plant. Leaves 5–12in across, rounded, and dissected to leaf stalk; floating, green
above, reddish below. Flowers 4–5in across, fragrant with numerous whitish or pinkish
petals (Jun–Sep). Ponds and backwaters. Throughout North America.

COMMON BARBERRY *Berberis vulgaris*   Height up to 8ft
Spiny-stemmed shrub. Leaves 2–3in long, ovate, and in clusters. Flowers ¼in across, yel-
low with 6 sepals and 6 petals; in pendant clusters (May–June). Fruits ovoid, ripening red.
Scrub habitats. NE US and SE Canada.

RED BANEBERRY *Actaea rubra*   Height up to 2ft
Much-divided plant. Leaves pinnately divided into numerous ovate to maplelike, toothed
leaflets each 2–3in long. Flowers ¼in across with whitish petals that soon drop (May–Jul).
Clusters of red berries in fall. NE US and Pacific states.

CANADA ANEMONE (MEADOW ANEMONE) *Anemone canadensis* Height up to 9in
Attractive upright plant. Leaves 1–2in long, deeply divided, arising from base. Flowers
1–2in across with 5 white petal-like sepals and numerous yellow stamens (Apr–May).
Prairies. E of Rocky Mountains, E to NJ and QU, S to NM.

PASQUEFLOWER *Anemone patens*   Height up to 8–14in
Upright silky-hairy plant. Leaves up to 3in long, palmately divided into fine segments.
Flowers 2–3in across with 5–7 purplish white petal-like sepals (Apr–Jun). Fruits are feath-
ery. Meadows across E half of North America.

WOOD ANEMONE *Anemone quinquefolia*   Height up to 8in
Delicate woodland flower often forming carpets. Leaves palmate with 3 or 5 toothed segments, each 1½in long. Flowers 1in across with 4–9 white petal-like sepals; solitary and
stalked (Apr–Jun). Fruits hairy. Open woodland. E of North America.

WILD COLUMBINE *Aquilegia canadensis*   Height up to 2ft
Attractive bushy plant. Leaves 5–6in across, divided into numerous 3-lobed leaflets. Flowers 1–2in long, red with 5 spurred petals and 5 sepals (Apr–Jul). Fruits podlike. Wooded,
rocky ground. SE Canada and E US, S to WI.

BLUE COLUMBINE *Aquilegia coerulea*   Height up to 3ft
Attractive bushy plant. Leaves much divided into lobed leaflets, each 1in long. Flowers
2–3in across with 5 petal-like pale blue sepals and 5 whitish petals (Jun–Aug). Upland
woodlands. Mountains from Rockies S to AZ.

MARSH MARIGOLD *Caltha palustris* Height up to 2ft
Attractive perennial with stout stems. Leaves 3–7in across, kidney- to heart-shaped, and glossy. Flowers 1–2in across with 5 yellow petal-like sepals (Apr–Jun). Damp woodland, marshes, and wet meadows. Throughout Canada and NE US.

VIRGIN'S BOWER *Clematis virginiana* Climbing
Twining, vinelike plant. Leaves divided into 3 leaflets, each toothed and 1–2in long. Flowers 1in across with 4–5 whitish petal-like sepals and numerous stamens (Jul–Sep). Fruits are feathery-tailed seeds. Margins of woods and scrub. E of North America.

 MOUSETAIL *Myosurus minimus* Height up to 5in
Curious, tufted buttercup-relative. Leaves 2–3in long, narrow, and arising from base. Spikelike flowers resemble miniature plantain heads but with 5 petals and 5 sepals at base (Apr–Jun). Margins of tillable fields. Throughout most of North America.

 ROUND-LOBED HEPATICA *Hepatica americana* Height up to 6in
Charming woodland floor plant. Leaves 2in across with 3 round lobes. Flowers 1in across with 5–9 purple petal-like sepals; borne on hairy stalks (Mar–Jun). Dry woodland, usually on rocks. E half of North America.

 COMMON BUTTERCUP *Ranunculus acris* Height up to 3ft
Branched and hairy perennial. Lower leaves 2–4in long, rounded, and divided into 3–7 lobes; upper leaves unstalked and smaller. Flowers 1in across with 5 shiny yellow petals and 5 green sepals (May–Sep). Grassland and disturbed areas throughout North America.

 BULBOUS BUTTERCUP *Ranunculus bulbosus* Height up to 1½ft
Hairy and branching perennial. Leaves 2–4in across and divided into 3 lobes, each of which is stalked. Flowers 1in across with 5 yellow petals and 5 green, reflexed sepals (Apr–Jun). Grassland. Throughout much of North America.

 CURSED BUTTERCUP *Ranunculus sceleratus* Height up to 1½ft
Annual with fresh green appearance. Lower leaves 2–3in long, celerylike, and divided into 3 lobes. Flowers ½in across with 5 yellow petals; in clusters (May–Sep). Damp, often trampled ground. Widespread in W of North America.

AMERICAN GLOBEFLOWER *Trollius laxus* Height up to 1½ft
Attractive upright perennial. Leaves 2–4in across and palmately divided into toothed lobes. Flowers 1in across with 5 yellow petal-like sepals and many small petals (Apr–Jun). Damp meadows and marshes. Local, BC, WA, and Rockies; also NE US.

HAIRLEAF WATER BUTTERCUP *Ranunculus aquatilis* Aquatic
Floating annual or perennial. Has threadlike submerged leaves and floating ones that are 1in across with toothed lobes. Flowers ½in across with 5 white petals (Apr–Aug). Slow-flowing and still waters. Throughout most of North America.

WESTERN MONKSHOOD *Aconitum columbianum* Height up to 6ft
Upright perennial. Leaves 3–8in across, palmately lobed, and toothed. Flowers 1in long, bluish purple, and hooded comprising 5 petal-like sepals (Jun–Aug). Damp woodland and mountain meadows. Pacific states and provinces; also Rocky Mountains.

TALL MEADOWRUE *Thalictrum polygamum* Height up to 8ft
Impressive waterside plant. Leaves bluish green and pinnately divided into 3-lobed leaflets, each 1in long. Flowers ¼in across with whitish sepals that fall and no petals (Jun–Aug). Marshes, margins of rivers. E of North America, W to ON, S to GA.

CELANDINE *Chelidonium majus* Height up to 3ft
Upright, brittle-stemmed perennial. Leaves 5–8in long, gray-green, and pinnately divided. Flowers ¾in across with 4 bright yellow, non-overlapping petals (Apr–Aug). Margins of woodland and roadsides. Non-native, widespread in E of North America.

 CALIFORNIA POPPY *Eschscholzia californica* Height up to 2ft
Attractive wayside plant. Leaves 1–2in long, blue-green, and divided into narrow segments. Flowers 1–2in across with 4 yellow or orange-yellow petals; open fully only in bright sunlight (Feb–Aug). CA, OR, and WA. Also widely cultivated.

 YELLOW HORNED-POPPY *Glaucium flavum* Height up to 2ft
Clump-forming blue-gray perennial. Leaves 4–6in long and pinnately divided; upper ones clasping and lobed. Flowers 2–3in across with 4 yellow petals (Jun–Aug). Seedpods curved and 6–12in long. Coastal shingle, Atlantic and Pacific US.

 CORN POPPY *Papaver rhoeas* Height up to 2ft
Hairy annual weed. Leaves 2–4in long and much-divided. Flowers 2–3in across with 4 papery and overlapping scarlet petals (Jun–Aug). Ovoid seed capsule. Disturbed areas and tillable fields. Widespread across much of US and S Canada.

 DEVIL'S-FIG *Argemone mexicana* Height up to 3ft
Leafy blue-green plant. Leaves up to 7in long, lobed, and thistlelike. Flowers up to 3in across with 4–6 yellow petals (May–Sep); sepals drop as flower opens. Fruit is a spiny capsule. Disturbed areas and waste ground. SE US, W to TX.

 ARIZONA PRICKLY POPPY *Argemone platyceras* Height up to 2ft
Distinctive prickly perennial with yellow sap. Leaves 3–5in long, lobed, spiny, and thistlelike. Flowers 2–3in across with 4–6 white, papery petals and a yellow center (all year). Grassland and roadsides. Deserts of SW US.

 BLOODROOT *Sanguinaria canadensis* Height up to 1ft
Delicate woodland floor plant. Roots yield red juice. Leaves 4–6in long, bluish, and palmately divided into 5–9 lobes. Flowers 1–2in across with 8–10 white petals and yellow center. Damp woodlands. Canada and E US.

WILD BLEEDING HEART *Dicentra exima* Height up to 1½ft
Distinctive perennial. Leaves up to 9in long and much divided into narrow leaflets; all leaves basal. Flowers ¾in long, pendant, heart-shaped, and pinkish red; borne in rows (May–Aug). Rocky ground. E US.

DUTCHMAN'S BREECHES *Dicentra cucullaria* Height up to 1ft
Attractive plant. Leaves 3–6in long, gray-green, and much-divided into feathery leaflets. Flowers ¾in long, white, and angular heart-shaped; borne in clusters (Apr–May). Undisturbed woodlands. E Canada and mountains of E US, WA and OR.

BLACK MUSTARD *Brassica nigra*   Height up to 3ft
Robust and much-branched grayish green annual. Leaves 2–3in long, stalked, lower ones pinnately lobed, the terminal lobe largest. Flowers ½in across with 4 yellow petals; in clusters (May–Sep). Waste ground and fields. Throughout North America.

SEA ROCKET *Cakile maritima*   Height up to 1ft
Straggling, fleshy annual. Leaves 3–5in long, toothed, shiny, and lobed. Flowers ¼in across with 4 pale lilac petals; in dense clusters (Jun–Sep). Restricted to stabilized coastal shingle and sand. Atlantic and Pacific coasts of North America.

SHEPHERD'S-PURSE *Capsella bursa-pastoris*   Height up to 1½ft
Upright annual. Leaves vary from lobed to entire; basal ones 2–4in long, upper ones smaller and toothed. Flowers tiny with 4 white petals; in terminal clusters (Mar–Nov). Seedpods green and triangular. disturbed areas throughout North America.

WESTERN WALLFLOWER *Erysimum capitatum*   Height up to 3ft
Attractive upright plant. Leaves 2–5in long, narrow; in basal rosette and up lower stem. Flowers ¾in across with 4 orange or orange-yellow flowers; in terminal heads (Mar–Jul). Dry, open ground, often stony. W North America.

CUCKOOFLOWER *Cardamine pratensis*   Height up to 2ft
Variable upright perennial. Leaves 1–2in long, pinnately divided, and forming a basal rosette. Flowers ¾in across with 4 pinkish white or pale lilac petals; in terminal clusters (Apr–Jun). Damp meadows and woodlands. E half of North America.

SPRING-CRESS *Cardamine bulbosa*   Height up to 2ft
Elegant upright plant. Leaves 1–2in long; basal ones oval and stalked, stem leaves narrow and unstalked. Flowers ½in across with 4 white petals; in terminal clusters (Mar–Jun). Marshes and margins of rivers. E half of North America.

WHITLOW GRASS *Erophila verna*   Height up to 9in
Low-growing annual. Leaves up to 1in long, narrow, and toothed; form basal rosette. Flowers tiny with 4 white and deeply notched petals (Mar–Jun). Dry, bare places including margins of fields, and tracks. E US.

WATERCRESS *Rorippa nasturtium-aquaticum (Nasturtium officinale)*   Height up to 1ft
Aquatic and emergent water perennial. Leaves 1–5in long, pinnately divided into 5–9 segments. Flowers tiny with 4 white petals; in 1in wide terminal clusters (May–Oct). Streams and ditches. Introduced non-native. Widespread throughout North America.

HEDGE MUSTARD *Sisymbrium officinale*   Height up to 2ft
Tough, upright plant. Leaves 2–6in long; lower ones deeply divided, stem leaves narrow. Unbranched upper part has cylindrical pods pressed close to stem and terminal head of tiny yellow 4-petalled flowers. disturbed areas throughout North America.

CALIFORNIA PITCHER PLANT *Darlingtonia californica*   Height up to 3ft
Bizarre-looking carnivorous plant. Leaves 5–20in long, fresh green, tubular, with hooded tips. Flowers 2–3in long with 5 greenish sepals and 5 dark red petals; pendant on long stalk (Apr–Aug). Upland and coastal bogs. OR and N CA.

TRUMPETS *Sarracenia flava*   Height up to 3ft
Carnivorous plant with 1–3ft tall, hooded, and hollow leaves that collect water and trap
insects. Flowers 3–5in across with 5 sepals and 5 petals; on long stalks (Apr–May). Bogs
and saturated pine forest. SE US.

NORTHERN PITCHER PLANT *Sarracenia purpurea*   Height up to 1ft
Carnivorous plant with rosette of inflated and hollow, flagon-shaped, greenish-maroon
leaves that collect water and trap insects. Flowers 2in across and reddish purple with 5
petals; on long stalks (May–Aug). Bogs in E of North America.

ROUND-LEAVED SUNDEW *Drosera rotundifolia*   Height up to 8in
Distinctive insectivorous plant. Has a basal rosette of reddish, round leaves, ½in long, that
are stalked and covered in sticky hairs that trap insects. Flowers ¼in across with 5 white
petals; on upright spikes (Jun–Aug). Bogs. Throughout North America.

NORTHERN SUNDEW *Drosera anglica*   Height up to 10in
Insectivorous plant with rosette of 1½in long, reddish, narrow leaves borne upright on long
stalks and covered in sticky, insect-trapping hairs. Flowers ¼in across with 5 white petals;
on tall stalks (Jun–Aug). Wet bogs. Canada and N US.

GRASS-OF-PARNASSUS *Parnassia palustris*   Height up to 1ft
Distinctive perennial. Basal leaves 2in across, heart-shaped, and stalked. Flowers ½–1in
across with 5 white petals; solitary on erect stalks with clasping leaves (Jun–Sep). Damp,
usually lime-rich, meadows. NE North America.

ROSEROOT *Sedum rosea (Rhodiola rosea)*   Height up to 1ft
Succulent plant. Clusters of stout stems. Leaves ½–1in long, overlapping on stem, and
fleshy. Flowers tiny and yellow; in dense terminal and rounded clusters (Jun–Aug). Mountains and N coastal cliffs. Across N parts of North America, S to N US.

ROSE-CROWN *Sedum rhodanthum*   Height up to 1ft
Succulent plant with clusters of robust stems. Leaves up to 1in long, fleshy, and narrow-
ovate. Flowers up to ½in long, pinkish white with 4 sepals and 4 petals; in clusters
(May–Aug). Damp rocky places. Mountains in W of North America.

VENUS FLYTRAP *Dionaea muscipula*   Height up to 1ft
Bizarre insectivorous plant with rosette of 2–5in-long, folding, bristle-fringed, leaves that
snap shut in response to insects landing on them. Flowers 1in across, pale yellow with 5
petals (May–Jun). Sandy ground. Local, NC.

GOLDEN SAXIFRAGE *Saxifraga aizoides*   Height up to 5in
Attractive and clump-forming perennial. Leaves up to ½in long, narrow, fleshy, and light
green. Flowers ½in across with 5 narrow, yellow petals. Favors damp ground including
margins of streams. Arctic and sub-Arctic areas of AK and Canada.

TUFTED SAXIFRAGE *Saxifraga cespitosa*   Height up to 10in
Perennial with 3- or 5-lobed leaves arranged as tufted basal rosette. Flowers ¼–½in across,
cup-shaped with 5 white petals; borne in clusters on erect stalks (May–Sep). Rocky
ground. Arctic and sub-Arctic areas; also mountains in W US.

PURPLE SAXIFRAGE *Saxifraga oppositifolia*   Creeping
Mat-forming perennial. Trailing stems bearing opposite pairs of small, dark green leaves.
Flowers ½in across with 5 pinkish purple petals. Rocky slopes. Arctic and sub-Arctic
areas; also S in mountains through Canada to NE US.

WILD STRAWBERRY *Fragaria virginiana*   Height up to 6in
Creeping perennial with long, rooting runners. Long-stalked leaves 1in long, with 3 oval, toothed leaflets. Flowers ¾in across with 5 white petals (Apr–Jun). Fruits fleshy strawberries, studded with seeds. Woods and fields throughout North America.

SILVERWEED *Potentilla anserina*   Creeping
Creeping perennial with trailing stems that root at the nodes. Leaves up to 1in long, divided into up to 12 pairs of silvery leaflets with tiny ones between. Flowers 1in across with 5 yellow petals (Mar–Jun). Open places. Widespread in North America.

MARSH CINQUEFOIL *Potentilla palustris*   Height up to 2ft
Delicate perennial. Leaves 1–2in long, grayish, and divided into 3–5 toothed, oval leaflets. Flowers ¾in across, star-shaped with 5 reddish sepals and smaller purple petals (May–Jul). Bogs and damp meadows. Widespread except in S of North America.

SHRUBBY CINQUEFOIL *Potentilla fruticosa*   Height up to 3ft
Attractive shrubby perennial. Leaves ½in long, pinnate usually with 5 downy leaflets. Flowers 1in across with 5 yellow petals (Jun–Aug). All sorts of open habitats from tundra to grassy plains. Throughout North America.

MOUNTAIN AVENS *Dryas octopetala*   Height up to 3in
Low-growing, patch-forming plant. Leaves 1in long, dark green, oblong, and toothed. Flowers 1in across with 8 or more white petals and many yellow stamens (Jun–Jul). Tundra and mountains. Widespread in N of North America, S to OR and CO in W.

ARCTIC DRYAS *Dryas integrifolia*   Height up to 3in
Low-growing, patch-forming plant. Leaves 1in long, dark green, oblong, and untoothed. Flowers 1in across with 8 or more white petals and numerous yellow stamens (Jun–Jul). Arctic areas throughout North America and mountains S to MT and NF.

PRAIRIE SMOKE *Geum triflorum*   Height up to 15in
Attractive downy perennial. Leaves 4–8in long, pinnate with toothed leaflets. Flowers ¾in long with 5 pinkish petals (Apr–Jul). Fruits have long feathery plumes. Open woodland and prairies. Widespread across North America.

MULTIFLORA ROSE *Rosa multiflora*   Height up to 15ft
Scrambling perennial with arching stems and curved thorns. Leaves pinnate with 7–9 oval leaflets, each 1in long. Flowers 1in across with 5 white petals; in dense clusters (May–Jun). Fruits are fleshy hips. Margins of woods, and scrub. E US.

BAKED-APPLE BERRY *Rubus chamaemorus*   Height up to 1ft
Creeping perennial that lacks prickles. Has up to 3 leaves, each with 5–7 1in-long lobes. Flowers are ¾in across with 5 white petals (Jun–Aug). Mature fruit orange and berrylike. Open upland areas. Widespread Canada; mountains of NE US.

MEADOWSWEET *Spiraea latifolia*   Height up to 4ft
Attractive shrubby plant. Leaves pinnate with 7–15 toothed leaflets, each 2–3in long. Flowers small and white; in dense cylindrical spikes (Jun–Aug). Damp ground including meadows. Widespread in NE of North America, MI to NF, S to NC.

FEATHER PEABUSH *Dalea formosa* Height up to 3ft
Untidy-looking low shrub. Leaves ½in long with 7 or 9 leaflets. Flowers ½in across, purple except for yellow upper petal (Mar–May). Dry habitats including deserts and plains. Central S US.

CROWN VETCH *Securigera varia (Coronilla varia)* Height up to 3ft
Straggling perennial. Leaves pinnate with 7–12 pairs of oblong leaflets, each ½–1in long. Flowers pinkish white, in 1in wide heads of 10–20 flowers (Jun–Aug). Grassy places including roadsides. Non-native, but now widespread. E US.

BEACH PEA *Lathyrus japonicus* Height up to 8in
Trailing gray-green plant; stems to 3ft long. Leaves pinnate; 2–5 pairs of oval leaflets, each 1–2in long. Flowers ¾in long, bluish purple; in clusters (Jun–Aug). Coastal shingle. Atlantic S to NJ, Pacific N to BC; also Great Lakes.

BIRDSFOOT TREFOIL *Lotus corniculatus* Creeping
Trailing perennial. Leaves have 3 leaflets, each ½in long, and 2 leaflike stipules at base. Flowers yellow or orange; in heads ½–1in across (Jun–Sep). Pods arranged like a bird's foot. Grassy places. Widespread non-native.

WILD LUPINE *Lupinus perennis* Height up to 2ft
Elegant perennial. Leaves palmate with 7–11 narrow leaflets, each 1–2in long. Flowers ¾in long and blue; in tall spikes (Apr–Jul). Pods hairy. Dry grassy places and margins of woodland. E US.

ARCTIC LUPINE *Lupinus arcticus* Height up to 2ft
Attractive and showy perennial. Leaves long-stemmed and palmate with usually 5–6 ovate leaflets each 2–3in long. Flowers ½–1in long and bluish purple; in tall spikes (Jun–Jul). Pods hairy. Dry, open ground. Arctic areas.

WHITE SWEET CLOVER *Melilotus albus* Height up to 3ft
Attractive, bushy biennial. Leaves with 3 narrow leaflets, each ½–1in long. Flowers ¼in long and white; in tall spikes (Jun–Oct). Grassy places including roadsides. Non-native, but now widespread throughout North America.

YELLOW SWEET CLOVER *Melilotus officinalis* Height up to 4ft
Distinctive, branched biennial. Leaves comprise 3 oblong leaflets, each ½–1in long. Flowers ¼in long and yellow; in tall clustered spikes (May–Sep). Grassy areas and waste ground. Non-native, but now widespread throughout North America.

SIBBALDIA *Sibbaldia procumbens* Creeping
Prostrate and densely hairy perennial. Leaves ¼–½in long, bluish green, and trifoliate with wedge-shaped leaflets, toothed at tip. Flowers tiny with 5 narrow yellow petals (Jul–Aug). Arctic North America and mountain tops S to CA and NH.

NORTHERN OXYTROPE *Oxytropis campestris* Height up to 1ft
Tufted gray-green perennial. Leaves 2–4in long, hairy, and pinnate with 10–15 oval leaflets. Flowers ½in long and creamy white; in clusters (Jun–Jul). Dry stony places. Widespread in Arctic; widespread but local further S on mountains in W.

LOCOWEED *Oxytropis splendens* Height up to 1ft
Tufted and silkily hairy perennial. Leaves ½in long; in clusters, these are arranged in whorls. Flowers ½in long and pinkish lilac; in long-stalked spikes (Jun–Aug). Open, grassy places. Widespread across W of North America.

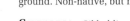

ALPINE MILKVETCH (ALPINE LOCOWEED) *Astragalus alpinus*   Height up to 1ft
Hairless, straggling upland perennial. Leaves 4–5in long with 13–23 oval, yellow-green leaflets. Flowers up to ½in long, white with reddish tips; in long-stalked clusters (Jun–Aug). Pods black and hairy. Mountains of BC and WA.

HOP CLOVER *Trifolium campestre*   Height up to 1½ft
Charming annual. Leaves trifoliate, each leaflet wedge-shaped and ½in long. Flowers ¼in long and yellow; in spherical heads of 20–30 flowers (Jun–Sep), which brown with age to resemble miniature hops. Roadsides and fields. Widespread non-native.

RABBIT'S-FOOT CLOVER *Trifolium arvense*   Height up to 1½ft
Distinctive annual. Leaves with 3 narrow leaflets, each ½in long. Flowers small and pale pink; in dense cylindrical heads up to 1in long (May–Sep). Grassy places on free-draining soils. Widespread throughout North America.

RED CLOVER *Trifolium pratense*   Height up to 2ft
Attractive perennial. Leaves with 3 oval leaflets, each 1–2in long with pale 'V' mark. Flowers ½in long and reddish; in dense, spherical heads (May–Sep). Grassy places. Throughout North America. Non-native, widely cultivated but also naturalized.

WHITE CLOVER *Trifolium repens*   Height up to 1ft
Distinctive perennial. Long-stalked leaves with 3 oval leaflets, each up to 1in long. Flowers up to ½in long and white or pale pink; in long-stalked, rounded clusters (May–Sep). Grassy places including lawns. Widespread non-native.

AMERICAN VETCH *Vicia americana*   Height up to 3ft
Attractive perennial. Leaves pinnate with 8–12 leaflets, each 1in long. Leaves end in coiling tendrils that aid plant's climbing progress. Flowers up to 1in long and bluish purple; in open clusters (May–Jul). Grassy places. Throughout North America.

COW VETCH *Vicia cracca*   Climbing
Climbing non-native. Stems 3–5ft long. Leaves pinnate with 8–12 narrow leaflets each 1in long. Leaves end in paired tendrils that aid plant's progress. Flowers ½in long and pinkish blue; in open spikes (May–Aug). Grassy places. S Canada and N US.

HAIRY VETCH *Vicia villosa*   Climbing
Climbing plant with stems 2–3ft long. Leaves pinnate with 5–10 narrow leaflets, each up to 1in long. Flowers ½in long and bluish pink; in one-sided spikes (May–Oct). Grassy places. Throughout North America; cultivated and naturalized.

LADY'S-FINGER *Anthyllis vulneraria*   Height up to 1ft
Patch-forming hairy perennial. Leaves pinnate with 1–13 leaflets, each up to 1in long. Flowers up to ½in long; in paired heads, the pairs kidney-shaped (May–Jul). Grassy places, usually base-rich soils. Local in NE US and SE Canada.

YELLOW WOOD SORREL *Oxalis europaea*   Height up to 1ft
Attractive, spreading perennial. Leaves shamrocklike with 3 leaflets, each ½in long. Leaves open only during daylight hours. Flowers ½in across with 5 yellow petals (May–Sep). Open ground. Widespread in North America.

COMMON WOOD SORREL *Oxalis montana*   Height up to 6in
Delicate, creeping woodland flower. Leaves ½in across and shamrocklike with heart-shaped leaflets. Flower ¾in across with 5 white or pale pink petals (May–Jul). Damp woodland soils. Widespread in E of North America.

WILD FLAX *Linum perenne*   Height up to 2ft
Attractive, tufted perennial. Leaves ½in long and narrow. Flowers 1in across with 5 pale blue flowers; borne in branched clusters (May–Jul). Dry grassy places including prairies. Widespread in W of North America.

STORKSBILL *Erodium cicutarium*   Height up to 1ft
Tufted, low-growing perennial. Leaves deeply divided and fernlike; form a basal rosette. Flowers ½in across with 5 pink petals; in open clusters (Apr–Sep). Fruit resembles a bird's beak. Disturbed areas. Widespread non-native.

WILD GERANIUM *Geranium maculatum*   Height up to 2ft
Attractive, branched plant. Leaves 3–6in across and deeply divided into 5 toothed lobes. Flowers 1in across with 5 pinkish lilac flowers; in open clusters (Apr–Jun). Open woods and meadows. Locally common in E of North America, S to GA.

HERB ROBERT *Geranium robertianum*   Height up to 2ft
Straggly, shade-loving plant; stems and leaves often tinged red. Leaves 2–3in across and palmate with 3–5 toothed lobes. Flowers ½in across with 5 pink petals; stalked and in clusters (May–Oct). Shady woodland. SE Canada and NE US.

WILD POINSETTIA *Euphorbia heterophylla*   Height up to 3ft
Distinctive perennial. Broken stems exude milky sap. Leaves 2–3in long, ovate, and often lobed. Flowers small and green; surrounded by 1in long reddish leaflike bracts (Aug–Sep). Open woods on free-draining soils. SE US.

CYPRESS SPURGE *Euphorbia cyparissias*   Height up to 1ft
Tufted plant with milky sap. Leaves 1in long and narrow; densely crowded on stems. Flowers inconspicuous and tiny but surrounded by glands and yellowish petal-like bracts (Mar–Jul). Disturbed areas. Non-native, but now widespread throughout North America.

CROWBERRY *Empetrum nigrum*   Height up to 6in
Creeping woody plant. Leaves ¼in long, narrow, stiff, and needlelike; densely crowded on stems. Flowers tiny with 3 sepals and no petals. Fruits ripen to a black berry. Alpine heathland and tundra, usually on acid soils. Arctic areas.

SPOTTED TOUCH-ME-NOT (JEWELWEED) *Impatiens capensis*   Height up to 5ft
Bushy, branched plant. Leaves 2–3in long and ovate. Flowers 1in long, helmet-shaped with wide mouth; orange with dark red spots (Jul–Oct). Ripe fruits explode when touched. Damp ground. Widespread in N; S to OR and FL.

SWAMP CURRANT *Ribes lacustre*   Height up to 3ft
Much-branched woody shrub with prickly stems. Leaves 1–2in long, palmate with 3–5 toothed lobes. Flowers small, red, and pendant. Fruits are black, hairy berries. Damp margins of woodland, and meadows. Widespread in N of North America.

HIBISCUS *Hibiscus coccineus* Height up to 10ft
Attractive, shrubby plant. Leaves palmate with narrow lobes, each up to 9in long. Flowers 6–8in across with 5 bright red petals (Jun–Sep). Wetlands; tolerates brackish conditions. SE US only.

 MUSK MALLOW *Malva moschata* Height up to 2ft
Attractive perennial. Leaves 4in across, palmate with pointed, toothed lobes. Flowers 1–2in across with 5 pale pink petals; musk-scented (Jun–Oct). Grassy and disturbed places. Non-native, but widely naturalized in E of North America.

 MARSH MALLOW *Althaea officinalis* Height up to 3ft
Downy and upright gray-green perennial. Leaves variable but mostly 2–4in long, triangular to heart-shaped with shallow toothed lobes. Flowers 1–2in across with 5 pink petals (Aug–Oct). Margins of wetlands. Atlantic coast of US, S to VA.

 COMMON ST JOHN'S-WORT *Hypericum perforatum* Height up to 2ft
Much-branched perennial. Leaves 1–2in long, elliptical with translucent dots. Flowers 1in across with 5 yellow petals that have black dots on margins; borne in clusters (Jun–Sep). Grassy areas and waste ground. Non-native, now widespread.

 MARSH ST JOHN'S-WORT *Hypericum virginicum* Height up to 2ft
Delicate perennial. Leaves 1–2in long, ovate with translucent dots; in opposite pairs. Flowers ½in across with 5 pink petals; in clusters (Jul–Aug). Damp ground. Widespread along Atlantic coast from NS to FL. Local inland in E.

 WESTERN CANADA VIOLET *Viola canadensis* Height up to 1ft
Charming perennial. Leaves 2–3in long, heart-shaped, and stalked. Flowers up to 1in across with five white petals and a backward-projecting spur; on stalks (May–Jul). Damp woodland. Pacific states and provinces; also Rocky Mountains.

 BLUE VIOLET (HOOKED-SPUR VIOLET) *Viola adunca* Height up to 5in
Low-growing plant. Leaves up to 1in long, stalked, and heart-shaped or ovate. Flowers ½in across with 5 bluish violet petals and backward-pointing spur (May–Aug). Open grassy places. Widespread in Canada; S to ME in E, CA in W.

DOWNY YELLOW VIOLET *Viola pubescens* Height up to 1ft
Delicate, downy plant. Leaves 2–3in across, toothed, and heart-shaped. Flowers up to ¾in across with 5 yellow petals, the lower 3 with dark veins (May–Jun). Undisturbed woodlands. NE of North America.

COMMON BLUE VIOLET *Viola papilionacea* Height up to 8in
Delicate, low-growing plant. Leaves 3–5in across, heart-shaped, and toothed. Flowers ½in across, blue or white with 5 veined petals (Mar–Jun). Damp grassland and woodland. Widespread in E of North America, S to TX.

PARRY'S PRIMROSE *Primula parryi*   Height up to 15in
Distinctive upland perennial. Leaves up to 10in long and oblong; form a basal rosette. Carrion-scented flowers 1in across with 5 pinkish red lobes; in clusters on leafless stalk (Jun–Aug). Uplands. Rocky Mountains, S to AZ and NM.

FEW-FLOWERED SHOOTING STAR *Dodecatheon pulchellum*   Height up to 2ft
Delicate plant. Leaves 3–15in long and lanceolate; form a basal rosette. Flowers 1in long with 5 backward-pointing deep pink petals and projecting stamens; in terminal clusters on tall stalk (Apr–Aug). Grassy places. Widespread in W.

FRINGED LOOSESTRIFE *Lysimachia ciliata*   Height up to 4ft
Attractive perennial. Leaves 3–5in long, narrow ovate, and in opposite pairs; stalks fringed with hairs. Flowers ¾in across with 5 yellow petals; on stalks from leaf axils (Jun–Aug). Damp woods and margins of water. Widespread throughout North America.

TUFTED LOOSESTRIFE *Lysimachia thyrsiflora*   Height up to 3ft
Upright wetland plant. Leaves 2–6in long, lanceolate, and in opposite pairs. Flowers comprise 5 narrow yellow lobes; in dense, stalked clusters arising from leaf axils (May–Jul). Wetlands. Widespread throughout much of North America.

MONEYWORT *Lysimachia nummularia*   Creeping
Low-growing, trailing plant. Leaves up to 1in across and rounded; borne in pairs. Flowers 1in across with 5 yellow petals; on stalks arising from leaf axils (Jun–Aug). Areas of short grass on damp ground. Non-native, but now widespread in NE.

STARFLOWER *Trientalis arctica*   Height up to 6in
Low-growing perennial. Leaves 2–3in long, lanceolate; in whorls of 5–9 around the stem. Flowers ½in across with (usually) 7 white petals and yellow anthers; solitary atop upright stem (Jun–Jul). Woods and upland slopes. AK and N Canada.

FIREWEED *Chamerion angustifolium (Epilobium angustifolium)*   Height up to 5ft
Patch-forming perennial. Leaves 5–8in long and lanceolate. Flowers 1in across with 4 pink petals; in terminal spikes (Jul–Sep). Seeds silky and wind-dispersed. Disturbed, cleared, and burned ground. Widespread in N, S to CA in W, NC in E.

HAIRY WILLOWHERB *Epilobium hirsutum*   Height up to 5ft
Hairy-stemmed perennial. Leaves 2–4in long, lanceolate, toothed, and hairy. Flowers 1in across with 4 notched and pinkish purple petals; on stalks from axils of upper leaves (Jul–Sep). Grassy and waste areas. NE North America.

AMERICAN WILLOWHERB *Epilobium ciliatum (Epilobium adenocaulon)*   Height up to 2ft
Upright perennial. Leaves 2–4 in long and lanceolate; in opposite pairs, often pressed close to stem. Flowers ½in across with 4 notched, pink petals from axils of upper leaves (Jun–Aug). Disturbed areas. Widespread in N of North America.

ARCTIC RIVER BEAUTY *Epilobium latifolium*   Height up to 1½ft
Sprawling perennial. Leaves 1–2in long and oval. Flowers 1–2in across with 4 pink, oval petals; on stalks from axils of upper leaves (Jul–Aug). Shingle bars in rivers and scree slopes. Widespread in N of North America; S to NF in E and CO in W.

MARSH-PURSLANE *Ludwigia palustris*   Creeping
Spreading waterside plant. Stems and leaves often reddish. Leaves ½in long and in opposite pairs. Flowers ¼in long, greenish, and bell-shaped with 4 sepals with spreading, pointed tips; in leaf axils (Jun–Sep). Margins of water. Widespread in North America.

PURPLE LOOSESTRIFE *Lythrum salicaria*   Height up to 4ft
Attractive upright perennial. Leaves 2–4in long and lanceolate. Flowers up to ¾in across with 4–6 pinkish purple, wrinkled petals; in spikes (Jun–Sep). Wetlands. Invasive and generally unwelcome non-native. Widespread in NE of North America.

EVENING-PRIMROSE *Oenothera biennis*   Height up to 5ft
Branched and upright biennial. Leaves 5–8in long and lanceolate; form basal rosette in
first year, in second year borne up stem. Flowers 1–2in across with 4 yellow petals; open
at night and in dull weather (Jun–Sep). Grassy places. Widespread in North America.

SEASIDE EVENING-PRIMROSE *Oenothera humifusa*   Height up to 2ft
Branched and hairy plant. Leaves 2–5in long; basal leaves with pinnate lobes, stem leaves
narrow and entire. Flowers up to 1in across with 4 pale yellow petals (Jun–Sep). Coastal
sand dunes. Atlantic coast, mainly NJ, S to FL.

SHOWY EVENING-PRIMROSE *Oenothera speciosa*   Height up to 2ft
Patch-forming stiffly hairy plant. Leaves 2–4in long, lanceolate with wavy-lobed margins.
Flowers 2–3in across with 4 white or pale pink petals (May–Jul). Dry grassy places includ-
ing roadsides. E central US.

YELLOW DESERT EVENING-PRIMROSE *Oenothera primiveris*   Height up to 2ft
Attractive, low-growing plant. Leaves 2–5in long, narrow and usually deeply lobed; in a
basal rosette. Flowers 1–3in across with 4 yellow petals fading reddish; on upright stalks
(Mar–May). Deserts from S CA to TX.

SCARLET GAURA *Gaura coccinea*   Height up to 2ft
Upright, much-branched plant. Leaves 1–2in long, narrow-lanceolate, and crowded up
stem. Flowers ½in across with 4 petals, turning white to deep pink after dawn (May–Sep).
Dry grassy places. W of North America, N to S central Canada.

FENNEL *Foeniculum vulgare*   Height up to 8ft
Distinctive gray-green perennial. Leaves up to 1ft long, divided into threadlike leaflets.
Flowers small and yellow; in compound umbels up to 6in across (July–Sep). Grassy
places. Non-native; widespread in temperate parts of North America.

POISON HEMLOCK *Conium maculatum*   Height up to 8ft
Highly poisonous biennial; purple-blotched stems. Leaves up to 1ft long, 2–4 times pinnately divided into fine leaflets. Flowers small and white; in domed umbels up to 8in
across (Jun–Jul). Damp wayside ground. Widespread in North America.

QUEEN ANNE'S LACE *Daucus carota*   Height up to 3ft
Distinctive, hairy plant. Leaves 4–8in long, 2–3 times pinnately divided into narrow
leaflets. Flowers small, pinkish in bud, white in flower; in flat-topped umbels 4–6in
across, central flower red (May–Sep). Grassland. Widespread in North America.

COW PARSNIP *Heracleum lanatum*   Height up to 8ft
Robust perennial with hollow, grooved, and hairy stems. Leaves up to 2ft long, broad, and
in 3 segments. Flowers small and off-white with unequal petals; in domed umbels up to
8in across (May–Aug). Damp ground. Widespread Canada and N US.

WILD CELERY *Apium graveolens*   Height up to 3ft
Branched biennial smelling strongly of celery. Leaves up to 6in long and 1–2 times pinnate. Flowers small and greenish white; in umbels 1–2in across (May–Jul). Damp grassy
places. Widespread in CA.

SHEPHERD'S-NEEDLE *Scandix pecten-veneris*   Height up to 1ft
Low-growing plant covered in bristly hairs. Leaves 2–4in long, pinnate into numerous
small leaflets. Flowers tiny and white; in umbels up to 1in across (Apr–Jul). Fruits needlelike and 1in long. Disturbed areas. Widespread in US and BC.

GINSENG *Panax quinquefolium*   Height up to 2ft
Delicate woodland plant. Leaves 6–12in long with 5 oval, toothed leaflets; in whorls of 3.
Flowers tiny and greenish white; in umbels 1in across (May–Aug). Fruits are red berries.
Damp woodlands. E of North America, N to MB and QC.

 BUNCHBERRY *Cornus canadensis*   Height up to 6in
Patch-forming plant. Leaves 2–3in long and ovate; in whorls near top of stem. Flowers tiny
and yellowish; in cluster surrounded by whorl of white bracts, 1½in across (May–Jul).
Fruits are red and berrylike. Damp woods. Canada, AK, and NE US.

PIPISSEWA *Chimaphila umbellata*   Height up to 1ft
Attractive woodland plant. Leaves 1–2in long, oval, toothed, dark green, and shiny; in
whorls of 3–6 up stem. Flowers ½in across with 5 waxy pink petals; in terminal clusters
(Jun–Aug). Dry woodland. Canada and AK, S to GA in E and CA in W.

LESSER WINTERGREEN *Pyrola minor*   Height up to 8in
Distinctive perennial. Leaves 1–2in long and rounded to oval; on stalks and in a basal
rosette. Flowers up to ½in across with 5 white or pinkish petals; stalked, pendant and in
terminal spikes (Jun–Aug). Conifer woods. Canada, AK, and NE US.

ONE-SIDED WINTERGREEN *Orthilia (Pyrola) secunda*   Height up to 8in
Patch-forming evergreen. Leaves 1–2in long, rounded to ovate; in a basal rosette. Flowers
¼in across with 5 whitish petals; in a one-sided spike (Jun–Aug). Conifer woodland. Widespread Canada, AK, and N US.

ONE-FLOWERED WINTERGREEN *Moneses uniflora*   Height up to 5in
Distinctive perennial. Leaves rounded to ovate and toothed; in whorls near base of stem.
Flowers ¾in across, solitary and disclike with 5 pale pink or white petals. Conifer wood-
lands. Widespread Canada and AK; S in mountains to CA and NM.

PINESAP *Monotropa hypopitys*   Height up to 1ft
Waxy, parasitic plant. Has upright reddish stem that is curved at tip; leaves reduced to
scales pressed close to stem. Flowers ¼in long and yellowish or red; terminal and pendant
(Jun–Sep). Shady woods. Canada, AK, and S in US mountains.

BEARBERRY (KINNIKINNIK) *Arctostaphylos uva-ursi*   Creeping
Low-growing, trailing, and mat-forming perennial. Leaves up to 1in long and oblong.
Flowers ¼in long, bell-shaped, and white; stalked, pendant, and terminal groups
(Mar–Jun). Open heathlands, tundra and mountains. Canada and AK; further S in US
mountains.

LAPLAND HEATHER *Cassiope tetragona*   Height up to 8in
Low-growing, woody plant. Leaves up to ¼in long, narrow-oval, and overlapping on stem.
Flowers ¼in long, white, and bell-shaped with 5 spreading lobes at mouth; stalked and
pendant (Jul–Aug). Arctic heathlands and mountains. AK, Canada, and Rocky Mts.

LABRADOR TEA *Ledum groenlandicum (palustre)*   Height up to 2½ft
Dwarf woody shrub. Reddish downy hairs on stem and leaf underside. Leaves 1–2in long
and ovate; margins inrolled. Flowers ¼in across with 5 white petals; in terminal clusters
(Jun–Jul). Heathlands and mountains. AK and Canada; S to OR in W.

ALPINE AZALEA *Loiseleuria procumbens*   Creeping
Branched, mat-forming shrub. Leaves tiny, evergreen and elliptical; in opposite pairs.
Flowers ¼in across with 5 pinkish purple spreading petals (Jun–Aug). Heathlands and
mountains on peaty soil. Widespread AK and Canada; S to NH in NE US.

SMALL CRANBERRY *Vaccinium oxycoccos*   Height up to 4in
Trailing evergreen shrub. Leaves ¼in long, ovate with inrolled margins. Flowers ½in long,
recall tiny Fuchsia flowers with 4 reflexed pale pink petals and projecting anthers
(Jun–Aug). Fruits are red berries. Bogs. E Canada and NE US. Cranberry (*Vaccinium macro-
carpon*) has larger paler flowers, larger flat leaves, and produces luscoius red berries.
Range similar to Small cranberry.

MOUNTAIN CRANBERRY *Vaccinium vitis-idaea*   Creeping
Evergreen shrub. Leaves ½in long, oval and leathery with black dots on underside. Flowers ¼in long, pink and bell-shaped; in terminal clusters on upright stems (Jun–Jul). Fruits
are dark red berries. Heathlands and bogs. AK, Canada, and ME.

BOG ROSEMARY *Andromeda polifolia*   Height up to 8in
Low-growing evergreen shrub. Leaves ½in long, narrow, gray-green above, and whitish
below with inrolled margins. Flowers ¼in long, urn-shaped; stalked, pendant, and in terminal clusters (Jun–Jul). Bogs. AK and N Canada.

DIAPENSIA *Diapensia lapponica*   Creeping
Mat-forming evergreen plant. Leaves ½in long, leathery, narrow and blunt. Flowers ½in
across with 5 white spreading lobes (Jun–Jul). Bare stony ground and mountain tops. AK,
Arctic Canada, and mountains of SE Canada and NE US.

SCARLET PIMPERNEL *Anagallis arvensis*   Creeping
Trailing, hairless annual. Leaves ¼–½in long, oval, and in opposite pairs. Flowers ¼in
across with 5 petal lobes, usually red but also blue or white; on stalks, opening only in sun
(Jun–Aug). Disturbed areas. Non-native but now widespread.

SEA MILKWORT *Glaux maritima*   Height up to 10in
Low-growing succulent plant. Leaves up to ½in long, oval, and fleshy; in opposite pairs.
Flowers ¼in across with 5 pink sepals; in leaf axils (May–Sep). Coastal salt marshes.
Atlantic and Pacific coasts.

THRIFT *Armeria maritima*   Height up to 10in
Cushion-forming perennial. Leaves 2–4in long, dark green, and grasslike. Flowers 5-lobed
and pink; in globular heads up to 1in across and on stalks 6–8in long (Apr–Aug). Coastal
cliffs and Arctic. Pacific coast, NE Atlantic coast, and Arctic NA.

NORTHERN GENTIAN *Gentianella (Gentiana) amarella*   Height up to 1ft
Upright biennial. Leaves up to 1½in long and oblong; form basal rosette in 1st year which withers before flowering stem appears in 2nd year. Flowers ½in long, purple, and 4- or 5-lobed; in clusters (Jun–Sep). Grassy places. N and W of North America.

BUCKBEAN *Menyanthes trifoliata*   Height up to 9in
Aquatic perennial. Emergent leaves 4–10in long, trifoliate, and resemble those of broad bean. Flowers ½in across, star-shaped, pinkish white, and fringed; in open spikes (May–Jul). Shallow water and bogs. AK, Canada and mountains in W US.

YELLOW FLOATING HEARTS *Nymphoides peltata*   Floating
Aquatic plant. Leaves 2–4in across, round and floating. Flowers 1in across with 5 yellow finged petal lobes; (Jul–Sep). Slow-flowing and still water. Naturalised in E USA. Similar Floating Hearts Nymphoides aquatica has similar range but white flowers.

SALT-MARSH PINK *Sabatia stellaris*   Height up to 1½ft
Delicate, slender plant. Leaves 1in long, narrow, and in opposite pairs. Flowers 1in across, star-shaped with 5 pink petals and yellow stamens (Jul–Sep). Coastal brackish grassland and marshes. Atlantic coast N to MA.

SPREADING DOGBANE *Apocynum androsaemifolium*   Height up to 2ft
Poisonous branched plant with milky sap. Leaves 2–4in long, ovate and opposite. Flowers ½in long, pink, trumpet-shaped with 5 spreading lobes at mouth; in clusters (Jun–Aug). Grassy places. Widespread across US and S Canada.

PERIWINKLE (MYRTLE) *Vinca minor*   Height up to 9in
Creeping, trailing evergreen. Leaves 1in long, oblong to ovate, glossy, and in opposite pairs. Flowers 1in across, bluish purple with 5 lobes (Apr–May). Roadsides and margins of woodland. Non-native. Now widespread in US and S Canada.

SWAMP MILKWEED *Asclepias incarnata*   Height up to 4ft
Branched leafy plant with milky sap. Leaves 2–4in long, narrow ovate, and opposite. Flowers ¼in across, flesh pink with 5 petals with reflexed lobes; in clustered heads (Jun–Aug). Wetlands. E of North America, N to MB and NS.

COMMON MILKWEED *Asclepias syriaca*   Height up to 6ft
Branched woolly plant with milky sap. Leaves 5–10in long, oblong and opposite. Flowers ½in across with 5 reflexed pink petals and whitish central 'crown'; in clustered heads (Jun–Aug). Dry, grassy places. S Canada and N US, W to SK and IA.

BUTTERFLY WEED *Asclepias tuberosa*   Height up to 3ft
Attractive hairy plant; flowers popular with insects. Leaves 3–6in long, ovate and opposite. Flowers ½in across, orange with 5 reflexed petals and projecting crown; in heads (Jun–Sep). Free-draining soils. SE Canada and E US, W to CO.

HEDGE BINDWEED *Calystegia sepium*   Climbing
Twining plant with stems up to 9ft long. Leaves 4–6in long and arrowhead-shaped. Flowers 1–2in across, white, and funnel-shaped; on stalks arising from leaf axils (Jun–Sep). Hedgerows and margins of woods. Widespread in temperate parts of North America.

SEA BINDWEED (BEACH MORNING GLORY) *Calystegia soldanella*   Creeping
Attractive coastal perennial. Leaves 1–2in across, kidney-shaped, and long-stalked. Flowers 2in across, funnel-shaped, and pink with white stripes (Apr–Sep). Coastal sand dunes. Pacific coast, from CA, N to BC.

FIELD BINDWEED *Convolvulus arvensis*   Creeping or climbing
Perennial that twists around other plants to assist its progress; stems up to 9ft long. Leaves 1–2in long, arrowhead-shaped and long-stalked. Flowers up to 1in across, funnel-shaped, and pale pink with white stripes (May–Sep). S Canada and US.

COMMON MORNING GLORY *Ipomoea purpurea* Climbing
Twining plant with stems up to 10ft long. Leaves 2–4in long, heart-shaped and stalked. Flowers 2in across, trumpet-shaped, and red, blue, purple, or white (Jun–Nov). Disturbed and cultivated ground. Non-native, now widespread.

VIRGINIA CREEPER *Parthenocissus quinquefolia* Climbing
Familiar twining perennial. Leaves 2–5in long and vine- or maplelike; fresh green in spring, turning red in autumn. Flowers tiny, greenish and clustered (May–Jun). Fruits are small bluish berries. Woods. E of North America. Also planted.

JACOB'S-LADDER OR SHOWY POLEMONIUM *Polemonium pulcherrimum* Height up to 1ft
Attractive upright perennial. Leaves 3–5in long, pinnate with 11–23 narrow-ovate leaflets; stickily hairy. Flowers ½in cross with 5 pale blue petal lobes; in terminal clusters (May–Aug). Upland grassy places. Pacific states.

GREEK-VALERIAN *Polemonium caeruleum* Height up to 3ft
Attractive perennial. Leaves 6–8in long and pinnate with 7–15 ovate lobes. Flowers ½in across, purplish blue with 5 lobes; in clusters (May–Jun). Found in upland meadows and grassy places. Widespread in W US and Canada.

WILD BLUE PHLOX *Phlox divaricata* Height up to 1½ft
Attractive spreading plant. Stems sticky. Leaves 1–2in long, ovate, and opposite. Flowers 1in across with 5 pale blue petals; in clusters (Apr–Jun). Grassy places and open woodlands. SE Canada and E half of US except far S.

SPREADING PHLOX *Phlox diffusa* Height up to 1ft
Low-growing, mat-forming plant. Leaves ½–1in long, needlelike, yellowish, and often pressed close to stem. Flowers ½in across with 5 pale pink petal lobes; terminal on leafy stems (May–Aug). Mountain slopes. Pacific states.

TRUMPET CREEPER *Campsis radicans* Climbing
Vinelike plant. Leaves 3–5in long, pinnate with 7–11 ovate and toothed leaflets. Flowers 2–3in long, orange, and trumpetlike; in clusters (Jul–Sep). Margins of woods, and scrub. E US; cultivated and naturalized elsewhere.

VIPER'S-BUGLOSS *Echium vulgare* Height up to 2ft
Upright biennial covered with stiff hairs. Leaves 2–5in long, narrow, and pointed; basal leaves stalked. Flowers ¾in long, blue, and funnel-shaped with protruding red stamens; in clusters (Jun–Oct). Dry, sandy, or calcareous soil. E US.

VIRGINIA BLUEBELLS *Mertensia virginica* Height up to 2ft
Attractive upright plant. Leaves 2–7 in long, ovate, fleshy, and grayish green. Flowers 1in long, trumpet-shaped, and blue (pink in bud); in clusters (Mar–Jun). Damp woodlands. SE Canada and NE US, S to VA and AR.

SEA LUNGWORT *Mertensia maritima* Creeping
Trailing plant with stems up to 2ft. Leaves up to 1in long, ovate, gray-green, and fleshy. Flowers ¼in across, bell-shaped, and blue (pink in bud); in clusters (Jun–Aug). High tide line on shingle and sandy beaches. Atlantic coast, S to MA.

TRUE FORGET-ME-NOT *Myosotis scorpioides* Height up to 1ft
Creeping perennial with upright flowering shoots. Leaves 1–2in long, narrow, and oblong. Flowers ¼in across, sky-blue, and 5-lobed; in clusters (May–Sep). Watery habitats. Non-native but now widespread in E of North America.

BLUE VERVAIN *Verbena hastata* Height up to 5ft
Upright, branched plant. Leaves 4–5in long, narrow, and opposite. Flowers tiny, bluish, and 5-petalled; in spikes with only a few flowers opening at a time (Jul–Sep). Damp grassy places. Widespread in E. Similar species elsewhere in North America.

GROUND-IVY *Glechoma hederacea*   Height up to 6in
Softly hairy, strong-smelling perennial. Creeping stems root regularly. Leaves ½–1in long, kidney-shaped, stalked. Flowers ½–1in long and violet; in whorls of 2–4 (Mar–Jun). Grassy places. Non-native; widespread, except in central and N North America.

HENBIT *Lamium amplexicaule*   Height up to 9in
Annual that often trails on ground. Leaves 1in long, rounded, and toothed; clasp stems in pairs. Flowers ½in long, pinkish purple; in clusters (Feb–Oct). Cultivated and disturbed areas. Widespread throughout much of North America.

MOTHERWORT *Leonurus cardiaca*   Height up to 3ft
Hairy perennial. Lower leaves 2–4in long, palmate with 3–7 lobes; upper ones shorter and 3-lobed. Flowers ½in long, pink or white; in whorls with conspicuous bracts (Mar–Nov). Disturbed grassy places. Temperate E half of North America.

WOUNDWORT *Stachys palustris*   Height up to 3ft
Downy perennial. Leaves ½–1in long, narrow-oblong, and most unstalked. Flowers ½–1in long, pinkish purple with white markings; in spikes (Jul–Sep). Roadsides and grassy places, usually on damp ground. Widespread in E of North America.

MARSH SKULLCAP *Scutellaria galericulata*   Height up to 2ft
An often hairy perennial with square stems. Leaves 1–2in long, oval, stalked, and toothed. Flowers ½in long and bluish violet; on upright leafy stems (Jun–Sep). Damp ground, often beside streams. W of North America, in suitable habitats.

WILD MINT *Mentha arvensis*   Height up to 2ft
Mint-scented perennial. Leaves 1–2in long, oval, and short-stalked. Flowers ¼in long and lilac; in dense whorls at intervals up stems (Jul–Sep). Damp tillable land, paths, and disturbed areas. Throughout except SE of North America.

PENNYROYAL *Mentha pulegium*   Height up to 1ft
An often creeping perennial. Leaves 1in long, oval and toothed. Flowers ¼in long and pink; in dense and discretely separated whorls along stems (Jun–Sep). Damp grassy, and sometimes grazed, places. CA and OR.

BEE BALM *Monarda didyma*   Height up to 5ft
Upright perennial with a square stem. Leaves 3–5in long, ovate, toothed and opposite. Flowers 1½in long, red, and tubular; in terminal clusters above whorl of bracts (Jun–Aug). Damp woods and margins of streams. NE US. Also widely cultivated.

CATNIP *Nepeta cataria*   Height up to 3ft
Grayish white downy perennial. Leaves 1–2in long, heart-shaped, toothed, stalked, and opposite. Flowers ½in long and pale lilac; in terminal clusters (Jun–Sep). Waysides and roadsides. Non-native but now widespread. Widely cultivated.

HEAL-ALL (SELF-HEAL) *Prunella vulgaris*   Height up to 1½ft
Creeping, downy perennial. Leaves 1–2in long, oval and paired. Flowers ½in long and bluish violet; in dense clusters with hairy bracts on leafy stems (May–Sep). Areas of short grassland, including lawns. Non-native, now widespread.

SALVIA *Salvia coccinea*   Height up to 3ft
Attractive perennial with a square stem. Leaves up to 2in long, oval with lobed margin. Flowers 1in long, bright red; in whorls forming an open spike (May–Oct). Open woods on free-draining soils. Coastal SE US.

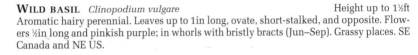

WILD BASIL *Clinopodium vulgare*   Height up to 1½ft
Aromatic hairy perennial. Leaves up to 1in long, ovate, short-stalked, and opposite. Flowers ½in long and pinkish purple; in whorls with bristly bracts (Jun–Sep). Grassy places. SE Canada and NE US.

WOOD SAGE *Teucrium canadense*   Height up to 3ft
Striking, showy perennial. Leaves 3–4in, narrow-oval; lower leaves broader than upper ones, toothed. Flowers up to ½in across, pinkish-blue with lobed lip; in tall, terminal spikes (Jun–Aug). Favors shady woodland rides and clearings. Widespread in E of North America.

BITTERSWEET NIGHTSHADE *Solanum dulcamara*   Height up to 4ft
Branched, climbing perennial. Leaves 1–3in long, oval, with narrow basal lobes or leaflets. Flowers ½in across, purplish with yellow stamens; in clusters (Jun–Sep). Berries red. Widespread non-native of grassland, scrub and margins of woods.

INDIAN PAINTBRUSH *Castilleja coccinea*   Height up to 2ft
Upright plant. Lower leaves 2–3in long, oblong; in a basal rosette. Stem leaves shorter and 3–5 lobed. Flowers green and tubular, hidden by scarlet, lobed bracts 1in long; in terminal spikes (May–Jul). Grassland. E of North America, N to S Canada.

DESERT PAINTBRUSH *Castilleja chromosa*   Height up to 2ft
Upright plant. Leaves up to 2in long; lower ones lanceolate, upper ones divided into 3 or 5 narrow lobes. Flowers 1in long and pinkish; in spikes with red, 5-lobed bracts (Apr–Aug). Deserts. SW US.

COMMON LOUSEWORT *Pedicularis canadensis*   Height up to 1½ft
Upright hairy plant. Leaves 2–4in long, oblong in outline but deeply divided into toothed lobes; often tinged red. Flowers ¾in long, tubular, hooded, and red or yellow; in terminal clusters (Apr–Jun). Open woodland. E US and S Canada.

YELLOW-RATTLE *Rhinanthus crista-galli*   Height up to 1½ft
Upright plant. Leaves 1–2in long, ovate, toothed, and opposite. Flowers ½in long, hooded, and yellow with inflated green calyx at base; in spikes (Jun–Sep). Seeds rattle in pods. Grassland. Widespread in AK and Canada; local NE US.

TURTLEHEAD *Chelone glabra*   Height up to 4ft
Upright, branched plant. Leaves 3–5in long, lanceolate, toothed, and opposite. Flowers 1in long, tubular, white and pink with fanciful resemblance to a turtle's head; in terminal clusters (Jul–Sep). Damp ground. AK and S Canada; also NE US.

MUDWORT *Limosella aquatica*   Height up to 6in
Hairless annual with creeping runners. Leaves 2–5in long, narrow spoon-shaped, and long-stalked or linear; form a basal rosette. Flowers tiny, 5-lobed, and white; on stalks at plant base (May–Aug). Bare mud beside lakes and streams. W of North America.

EYEBRIGHT *Euphrasia sp.*   Height up to 1½ft
Variable upright plant; several similar species. Leaves up to ½in long, ovate, toothed, and opposite. Flowers ¼–½in long, white with purple and orange marks; in spikes with toothed bracts (Jun–Sep). Grassland. Widespread in N of North America.

BLUE TOADFLAX *Linaria canadensis*   Height up to 2ft
Slender upright plant. Leaves 1–2in long and grasslike. Flowers ½in long, bluish, 2-lipped, and spurred; in spikes (Mar–Jul). Grassy places on sandy soil. Widespread across much of North America.

BUTTER-AND-EGGS *Linaria vulgaris*   Height up to 4ft
Upright and branched gray-green perennial. Leaves 1–2in long and grasslike. Flowers 1in long, long-spurred, yellow but orange-centered; in terminal clusters (May–Sep). Grassy places. Non-native, now widespread in temperate parts of North America.

COW WHEAT *Melampyrum lineare*   Height up to 1½ft
Upright, branched plant. Leaves 1–2in long, lanceolate, and paired. Flowers ½in long, tubular, 2-lipped, and whitish; from upper leaf axils (Jun–Aug). Wooded and open ground. Widespread in Canada; also in mountains of NE and W US.

YELLOW MONKEYFLOWER *Mimulus guttatus*   Height up to 2ft
Upright perennial. Leaves 1–2in long, ovate, and opposite. Flowers 1–2in across, 2-lipped and yellow marked with red spots on throat (Jun–Sep). Margins of rivers, and wetlands. Native to W half of North America but naturalized elsewhere.

MUSKFLOWER *Mimulus moschatus*   Height up to 1ft
Stickily hairy perennial. Leaves 1–2in across, ovate, and opposite. Flowers ¾in long, 2-lipped, and yellow; from leaf axils (Jun–Sep). Margins of rivers, and damp ground. E Canada and NE US; in W, found from BC to CA and Rocky Mountains.

CLIFF PENSTEMON *Penstemon rupicola*   Creeping
Charming patch-forming perennial. Leaves up to ¾in long, ovate, and opposite. Flowers up to ¾in long, pink, tubular, and 2-lipped, lower lip 3-lobed, upper 2-lobed; on stalks 3–4in tall (May–Aug). Rocky places. WA, OR, and N CA.

GRAY BEARDTONGUE *Penstemon canescens*   Height up to 3ft
Attractive downy perennial. Leaves 3–5in long, ovate, and opposite. Flowers up to 1¼in long, pinkish purple, tubular, and 2-lipped, lower lip 3-lobed, upper 2-lobed; in clusters (May–Jul). Woodland. E US, from IN to PA, S to GA.

COMMON MULLEIN *Verbascum thapsus*   Height up to 6ft
Upright plant covered in white, woolly hairs. Leaves 4–15in long and ovate; form basal rosette in 1st year, tall leafy stalks appearing in 2nd year. Flowers 1in across and yellow; in dense spikes (Jun–Aug). Open ground. Throughout North America.

COMMON SPEEDWELL *Veronica officinalis*   Creeping
Mat-forming perennial. Prostrate stems are hairy and root at nodes. Leaves 1–2in long, elliptical, and opposite. Flowers ¼in across, with 4 pale bluish lilac petals; from leaf axils (May–Jul). Open grassy places. NE of North America, S to TN.

BROOMRAPE *Orobanche fasciculata*   Height up to 6in
Upright root parasite; plant is yellowish brown and lacks chlorophyll. Leaves reduced to 5–10 tiny scales. Flowers ½in long, yellow or purple; 5–10 on 1in-long stalks (Apr–Aug). Woodland. W of North America.

GREATER BLADDERWORT *Utricularia vulgaris*   Aquatic
Unusual freshwater plant. Submerged stems have finely divided leaves and small, flask-shaped bladders that trap tiny invertebrates. Flowers ½in long, spurred, and yellow; on emergent stalks 4–6in long (Jun–Aug). Still waters. Throughout North America.

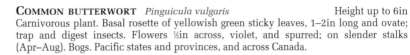

COMMON BUTTERWORT *Pinguicula vulgaris*   Height up to 6in
Carnivorous plant. Basal rosette of yellowish green sticky leaves, 1–2in long and ovate; trap and digest insects. Flowers ½in across, violet, and spurred; on slender stalks (Apr–Aug). Bogs. Pacific states and provinces, and across Canada.

DUCKWEED *Lemna* sp.   Aquatic
Floating, perennial freshwater plant. Often forms a carpet over the surface of suitable ponds and lakes by summer months. Leaflike thallus, up to ¼in across, has a single, dangling root. Multiplies by division. Still waters. Widespread in North America.

WATERWEED *Elodea canadensis*   Aquatic
Fast-growing freshwater plant. Submerged and rather brittle stems carry narrow, back-curved unstalked leaves, each up to ½in long, in whorls of 3. Flowers are tiny and seldom seen. Still waters. Widespread in temperate parts of North America.

HORNWORT *Ceratophyllum demersum*   Aquatic
Freshwater perennial. Long stems carry whorls of dark green, rigid, and minutely toothed leaves; each is divided 1 or 2 times into narrow segments up to 1in long. Flowers tiny and at leaf nodes (Jul–Sep). Still waters. NE of North America.

WATER-STARWORT *Callitriche* sp.   Aquatic
Variable freshwater and marginal plant. Appearance varies with growing site. Leaves up to ¾in long, ovate to elliptical; upper ones form a rosette. Flowers minute and at leaf axils (Apr–Sep). Ponds and mud. Widespread in temperate North America.

MARE'S-TAIL *Hippuris vulgaris*   Aquatic
Distinctive freshwater plant. Submerged part of plant produce emergent stems, up to 1ft tall, that carry narrow leaves in whorls or 6–12; each leaf is up to ¾in long. Flowers minute. Ponds and lakes; avoids acid waters. Widespread in North America.

LIZARD'S TAIL *Saururus cernuus*   Height up to 5ft
Distinctive wetland plant. Leaves up to 6in long and heart-shaped. Flowers tiny and white; in a narrow spike, up to 6in long, with a drooping tip (Jun–Sep). Margins of water. E US and S ON.

SALTMARSH ARROWGRASS *Triglochin maritima*   Height up to 1½ft
Plantainlike tufted perennial. Leaves are up to 1ft long, narrow, and unveined. Flowers are tiny and 3-petalled; borne in a long narrow spike, up to 6in long, which is itself long-stalked (May–Sep). Salt marshes. Pacific coast.

MARSH ARROWGRASS *Triglochin palustris*   Height up to 1½ft
Very similar to saltmarsh arrowgrass but leaves, which are up to 1ft long, are deeply furrowed at base. Flowers are tiny and 3-petalled; borne in tall spikes, up to 6in long (Jun–Aug). Marshes and wet meadows. N of North America.

POKEWEED *Phytolacca americana*   Height up to 9ft
Upright, branched plant with reddish stems. Leaves up to 1ft long. Flowers ½in across with 5 white petal-like sepals; in clustered spikes (Jul–Sep). Fruits are poisonous blackish-purple berries. Woods. E of North America.

HOARY PLANTAIN *Plantago media*   Height up to 1ft
Low-growing perennial. Leaves 2–4in long, elliptical, short-stalked with downy gray hairs; form a flat basal rosette. Flowers tiny; borne in dense cylindrical spikes up to 1ft long (Jun–Aug). Dry grassy places. E of North America.

ENGLISH PLANTAIN *Plantago lanceolata*   Height up to 1½ft
Familiar, and usually unwelcome perennial. Leaves up to 1ft long, narrow and ribbed. Flowers tiny and greenish white; borne in dense cylindrical spikes up to 1½ft long (Apr–Oct). Grassy places; a lawn weed. Non-native but now widespread.

SEA PLANTAIN *Plantago maritima*   Height up to 2ft
Distinctive perennial. Leaves up to 1ft long, narrow and linear with 3–5 veins; in upright basal rosette. Flower tiny and greenish white; in dense cylindrical spikes up to 1½ft long (Jun–Aug). Coastal cliffs and salt marshes. NE of North America.

COMMON PLANTAIN *Plantago major*   Height up to 1ft
Persistent perennial weed. Leaves up to 1ft long, broad, and oval with 3–9 veins; form a basal rosette. Flowers tiny and greenish; in dense cylindrical and long-stalked spikes 4–8in long (Jun–Oct). Disturbed areas and lawns. Widespread non-native.

CLEAVERS *Galium aparine*   Height up to 4ft
Sprawling annual. Prickles aid plant's scrambling progress. Leaves 1–3in long and lanceolate; in whorls of 6–8. Flowers tiny and white; from leaf axils (May–Jul). Fruits have hooked bristles. Widespread in E and Pacific states.

NORTHERN SNOW BEDSTRAW *Galium boreale*   Height up to 3ft
Scrambling perennial with smooth stems. Leaves 1–2in long and lanceolate; in whorls of 4. Flowers ¼in across, white, and 4-lobed; in terminal clusters (Jun–Aug). Rocky ground. Widespread AK and Canada; found S in mountains to CA in W.

WILD MADDER *Galium mollugo*   Height up to 4ft
Scrambling perennial. Stems smooth and oval. Leaves up to 1in long, narrow-oval, pointed-tipped with a single vein; in whorls of 6–8. Flowers tiny, white, and 4-lobed; in terminal clusters (Jun–Sep). Grassy places. NE of North America.

BUSH-HONEYSUCKLE *Diervilla sessilifolia*   Height up to 5ft
Bushy shrub. Leaves 3–5in long, ovate, toothed, and opposite. Flowers ¾in long, tubular, 5-lobed, and yellow; in clusters (Jun–Aug). Upland woodlands. SE of North America. Similar northern bush-honeysuckle *L. lonicera* found in NE of North America.

TWINFLOWER *Linnaea borealis*   Creeping
Delicate mat-forming perennial. Leaves ½–1in long, ovate or rounded, and on long, wiry stems. Flowers ½in long and bell-shaped; in nodding pairs on slender stalks (Jun–Aug). Conifer woods. Widespread AK and Canada; further S in US mountains.

AMERICAN FLY HONEYSUCKLE *Lonicera canadensis*   Height up to 5ft
Bushy shrub. Leaves 1–2in long, oblong, opposite, and short-stalked. Flowers 1in long, tubular, and yellow (Jun–Aug). Fruits are blue berries. Woodland and scrub. Widespread across Canada and N US.

JAPANESE HONEYSUCKLE *Lonicera japonica*   Climbing
Vigorous woody vine. Leaves 2–3in long, ovate, opposite, and hairy. Flowers 1½in long, tubular, and whitish with projecting stamens (Apr–Jul). Fruits are black berries. Woods, scrubs and roadsides. Non-native escape, now widespread in E of North America.

TRUMPET HONEYSUCKLE *Lonicera sempervirens*   Climbing
Vigorous but slender vine. Leaves 1–3in long and opposite; mainly fused and perfoliate, pierced by stem. Flowers 1–2in long, tubular, and red on outside, yellow inside; in terminal whorls (Apr–Aug). Red berries. Woods. E of North America.

SNOWBERRY *Symphoricarpos albus* Height up to 4ft
Much-branched shrub. Leaves 1–2in long, ovate, and opposite. Flowers ¼in long, pale pink, and bell-shaped, the mouth 5-lobed. Fruits ½in across, white, and berrylike. Scrub and roadsides. A garden escape, mostly in NE of North America.

MOSCHATEL *Adoxa moschatellina* Height up to 4in
Delicate and charming, low-growing perennial. Leaves ½–1in long and 3-lobed; basal leaves form a carpet, stem leaves in opposite pairs. Flowers tiny and greenish; in stalked heads of 5 (Jun–Jul). Shady woods. Widespread in N of North America.

TEASEL *Dipsacus fullonum* Height up to 6ft
Biennial. Leaves 5–15in long and spiny; as basal rosette in 1st year, paired and fused around stem in 2nd year. Flowers tiny, numerous, and purple; in ovoid spiny clusters 1–3in long, on tall stems (Jul–Oct). Disturbed areas. NE US.

HAREBELL *Campanula rotundifolia* Height up to 2ft
Delicate perennial. Rounded basal leaves soon wither; stem leaves 1–2in long and narrow. Flowers ½–1in long, bell-shaped, nodding, and blue; in clusters (Jun–Sep). Dry grassy places. Widespread in N; S in uplands to OR in W and NJ in E.

CARDINAL FLOWER *Lobelia cardinalis* Height up to 3ft
Attractive upright perennial. Leaves 2–4in long, lanceolate, and toothed. Flowers 1–2in long and scarlet; in tall spikes up to 1½ft tall (Jul–Oct). Damp ground and shady places. Widespread in E and S of North America.

YARROW *Achillea millefolium* Height up to 3ft
Strong-smelling perennial. Leaves up to 6in long, dark green, finely divided, and feathery. Flower heads ¼in across comprise yellowish disc florets and whitish pink ray florets; in flat-topped clusters (Jun–Oct). Grassy places. Widespread in North America.

COMMON RAGWEED *Ambrosia artemisiifolia* Height up to 5ft
Branched and hairy annual. Leaves 2–4in long and finely divided. Flowers tiny, greenish, and nodding; males in tall clustered spikes, females in clusters in leaf axils (Jul–Oct). Disturbed areas. Widespread in E of North America.

ABSINTHE WORMWOOD *Artemisia absinthium* Height up to 3ft
Highly aromatic, upright perennial. Leaves ½–1in long, pinnate, and silvery hairy on both surfaces. Flower heads ¼in across, yellowish, bell-shaped, and nodding; in spikes (Jul–Sep). Disturbed areas. S Canada and NE US.

BIG SAGEBRUSH *Artemisia tridentata* Height up to 9ft
Branched, silvery gray, and aromatic evergreen shrub with a short trunk. Leaves up to ½in long, triangular with blunt teeth. Flowers tiny and greenish; in upright spikes (Aug–Oct). A dominant species in Great Basin deserts.

PEARLY EVERLASTING *Anaphalis margaritacea* Height up to 3ft
Upright, white-woolly plant. Leaves 3–4in long and narrow. Flower heads ¼in across with whitish disc florets and pearly bracts only; in flat clusters (Jul–Sep). Free-draining soils. Widespread AK and Canada; in mountains further S.

MAYWEED *Anthemis cotula*   Height up to 2ft
Unpleasant-smelling annual. Leaves 1–2in long, oval in overall outline but finely divided. Flower heads 1in across and daisylike with yellow disc florets and white ray florets; long-stalked and solitary (Jun–Oct). Disturbed areas. Widespread in North America.

PINEAPPLE WEED *Matricaria discoidea (M. matricarioides)*   Height up to 1ft
Pineapple-scented perennial. Leaves 1–2m long, finely divided, and feathery. Flower heads up to ½in long and ovoid, comprising yellow disc florets only; on stalks (May–Nov). Disturbed areas, paths and tracks. Widespread in North America.

BRASS BUTTONS *Cotula coronopifolia*   Height up to 1ft
Attractive non-native plant. Leaves 1–2in long, varying from lanceolate to divided with narrow lobes. Flower heads ¼in across, yellow, and buttonlike; on stalks (all year). Tidal mud banks and salt marshes. Pacific coast; locally New England.

COMMON BURDOCK *Arctium minus*   Height up to 3ft
Branched biennial. Leaves up to 1½ft, downy, and heart-shaped. Flower heads up to 1in long, ovoid, prickly, and purplish; in open clusters (Jul–Oct). Seed heads prickly. Road-sides, woods and disturbed areas. Widespread in Canada and E US.

ENGLISH DAISY *Bellis perennis*   Height up to 6in
Attractive perennial. Leaves 1in long and spoon-shaped; form prostrate rosette from which flower stalk arises. Flower heads ½–1in across; white ray florets and yellow disc florets (Mar–Oct). Lawns and short grass. Widespread but local.

WHITE WOOD ASTER *Aster divaricatus*   Height up to 3ft
Upright perennial. Leaves 2–6in long, heart-shaped, and stalked. Flower heads 1in across with whitish ray florets and disc florets yellow, turning purple; in flat-topped clusters (Jul–Oct). Dry woodland. Canada and NE US.

ALPINE ASTER *Aster alpinus*   Height up to 10in
Low-growing plant. Leaves 1–3in long; basal leaves lanceolate, stem leaves becoming narrower. Flower heads 1in across with pinkish purple ray florets and yellow disc florets; solitary (Jul–Aug). Grassy tundra. AK and N Canada.

LEAFY ASTER *Aster foliaceus*   Height up to 1½ft
Clump-forming perennial. Leaves 4–8in long; lanceolate at base, becoming narrower up stem. Flower heads 1–2in across with pinkish purple ray florets and yellow disc florets; in clusters (Jul–Sep). Damp woodland. W of North America.

SALT-MARSH ASTER *Aster tenuifolius*   Height up to 2ft
Delicate, straggling plant. Leaves 2–5in long, narrow, and fleshy. Flowers up to 1in across with pale pinkish purple ray florets and yellow disc florets (Aug–Sep). Coastal salt marshes. Atlantic coast of US.

NODDING THISTLE *Carduus nutans*   Height up to 3ft
Upright biennial. Stems winged, spiny, and cottony. Leaves 2–9in long, pinnate, and spiny. Flower heads 1–2in across with pinkish purple florets and purple spiny bracts; stalked and nodding (Jun–Oct). Dry grassland. Local, US and S Canada.

OXEYE DAISY *Leucanthemum vulgare (Chrysanthemum leucanthemum)* Height up to 2½ft
Attractive perennial. Leaves 3–6in long; spoon-shaped at base and form a rosette, pinnately lobed and smaller on stem. Flower heads 1–2in across; white ray florets and yellow disc florets (Jun–Oct). Dry grassland. Temperate parts of North America.

CHICORY *Cichorum intybus*   Height up to 3ft
Branched and stiff perennial. Lower leaves 2–5in long, stalked, and lobed; upper ones smaller, narrow, and clasping. Flower heads 1–2in across and sky blue (Jun–Sep). Bare grassy places and roadsides. Non-native, now locally common throughout North America.

CANADA THISTLE *Cirsium arvense*   Height up to 3ft
Creeping perennial with upright, unwinged stems. Leaves 5–7in long, pinnately lobed, and spiny. Flower heads 1in across and pinkish lilac; in clusters (Jun–Sep). Flowers popular with insects. Grassland and disturbed areas. Throughout North America.

BULL THISTLE *Cirsium vulgare*   Height up to 3ft
Attractive biennial. Stems cottony, winged, and spiny between leaves. Leaves 3–6in long, pinnately lobed, and spiny. Flower heads 1–2in across, with purple florets topping ball of spiny bracts (Jul–Sep). Disturbed areas. Throughout North America.

YELLOW THISTLE *Cirsium horridulum*   Height up to 4ft
Branched, spiny plant. Leaves 6–9in long, pinnately lobed, spiny, and clasping. Flower heads 2–3in across with yellow florets topping ball cloaked in spiny bractlike leaves (May–Aug). Sandy and peaty soil. Atlantic and Gulf coasts of US.

DAISY FLEABANE *Erigeron annuus*   Height up to 4ft
Branched, hairy plant. Leaves 2–5in long, lanceolate, and toothed. Flower heads ½in across, daisylike with pale pink ray florets and yellow disc florets (Jun–Sep). Grassy places and disturbed areas. Widespread in E of North America.

HORSEWEED *Erigeron canadensis*   Height up to 6ft
Much-branched upright plant. Leaves 1–3in long, narrow, hairy, and toothed. Flower heads up to ¼in across, greenish white with insignificant white ray florets (Jul–Oct). Grassy places and disturbed areas. Widespread in E of North America.

COMMON FLEABANE *Erigeron philadelphicus*   Height up to 3ft
Branched, downy plant. Leaves 2–5in long, oblong, and clasping. Flower heads up to 1in across, daisylike with pale pink ray florets and yellow disc florets (Apr–Jul). Woods and grassland. Widespread across much of the North America.

SPOTTED JOE-PYE WEED *Eupatorium maculatum*   Height up to 6ft
Upright perennial. Stems usually purple spotted. Leaves 3–7in long, lanceolate, toothed; in whorls of 4–5. Pinkish flowers in terminal heads 4–6in across (Jul–Sep). Damp grassland, lime-rich soils. S Canada, N US; further S in mountains.

TICKSEED *Coreopsis tinctoria*   Height up to 4ft
Branched upright plant. Leaves 2–4in long, highly divided into narrow segments. Flower heads 1–2in across with yellow ray florets and reddish purple disc florets (Jun–Sep). Grassy places. Central plains and W of North America; garden escape in E.

DESERT MARIGOLD *Baileya multiradiata*   Height up to 1ft
Attractive and woolly desert plant. Leaves 2–3in long, pinnately divided, the lobes toothed. Flower heads 2in across with both the ray and disc florets bright yellow (Apr–Oct). Dry ground, especially roadsides. From S CA to TX.

INDIAN BLANKET *Gaillardia pulchella*   Height up to 2ft
Upright, branched plant. Leaves 1–3in long, narrow, and toothed. Flower heads 2in across with reddish disc florets and yellow ray florets (May–Jul). Deserts and free-draining soils. From NE and E CO, S to AZ and TX.

BLANKET-FLOWER *Gaillardia aristata*   Height up to 2ft
Upright hairy plant. Leaves 1–3in long, narrow, and lobed. Flowers 3–4in across with a domed array of red disc florets and yellow ray florets (May–Sep). Prairies and dry grassland. From BC, S to UT and CO.

COMMON SUNFLOWER *Helianthus annuus*   Height up to 12ft
Familiar upright annual. Leaves up to 1ft long, ovate to heart-shaped, stalked, and alternate. Flower heads up to 6in across with bright yellow ray florets and darker disc florets (Jul–Nov). Open, grassy places. Widespread except in far N.

 GIANT SUNFLOWER *Helianthus giganteus*   Height up to 10ft
Roughly hairy plant. Leaves 3–6in long, lanceolate, toothed, and usually stalkless. Flower heads 2–3in across with bright yellow ray florets and darker disc florets (Jul–Oct). Damp grassland and marshes. Widespread in E of North America.

 PRAIRIE SUNFLOWER *Helianthus petiolaris*   Height up to 3ft
Coarsely hairy plant. Leaves up to 5in long, narrow ovate to narrow heart-shaped, long-stalked, and untoothed. Flower heads 3–4in across with bright yellow ray florets and darker disc florets (Jun–Sep). Prairies. Central parts of North America.

 ORANGE HAWKWEED *Pilosella aurantiaca (Hieracium aurantiacum)* Height up to 2ft
Delicate, hairy plant. Leaves 2–4in long and narrow; form a basal rosette. Flower heads ¾in across, orange, ray florets only (Jun–Aug). Grassy places including roadsides. Non-native, now found in NE of North America and locally in Pacific northwest.

 MOUSE-EAR HAWKWEED *Pilosella officinarum (Hieracium pilosella)* Height up to 1ft
Spreading perennial. Leaves 1–4in long, spoon-shaped, green and hairy above, white downy below; form a basal rosette. Flower heads 1in across, pale yellow with red stripes below (Jun–Sep). Grassy places. Non-native; now found in NE of North America.

 RATTLESNAKE WEED *Hieracium venosum*   Height up to 2ft
Upright plant. Leaves 2–6in long, spoon-shaped to elliptical, green with reddish veins; form a basal rosette. Flowers up to ¾in across and yellow; in open clusters (May–Sep). Open woodland. Widespread in NE US.

BLACK-EYED SUSAN *Rudbeckia hirta*   Height up to 3ft
Roughly hairy biennial. Leaves 2–3in long, ovate to lanceolate, and hairy. Flower heads 2–3in across with orange-yellow ray florets and chocolate brown disc florets (Jun–Oct). Grassy places. Widespread in US and S Canada.

PURPLE CONEFLOWER *Echinacea angustifolia*   Height up to 1½ft
Robust upright plant. Leaves 1–2in long, narrow, and tapering. Flower heads 1in across with 1in long swept-back pinkish ray florets and a dome of brown disc florets (Jun–Aug). Prairies. Central parts of North America, from TX, N to SK and MN.

PRAIRIE BLAZING STAR *Liatris pycnostachya*   Height up to 6ft
Attractive upright plant. Leaves 4–10in long, narrow and linear. Flower heads ½in across, comprising reddish purple disc florets only; in dense spikes (Jul–Oct). Damp grassland and prairies. Central parts of North America, from MN and WI, S to TX.

ARROWLEAF BALSAMROOT *Balsamorhiza sagittata* Height up to 2ft
Striking, open-country plant. Leaves up to 1ft long, ovate to arrowhead-shaped, long-stalked, and silvery downy. Flower heads 3–4in across with bright yellow ray florets and orange disc florets (May–Jul). Grassland. E of North America, N to BC.

GOLDEN RAGWORT *Senecio aureus* Height up to 2ft
Attractive creeping plant. Basal leaves 3–6in long, heart-shaped, and long-stalked; stem leaves shorter and pinnate. Flower heads 1in across with yellow ray florets and orange disc florets; in clusters (Apr–Jul). Damp ground. E of North America.

RAGWORT *Senecio jacobaea* Height up to 3ft
Poisonous non-native biennial or perennial. Leaves 2–6in long, pinnate with a blunt end lobe. Flower heads ½–1in across, yellow ray florets and orange disc florets; in clusters (Jul–Aug). Grassland. Coastal NE and Pacific NW of North America.

SOFT ARNICA *Arnica mollis* Height up to 2ft
Attractive hairy plant. Leaves 2–5in long, lanceolate to narrow ovate, and unstalked. Flower heads 2in across with yellow ray and disc florets (Jun–Sep). Damp upland ground. Mountains of Pacific states and provinces; E across Canada.

HEARTLEAF ARNICA *Arnica cordifolia* Height up to 2ft
Distinctive upland plant. Leaves 2–5in long, heart-shaped, and stalked; 2–3 pairs. Flower heads 2–3in across with yellow ray florets and orange disc florets (May–Aug). Shady woods. Widespread in mountains in W of North America.

CANADA GOLDENROD *Solidago canadensis* Height up to 5ft
Attractive upright plant. Leaves 3–5in long, lanceolate, and hairy. Flower heads small and yellowish; in clusters on curved branches (May–Sep). Grassland and woodland clearings. Widespread throughout much of the North America.

SEASIDE GOLDENROD *Solidago sempervirens* Height up to 8ft
Striking coastal plant. Leaves 3–8in long, oblong, and fleshy; becoming smaller up stem. Flower heads ¼in long and yellow; in curved clusters (Jul–Nov). Coastal salt marshes. Atlantic and Gulf coasts, from NF to TX.

COMMON TANSY *Tanacetum vulgare* Height up to 3ft
Aromatic, downy perennial. Leaves 4–8in long, pinnate with deeply cut lobes. Flower head ½in across and yellow; in flat-topped clusters up to 5in across (Jul–Sep). Disturbed areas. S Canada and much of US.

COMMON SOW-THISTLE *Sonchus oleraceus* Height up to 5ft
Upright annual. Broken stems exude milky sap. Leaves 5–8in long, fleshy, and pinnate with toothed margins and pointed basal lobes. Flowers heads 1in across and pale yellow; in clusters (May–Oct). Disturbed areas. S Canada and much of US.

COMMON DANDELION *Taraxacum officinale* Height up to 1½ft
Variable perennial. Leaves up to 1ft long, lobed, spoon-shaped and forming basal rosette. Flower heads 1–2in across and yellow; on hollow stems that yield milky sap if broken (Mar–Sep). Grassy places. Widespread except in far N and S.

HAWKSBEARD (SMOOTH HAWKSBEARD) *Crepis capillaris* Height up to 3ft
Hairless annual or biennial. Leaves up to 8in long; lower ones lobed, forming a basal rosette, upper ones arrow-shaped and clasping. Flower heads ½–1in across bright yellow; in branched clusters (May–Jul). Non-native, widespread in N US.

OYSTER PLANT (SALSIFY) *Tragopogon porrifolius* Height up to 4ft
Upright, hairless perennial. Leaves up to 9in long, narrow, and grasslike. Flower heads 1–2in across, reddish purple and opening in morning sunshine only (Apr–Jun). Rough grassy places. Widespread in S Canada and much of US.

COLTSFOOT *Tussilago farfara*   Height up to 1½ft
Creeping perennial. Leaves 5–8in across and heart-shaped; appear after flowers have bloomed. Flower heads 1in across and yellow; borne on scaly stems (Feb–May). Bare, often disturbed areas. NE of North America.

COCKLEBUR *Xanthium strumarium*   Height up to 5ft
Roughly hairy upright plant. Leaves 3–6in long, broadly triangular, maplelike and bristly. Flowers in egg-shaped burs, 1in long, armed with stiff hooked hairs. Disturbed areas. Widespread in both E and W.

POISON IVY *Rhus radicans*   Climbing
Spreading plant. Contact causes skin irritation. Leaves divided into 3 ovate, glossy leaflets each 2–3in long. Flowers small and yellowish; in clusters 2–5in long (May–Jul). Fruits are white berries. Woodland. Widespread in E.

 POISON SUMAC *Rhus vernix*   Height up to 15ft
Much-branched poisonous shrub. Leaves up to 1ft long with 6–12 pairs of oval leaflets and a terminal leaflet. Flowers small and yellowish; in open clusters 2–4in long (May–Jul). Fruits are white berries. Wetlands. E of North America.

 WINGED SUMAC *Rhus copallina*   Height up to 25ft
Branched shrub or small tree. Leaves pinnate with a winged midrib and ovate, pointed leaflets 2–3in long. Flowers small and greenish; in clusters 4–6in long (Jul–Sep). Dry woodland. E US.

 WATER PLANTAIN *Alisma plantago-aquatica*   Height up to 3ft
Aquatic perennial. Emergent leaves up to 6in long, oval, and long-stalked with parallel veins; submerged leaves shorter and narrower. Flowers up to ½in across with 3 pink petals; in branched whorls (Jun–Aug). Margins of water. Widespread in North America.

 WATER PLAINTAIN *Alisma subcordatum*   Height up to 3ft
Emergent aquatic perennial. Emergent leaves 2–5in long, elliptical, and parallel-veined; submerged ones narrow. Flowers tiny with 3 white petals; in much-branched whorls (Jun–Oct). Margins of water. Widespread except in far N.

ARROWHEAD *Sagittaria latifolia*   Height up to 3ft
Distinctive aquatic perennial. Emergent leaves arrowhead-shaped, floating leaves oval, and submerged ones narrow. Flowers 1in across with 3 white petals; in branched whorls (Jul–Sep). Widespread in North America, N to S Canada.

SWEETFLAG *Acorus calamus*   Height up to 4ft
Emergent aquatic perennial. Leaves up to 3ft long, narrow and stiff. Flowers small greenish; crowded into a dense clublike spadix 2–4in long (May–Aug). Wetlands. Widespread in E of North America; more local in central and W.

JACK-IN-THE-PULPIT *Arisaema triphyllum*   Height up to 3ft
Intriguing perennial. Leaves 2–4in long, ovate, and stalked; 1 or 2 only. Flowers 4–5in tall, with clublike spadix of densely packed flowers shrouded by hooded brown and green spathe (Apr–Jun). Fruits are red berries. Woods. E of North America.

 WATER ARUM *Calla palustris*   Height up to 1ft
Attractive wetland plant. Leaves 4–6in long, heart-shaped and long-stemmed. Flowers up to 2in tall with clublike spadix of densely packed greenish flowers shrouded by white spathe (Jun–Aug). Ponds and bogs. Widespread N half of North America.

WATER LETTUCE *Pistia stratiotes*   Floating
Fast-spreading aquatic plant. Leaves 3–9in long, fresh green, downy, and conspicuously ribbed; form a rosette. Flowers tiny and whitish; borne on a short spadix with a whitish spathe (Apr). Standing water. SE US.

SKUNK CABBAGE *Symplocarpus foetidus*   Height up to 2ft
Intriguing plant with a fetid odor. Leaves 1–2ft long; rolled, then flat and broadly ovate. Flowers comprise a 4–6in long spathe, mottled brown and green, shrouding a spherical spadix (Feb–May). Damp ground. S Canada and N US.

YELLOW SKUNK CABBAGE *Lysichiton americanum*   Height up to 1½ft
Distinctive clump-forming plant. Leaves up to 6in long, oval and stalked; in clusters. Flowers comprise yellow spathe and clublike spadix of tiny flowers; on stalks (Apr–Jul). Saturated ground. Pacific states and provinces; also CO and MT.

CLIMBING BITTERSWEET *Celastrus scandens*   Climbing
Vigorous, twining vine. Leaves 2–4in long and ovate. Flowers tiny and greenish; in terminal clusters 3–5in long (May–Jun). Orange fruits contain red berrylike seeds inside. Woodland. E of North America.

COMMON PIPEWORT *Eriocaulon septangulare*   Height up to 8in
Intriguing aquatic plant. Leaves 1–3in long, narrow, and pointed; form a submerged clump attached to substrate. Flower ½in long and white; in terminal heads with gray bracts, borne on leafless stems (Jul–Sep). Standing water. NE of North America.

YELLOW FLAG *Iris pseudacorus*   Height up to 4ft
Attractive, robust perennial. Leaves 3–4ft, gray-green, sword-shaped, and often wrinkled. Flowers 3–4in across and bright yellow; in clusters of 2–3 on tall stems (Jun–Aug). Margins of water, and marshes. SE Canada and E US, S to GA.

ROCKY MOUNTAIN IRIS *Iris missouriensis*   Height up to 1½ft
Impressive, clump-forming perennial. Leaves up to 1½ft long, sword-shaped and robust. Flowers 3–4in across and bluish purple; in clusters on leafless stems (May–Jul). Damp ground. From BC to CA, E to Rocky Mountain states.

SOUTHERN BLUE FLAG *Iris virginica*   Height up to 3ft
Attractive perennial. Leaves up to 2½ft long, straplike and tapering. Flowers 3–4in across with bluish-purple sepals and petals, the sepals yellow and veined towards the base; borne in stalked clusters (May–Jul). Favors marshes and damp grassland. Widespread in temperate E of North America.

BLUE-EYED GRASS *Sisyrinchium angustifolium*   Height up to 1½ft
Slender and delicate perennial. Leaves up to 1½ft long, grasslike, and tufted. Flowers ½in across, blue with a yellow center, the 6 petal-like parts all pointed-tipped (May–Jul). Damp grassy places. Widespread across North America.

YELLOW CLINTONIA *Clintonia borealis*   Height up to 1ft
Delicate, low-growing plant. Leaves 6–10in long, broadly ovate to oblong. Flowers 1in long, bell-shaped, and yellow; in nodding heads of 3–8 (May–Aug). Fruits are blue berries. Damp woodlands, often in uplands. NE of North America.

QUEEN CUP *Clintonia uniflora*   Height up to 6in
Delicate woodland plant. Leaves up to 6in long, broadly ovate to oblong. Flowers 1in long with 6 petal-like white segments; usually solitary on slender stalk (May–Aug). Damp conifer woods. Pacific states and provinces, E to MT.

COAST FLATSTEM ONION *Allium falcifolium*   Height up to 6in
Low-growing, bulbous perennial. Leaves up to 6in long, narrow, flat and tapering. Flowers up to 1in long and pinkish purple; borne on short, flattish stems (May–Jun). Bare, often stony ground, especially on base-rich soils near the sea. Coastal districts in W North America, mainly CA.

WILD LEEK *Allium tricoccum*   Height up to 1½ft
Delicate bulbous plant. Leaves 8–12in long, lanceolate, and basal; wither before flowers appear. Flowers ¼in across and white; in umbel-like clusters on tall stalk (Jun–Jul). Woods and rough grassland. SE Canada and NE US.

TROUT LILY *Erythronium americanum*   Height up to 10in
Attractive spring flower. Leaves 2–6in long, elliptical, and mottled brown; 2 only. Flowers 1in across, orange-yellow with 6 petal-like segments, recurved towards tips; nodding, on bare stalks (Mar–Jun). Woods. E of North America, S to GA.

YELLOW FAWN-LILY *Erythronium grandiflorum*   Height up to 1ft
Charming upland flower. Leaves (2 only) 4–6in long and narrow-ovate. Flowers 1–2in across, with 6 petal-like yellow segments and projecting stamens; stalked and nodding (Mar–Jul). Mountain woodland. W of North America, from BC to CA, E to CO and WY.

MEADOW DEATH CAMAS *Zigadenus venosus*   Height up to 2ft
Attractive, poisonous plant. Leaves up to 1½ft long, grasslike, and basal. Flowers ¼in across with 6 petal-like segments; in crowded spikes (May–Jul). Damp meadows. Widespread in W US.

DESERT LILY *Hesperocallis undulata*   Height up to 4ft
Showy, bulbous desert plant. Leaves up to 1½ft long, basal, and narrow with wavy margins. Flowers 2–3in long, trumpet-shaped, and white; in clustered spikes (Mar–May). Sandy desert soils. S CA and AZ.

SCARLET FRITILLARY *Fritillaria recurva*   Height up to 3ft
Striking perennial. Leaves 2–4in long, gray-green, narrow, and straplike. Flowers 1in long, scarlet, and bell-shaped with recurved segment tips; nodding, on upright stems (Mar–Jun). Wooded slopes. OR and CA.

CANADA LILY *Lilium canadense*   Height up to 6ft
Bulbous perennial. Leaves 3–6in long, narrow, and in whorls. Flowers 2–3in across, bell-shaped with 6 petal-like segments recurved at mouth, orange or red and dark-spotted inside; nodding, in open clusters (Jun–Aug). Damp ground. E of North America.

TURK'S-CAP LILY *Lilium superbum*   Height up to 7ft
Elegant bulbous perennial. Leaves 3–6in long, narrow, upper ones in whorls. Flowers 2–3in across with 6 orange, dark-spotted petal-like segments recurved so that flower can appear almost spherical (Jul–Sep). Damp ground. E US.

CANADA MAYFLOWER *Maianthemum canadense*   Height up to 1ft
Charming, patch-forming perennial. Leaves (1–3 only) 2–3in long and narrow heart-shaped. Flowers small, star-shaped, and white; in clustered spikes (May–Jun). Upland and northern woods. NE of North America, S to GA in mountains.

SMOOTH SOLOMON'S-SEAL *Polygonatum biflorum* Height up to 3ft
Elegant woodland perennial with arching stems. Leaves 2–5in long, ovate, and parallel-veined. Flowers ½in long, greenish white, and bell-shaped; nodding, single or paired from leaf axils (May–Jun). E of North America, N to ON.

FALSE SOLOMON'S-SEAL *Smilacina racemosa* Height up to 3ft
Perennial with arching stems. Leaves 3–7in long, ovate, and parallel-veined. Flowers tiny with 6 petal-like white segments; in branched, terminal spikes (Apr–Jul). Damp and shady wooded areas. Widespread throughout much of North America.

STAR-FLOWERED SOLOMON'S-SEAL *Smilacina stellata* Height up to 2ft
Perennial with arching stems. Leaves 3–6in long, ovate, parallel-veined, and clasping. Flowers ¼in across with 6 petal-like white segments; in terminal unbranched spikes (May–Jun). Shady woods. Pacific Coast, from AK to CA.

 GIANT TRILLIUM *Trillium chloropetalum* Height up to 2ft
Shade-loving plant. Leaves 3–5in long, mottled purple, and broadly ovate; 3, borne in a whorl on stout stem. Flowers 2in long and greenish with 3 upright petals; borne just above leaves (Feb–May). Damp woods. Coastal WA and OR, S to CA.

PURPLE TRILLIUM *Trillium erectum* Height up to 1ft
Foul-smelling plant. Leaves 3–6in long, broadly ovate, and net-veined; 3, in a whorl on stout stem. Flowers 2–3in across with 3 reddish purple petals and 3 green sepals (Apr–Jun). Shady woods. NE of North America, S to GA in mountains.

 WILD OATS *Uvularia sessilifolia* Height up to 1ft
Delicate-looking plant. Leaves 2–3in long, stemless, oblong and conspicuously veined. Flowers 1in long, creamy white and bell-shaped; 1 or 2, nodding at top of stem (Apr–Jun). Woods and shady places. SE Canada and NE US.

 FALSE HELLEBORINE *Veratrum viride* Height up to 6ft
Poisonous plant. Leaves 6–12in long, broadly ovate, parallel-veined and clasping. Flowers ½in across with 6 greenish petal-like segments; in branching, clustered spikes (May–Jul). Damp ground. N of North America; S in mountains to OR in W, GA in E.

 GRASS PINK *Calopogon pulchellus* Height up to 1½ft
Attractive little orchid. Single leaf, up to 1ft long, is basal and grasslike. Flowers 1in across with spreading pink petals and sepals and bearded lip; in spikes (mainly Apr–Aug). Saturated acid soils. E of North America.

YELLOW FRINGED ORCHID *Habenaria ciliaris* Height up to 3ft
Attractive upright plant. Leaves up to 10in long, lanceolate; largest at base, getting smaller up stem. Flowers ½in across, orange or yellow, with strikingly fringed lip; in clustered spikes (Jul–Sep). Damp ground. E US.

NORTHERN BOG ORCHID *Platanthera hyperborea* Height up to 1ft
Robust little northern plant. Leaves 2–4in long, narrow with parallel veins. Flowers ¼in across, greenish yellow, and sweet-scented; in clustered spikes (Jul–Aug). Damp grassy places. Widespread in Arctic and sub-Arctic North America.

FROG ORCHID *Coeloglossum viride* Height up to 10in
Intriguing orchid. Basal leaves 2–3in long, oval, and form basal rosette; stem leaves narrower, partly sheathing. Flowers ¼in across and reddish green; sepals and upper petals form a hood; in open spikes (Jun–Aug). Grassy places. N of North America.

YELLOW LADY'S-SLIPPER *Cypripedium calceolus* Height up to 2ft
Striking orchid. Leaves 3–8in long, broadly ovate with parallel veins. Flowers (usually 1)
1–2in across with inflated yellow lip petal, the other 2 petals and 3 sepals brown or green
(Apr–Jul). Woodland. S Canada and N US; S in mountains.

 CALYPSO FAIRY SLIPPER *Calypso bulbosa* Height up to 8in
Charming forest orchid. Single basal leaf, 3in long, ovate and stalked, appears in fall and
withers next spring. Flowers 1–2in across and pinkish, expanded lower lip with yellow
hairs; 1–2 on stalk (May–Jul). Conifer woods. Canada and N US.

 PINK LADY'S-SLIPPER *Cypripedium acaule* Height up to 1ft
Beautiful orchid. Leaves (1 pair) 6–8in long, basal, conspicuously veined, and ovate. Flow-
ers 2–3in across; inflated lip petal pinkish red, 2 other petals and 3 sepals brown or green
(Apr–Jul). Woodland. E of North America, S to GA and AL.

 STRIPED CORALROOT *Corallorhiza striata* Height up to 1½ft
Saprophytic pinkish orchid that lacks chlorophyll. Leaves reduced to tiny basal scales.
Flowers 1in long and reddish pink; in open spikes on naked stem (May–Aug). Shady
woodlands. S Canada and N US; further S in mountains to CA and TX.

 CORALROOT ORCHID *Corallorhiza trifida* Height up to 1ft
Saprophytic orchid that is buffish brown and lacks chlorophyll. Leaves reduced to tiny
basal scales. Flowers ½in long and brown; in open spikes on naked stems (May–Jul).
Upland woods. AK, Canada and N US; further S in mountains.

 LESSER TWAYBLADE *Listera cordata* Height up to 5in
Delicate and easily overlooked perennial. Leaves ½–1in long and heart-shaped; borne as a
single, basal pair. Flowers tiny and reddish green; in a small, terminal cluster (May–Jul).
Woods and heathlands. Widespread across N of North America.

SHOWY ORCHIS *Orchis spectabilis* Height up to 1ft
Attractive and fragrant perennial. Leaves 3–8in long, ovate, and sheathing. Flowers 1in
long with white lip and purple hood; in spikes (Apr–Jun). Damp ground, including woods.
E of North America, S to GA.

DWARF RATTLESNAKE PLANTAIN *Goodyera repens* Height up to 1ft
Creeping woodland orchid. Leaves 1–2in long, ovate, evergreen, and mainly basal. Flowers ¼in long, white, and barely opening; in a spirally twisted spike (Jul–Aug). Conifer
woodland. NE of North America, and further S in E US in mountains.

FEN ORCHID *Liparis loeselii* Height up to 1½ft
Upright perennial. Leaves (usually 2) 4–6in long, oblong, basal, and opposite. Flowers ½in
across and yellow-green; in spikes of 2–10 (Jun–Jul). In bogs and other saturated ground.
S Canada and NE US; in E, further S in mountains.

 HOODED LADY'S-TRESSES *Spiranthes romanzoffiana* Height up to 1½ft
Robust little orchid. Leaves up to 8in long, mainly basal but smaller ones up stem. Flowers ¼–½in long, white, and tubelike; in 3 spiral rows in crowded spike (Jul–Oct). Damp
meadows and bogs. AK and Canada; further S in US in mountains.

SEA OATS *Uniola paniculata*   Height up to 6ft
Striking, clump-forming grass of coastal sands. Leaves up to 10in long. Flowers in spikelets, borne in 1ft-long clusters on curved stems (Jun–Jul). Widespread on coasts of SE US. Also planted here and elsewhere to combat dune erosion.

QUACKGRASS *Elytrigia (Agropyron) repens*   Height up to 2½ft
Spreading, unbranched perennial. Important grassland component but also an aggressive invader of cultivated ground. Leaves narrow and mainly basal. Flowers flat and in clusters; in 10–12in-long spikes (May–Jul). Widespread throughout North America.

PACIFIC CORDGRASS *Spartina foliosa*   Height up to 3ft
Tufted perennial of mudflats and salt marshes. Tolerant of inundation by sea. Leaves gray-green and tough. Flowers in a yellowish green elongated cluster (Jun–Sep). Locally common in suitable habitats on Pacific coast.

INDIAN GRASS *Sorghastrum nutans*   Height up to 8ft
Attractive, clump-forming perennial. Important prairie species; sometimes forms pure stands. Leaves 1–2ft long and narrow. Flowers have twisted bristles; golden brown when flowering and in feathery heads (Aug–Sep). Widespread, except in W.

ORCHARD GRASS *Dactylis glomerata*   Height up to 4ft
Tufted, tussock-forming perennial. Non-native, grown for fodder, now naturalized in grassy places. Leaves rough with inrolled margins. Flowers in purplish inflorescence; heads spread to resemble a bird's foot (May–Sep). Widespread in North America.

TUFTED HAIRGRASS *Deschampsia cespitosa*   Height up to 3ft
Tufted, clump-forming perennial. Leaves dark green, wiry and narrow with rough edges. Spreading clusters of 2-flowered, silvery purple spikelets are borne in open inflorescences on tall stems (Jun–Aug). Damp grassy places. Widespread in North America.

CRINKLED HAIRGRASS *Deschampsia flexuosa*   Height up to 3ft
Tufted perennial, favoring dry ground and often acid soils. Leaves up to 10in long, inrolled, hairlike, and basal. Inflorescence has open clusters of purplish spikelets on paired branches (Jun–Jul). Open woodland and slopes. Widespread in North America.

ANNUAL BLUEGRASS *Poa annua*   Height up to 1ft
Annual or short-lived perennial of bare grassland and disturbed areas. Stems flattened. Leaves pale green, blunt-tipped and often wrinkled. Inflorescence 6–8in long, dense, and cylindrical; on tall, slender stems (Jun–Aug). Widespread in North America.

VELVET GRASS *Holcus lanatus*   Height up to 3ft
Tufted perennial that is gray-green with downy leaves and stems. Flower head up to 5in long, tightly packed at first, then spreading; comprises reddish-tipped, gray-green, 2-flowered spikelets (May–Aug). Meadows and disturbed areas. Widespread in North America.

COMMON REED *Phragmites communis*   Height up to 10ft
Spreading perennial of freshwater marshes and margins of brackish areas. Often forms vast stands. Robust stems carry 1½ft-long, broad leaves. Flowers in large, terminal purplish inflorescence (Aug–Sep). Plants turn brown and persist. Widespread in North America.

TIMOTHY *Phleum pratense*   Height up to 4ft
Tufted perennial of meadows, agricultural land and waysides. Often cultivated for hay. Leaves gray-green and flat. Inflorescence up to 10in long, dense, and cylindrical; on tall, slender stem (Jun–Aug). Widespread and common.

RED FESCUE *Festuca rubra*   Height up to 3ft
Clump-forming, tufted perennial. Leaves up to 1ft long, narrow, wiry, and stiff. Inflorescence 2–9in long, comprising spikelets that are usually reddish (May–Jul). Dry grassy places. Sometimes used in lawns. Widespread in North America.

BERMUDA GRASS *Cynodon dactylon*   Height up to 10in
Creeping perennial with narrow, flat leaves. Inflorescence comprises 3–6 fingerlike spikes bearing small spikelets; spikes spread in full flower (Mar–Oct). Cultivated and disturbed areas, lawns; often coastal. Widespread in S.

SWEET VERNAL GRASS *Anthoxanthum odoratum*   Height up to 1½ft
Tufted perennial that smells of new-mown hay when dry. Leaves 1–3in long. Inflorescence a spikelike array of spikelets, fresh green at first then reddish brown (Apr–Jun). Meadows and roadsides. Widespread except in hot, dry areas.

REDTOP *Agrostis gigantea (alba)*   Height up to 4ft
Creeping perennial; roots at nodes. Leaves up to 8in long and ¼in wide. Conical inflorescence of 1-flowered spikelets borne on spreading branches; reddish purple when in flower (Jun–Aug). Meadows, disturbed areas and lawns. Widespread in North America.

SLENDER COTTONGRASS *Eriophorum gracile*   Height up to 1½ft
Creeping perennial with 3-sided stems and very narrow leaves. Inflorescence comprises drooping, stalked clusters of spikelets (May–Jun). Most distinctive when in fruit, seeds having cottony hairs. Bogs and swamps. Widespread in N.

HARESTAIL COTTONGRASS *Eriophorum vaginatum*   Height up to 1ft
Tussock-forming perennial. Leaves very narrow. Upright, stalked flower spike emerges from inflated sheath (May–Jun). Fruits have white, cottony hairs. Acid bogs and peaty soil. Widespread in N of North America, including Arctic and sub-Arctic.

BEAKED SEDGE *Carex rostrata*   Height up to 3ft
Patch-forming plant. Stems 3-sided. Leaves 1–3ft long, yellow-green with rough edges. Inflorescence comprises 2–4 narrow brown spikes of male flowers above 2–5 greenish ovoid to sausage-shaped female ones (May–Jul). Swamps. Widespread in North America.

WATER SEDGE *Carex aquatilis*   Height up to 3ft
Creeping perennial. Stems brittle and 3-sided. Leaves yellowish green and 1–3ft long. Inflorescence comprises 2–3 spikes of reddish brown male flowers above 2–5 brown, sausage-shaped female flowers (May–Jul). Margins of water. Widespread in North America.

TOAD RUSH *Juncus bufonius*   Height up to 1½ft
Tufted and branching annual. Narrow, grooved leaves arise at base of plant and on stems. Inflorescence comprises short, spreading clusters along branches and in branch forks (May–Jul). Damp, bare ground including wheel ruts. Widespread in North America.

SOFT RUSH *Juncus effusus*   Height up to 4ft
Tall perennial. Stems green and smooth-looking. Pale brown flowers borne in a loose, rounded cluster topped by a narrow bract (May–Jul). Grassland, mostly on acid soils; often an indication of over-grazing. Widespread in North America.

WOODRUSH *Luzula multiflora*   Height up to 2ft
Tufted perennial with creeping runners. Leaves fresh green, fringed with downy white hairs. Inflorescence comprises a terminal clusters of 3–10 stalked, oval heads (May–Jun). Woods and dry grassy places, usually on acid soils. Widespread in North America.

BUR REED *Sparganium americanum*   Height up to 3ft
Sedgelike perennial. Leaves 2–3ft long, bright green, linear, and keeled. Small male flower heads above 5–9 spherical female flower heads 1in across (May–Jul). Margins of still and standing fresh water. Widespread in North America.

COMMON CATTAIL *Typha latifolia*   Height up to 9ft
Impressive sedgelike plant. Leaves gray-green, 1in wide, and very long. Flower spikes comprise brown, sausagelike array of female flowers with narrow spire of male flowers above (Jun–Aug). Margins of fresh water. Widespread in North America.

BRACKEN *Pteridium aquilinum* Height up to 6ft or more
North America's most common and widespread fern. Carpets woodland floors and covers hillsides. Favours dry, acid soils. Curled-tipped fronds appear in spring. Mature fronds green and 3-pinnate. Spore cases around leaf margins. Throughout North America.

DEER FERN *Blechnum spicant* Frond length up to 2ft
Distinctive fern of damp woods and shady banks, usually on acid soils. Bright green, sterile, overwintering fronds are 1-pinnate; form spreading clumps. Fertile fronds are erect with very narrow lobes. W of North America, mainly AK to CA.

ROYAL FERN *Osmunda regalis* Height up to 6ft
Large and impressive fern that forms sizeable clumps. Favors swamps and wet woodlands, usually on acid soils. Fronds up to 5ft long, 2-pinnate with oblong leaflets. Brown spore cases terminal on central fronds. E half of North America.

CRESTED WOOD FERN *Dryopteris cristata* Frond length up to 2ft
Creeping, tufted fern that favors shady, damp woods and bogs. Frond outline narrow and parallel-sided; 1- or 2-pinnate with triangular leaflets. Inner fertile fronds erect; outer sterile ones spreading. Canada and temperate US.

MALE FERN *Dryopteris filix-mas* Frond length up to 4ft
Robust, clump-forming fern of woods and shady banks. Fronds remain green through winter; broadly oval in outline, 2-pinnate with pale brown scales on stalk. Spore cases round. Widespread across Canada and temperate parts of US, except SE.

FRAGILE FERN *Cystopteris fragilis* Frond length up to 3ft
Delicate fern that grows in tufts arising from crevices in rocks and stone walls, mostly on limestone. Fronds 2- or 3-pinnate and appear Apr–Oct. Spore cases rounded. Widespread AK, Canada, and temperate parts of US.

HAYSCENTED FERN *Dennstaedtia punctilobula* Frond length up to 1½ft
Brittle-stemmed and spreading fern that often covers large patches. Favors dry woods and open slopes. Fronds yellowish green, 2- to 3-pinnate with narrow-oblong leaflets. Stalk darkening towards base. E Canada and NE US.

LADY FERN *Athyrium filix-femina* Frond length up to 4ft
Large but rather delicate-looking fern, forming large clumps in damp woods, on banks and on hillsides. Fronds pale green and 2-pinnate. Pinnules pointed and toothed. Spore cases curved, ripening in fall. Widespread in suitable habitats.

SOUTHERN MAIDENHAIR FERN *Adiantum capillus-veneris* Frond length up to 2ft
Distinctive tufted fern. Spreading, hairlike stems carry green leaflets that are broadly triangular and 2–3 lobed. Favors humid settings, often among limestone rocks dampened by seepage or splashed by water. S US, N to NC and CO.

WATER FERN *Azolla caroliniana* Aquatic
Surface-floating fern that sometimes carpets whole ponds or backwaters. Fronds are yellowish green, but often tinged red in bright light; comprise small, overlapping leaves. Locally common in SE US; occasionally further N.

MARSH FERN *Thelypteris palustris* Frond length up to 1½ft
Delicate, creeping fern of saturated ground in woods, wetland meadows, and margins of water. Fronds pale green and 2-pinnate. Spore cases rounded, under inrolled margins of pinnules. Widespread in E half of North America; locally common NE US.

OAK FERN *Gymnocarpium dryopteris* Frond length up to 1½ft
Delicate, creeping fern of damp woods, shady and cool banks, and mountains. Fronds bright green, broadly triangular in outline and 3-pinnate; held horizontally. Stalks darken towards base. Widespread AK, Canada, and cooler parts of US.

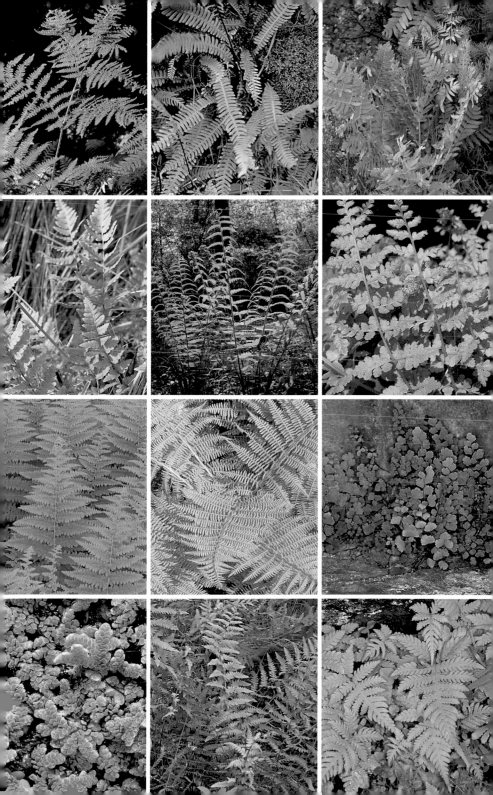

OSTRICH FERN *Matteuccia struthiopteris* Height up to 5ft
Distinctive fern. Often forms a shuttlecock array of dark green sterile fronds that are 2-pinnate; fancifully resemble ostrich plumes; fertile fronds are shorter, denser and brown. Wet woods and margins of rivers. AK, Canada, and NE US.

SENSITIVE FERN *Onoclea sensibilis* Height up to 2ft
Creeping fern of damp and shady woods, banks, and meadows. Sterile fronds broadly tri-angular in outline and pinnate with wavy-margined leaflets; fertile fronds shorter, more compact, and brown. Sensitive to frost. Central and E parts of North America.

RUSTY WOODSIA *Woodsia ilvensis* Height up to 6in
Tough, tufted fern. Fronds narrow-oblong in outline and 2-pinnate; undersurface hairy and stalks brown. Spore capsules rounded. Grows from crevices in acid rocks. Widespread AK, Canada, and cooler northern parts of US.

MOONWORT *Botrychium lunaria* Height up to 9in
Unusual fern of grassy uplands, mountain slopes, and undisturbed meadows. Single stalk bears a solitary frond, pinnately divided into 3–9 rounded lobes. Spores borne on divided, fertile spike. Widespread; absent from hot, dry parts of S.

QUILLWORT *Isoetes* sp. Height up to 8in
Aquatic or amphibious tufted perennial; several similar species in North America. Upright or spreading quill-like leaves arise from bulbous or cormlike base, attached to substrate. Widespread in shallow, clear water or margins of lakes.

FIELD HORSETAIL *Equisetum arvense* Height up to 2½ft
The commonest horsetail, forming spreading patches in dry, grassy places, and on dis-turbed areas. Sterile shoots have ridged stems and carry whorls of unbranched branches. Fertile stems appear in early spring and ripen in May. Throughout North America.

SWAMP HORSETAIL *Equisetum fluviatile* Height up to 3ft
Horsetail of marshes and margins of ponds and lakes. Tall, unbranched stems are jointed and thin with whorls of narrow, jointed branches. Spores in conelike structures at ends of fertile stems. AK, Canada, and N US.

SCOURING-RUSH *Equisetum hyemale* Height up to 4ft
Slender, unbranched horsetail forming large patches in suitable sites. Stems dark green with rough ridges. Cones pointed and ripe in early spring. Favours damp and saturated ground; often on river banks. Widespread throughout North America.

STIFF CLUBMOSS *Lycopodium annotinum* Height up to 1ft
Low-growing clubmoss with creeping stems and upright branches, these cloaked in spreading leaves and constricted at points along their length. Cones solitary and terminal, ripe Aug–Sep. Margins of drier swamps on acid soils. AK, Canada, and N US.

FIR CLUBMOSS *Lycopodium selago* Height up to 6in
Tufted, upright clubmoss with stems cloaked in green, needlelike leaves give plant more than a passing resemblance to a young conifer. Spore cases borne along stem. Dry, acid soils. AK and Canada; S in US in uplands.

ALPINE CLUBMOSS *Lycopodium alpinum* Prostrate
Low-growing clubmoss with flattened, creeping stems, branches cloaked in flat, scalelike leaves. Cones terminal, ripen brown (Aug–Sep). Mountains, tundra, and upland heath-lands on acid soils. Widespread AK and N Canada; further S in uplands.

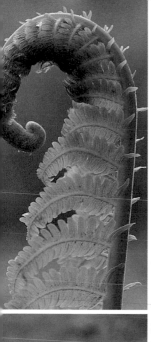

CUSHION MOSS *Leucobryum* sp.   Height up to 2in
A distinctive moss genus of damp woodland and bare upland slopes. Often forms large cushions on the ground, which are easily dislodged. Leaves narrow and gray-green; become almost white in dry weather. Widespread in suitable habitats.

SPHAGNUM MOSS (BOG MOSS) *Sphagnum* sp.   Height up to 2in
Widespread genus of mosses that favor boggy habitats or wet, peaty ground. Upright stems, clusters of branches, and terminal head are all cloaked in leaves that are fresh green and often look inflated. Throughout North America in suitable habitats.

FEATHER MOSS *Pleurozium* sp.   Height up to 2in
Tough little moss with reddish stems and branches that are cloaked in yellowish, oval, and translucent leaves that overlap one another. Cushion-forming in woods, usually on acid soils. Widespread in North America.

HAIRCAP MOSS *Polytrichum commune*   Height up to 9in
Upright moss of damp woods and open slopes, usually on acid soils. Leaves narrow, needlelike, and pointed; held almost at right-angles to stems creating clubmosslike appearance. Box-shaped spore capsules brown when ripe; on slender stems. Widespread across N North America

SPINELEAF MOSS *Atrichium undulatum*   Height up to 2in
Common and widespread moss of woodlands, found on most soil types except base-rich ones. Leaves long, narrow and dark green with wavy, toothed-edged margins. Curved brown spore capsules borne on long stalks and held at an angle. Widespread across N North America

CLADONIA LICHEN *Cladonia* sp.   Spreading
A widespread genus represented by numerous similar species found among low-growing vegetation in habitats ranging from coastal dunes to mountain tops. Form encrusting patches, cushions or mats covered with gray-white scales. Some species have erect stalks topped with red spore-producing bodies. Widespread across N North America

REINDEER MOSS *Cladonia rangiferina*   Height up to 4in
Cushion-forming gray lichen comprising interwoven curved branches. Widespread on tundra and Alpine heathlands of Arctic and sub-Arctic North America. Further S in mountains.

MAP LICHEN *Rhizocarpon geographicum*   Spreading
Encrusting lichen of rocks in uplands and mountains; also coastal in N. Surface yellowish, etched with black spore-producing bodies. Borders of neighboring colonies defined by black margins creating maplike appearance. Widespread in North America.

LICHEN *Ramalina* sp.   Tufts up to 2in long
A varied group of tufted lichens that grow attached to rocks (coastal and upland) or on bark, depending on species. All have a thallus that is strap-shaped, often twisted and uniformly gray or grayish-green on both sides. Widespread in North America.

BEARD-MOSS LICHEN *Usnea* sp.   Tufts up to 5in long
Widespread group of lichens that are much-branched and gray-green; the branches themselves are usually rather narrow, sometimes almost threadlike, and grooved in parts. Attached to, and often hanging from, tree bark or rocks. Widespread in North America.

LICHEN *Parmelia* sp.   Spreading
Encrusting, patch-forming lichens found on rock or mature tree bark, depending on the species. In most, patches are gray-green and comprise rounded lobes. Surface usually dotted with flat-topped, spore-producing discs. Widespread in North America.

 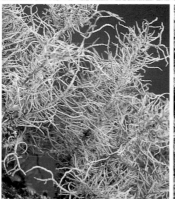 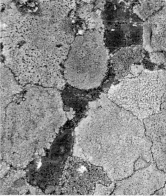

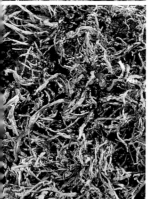 

LICHEN *Verrucaria* sp.   Spreading
Encrusting lichen found growing on rocks and stabilized shingle on the coast. Tolerant of periodic immersion in sea water as well as salt spray. Surface is sooty black and covered with a network of cracks. Widespread on N coasts.

ORANGE-YELLOW LICHEN *Xanthoria parietina*   Spreading
Colorful lichen. Forms bright orange-yellow patches on rocks, walls, brickwork, and the bark of some trees. Encrustation comprises leafy, narrow scales. Common on coasts; also on mountains and some inland lowland areas too. Widespread in North America.

GULFWEED *Sargassum* sp.   Length up to 2ft
Floating seaweed. Found far out to sea but frequently washed on to shores after gales. Comprises branched mass of narrow fronds, flattened towards tips and with pealike air bladders along length. Atlantic coast, mostly in S.

BLADDER ROCKWEED *Fucus vesiculosus*   Length up to 3ft
Tough seaweed found on middle shore attached to rocks. Frond olive- or greenish brown; branches regularly. Air bladders in groups of 2 or 3 along length. Spongy reproductive bodies occur at frond tips. Atlantic coast, S to VI. Similar *Fucus* species occur on Pacific coast.

KNOTTED ROCKWEED *Ascophyllum nodosum*   Length up to 4ft
Comprises greenish stems that are rough, leathery, and flat. Air bladders occur at regular intervals along stems, which branch repeatedly. Yellowish green reproductive bodies resemble sultanas. Atlantic coast, N from New England.

CORALLINE SEAWEED *Corallina* sp.   Spreading
Covers rocks with dense, short sward of jointed, cylindrical branches; tough and brittle due to calcium carbonate encrustation. Pink in life but bleaches white when detached and dead. Lower shore and rock pools. Pacific and NE Atlantic coasts.

GREEN ENTEROMORPHA *Enteromorpha* sp.   Length up to 3ft
Fronds membranous and green, forming long gutlike tubes that become inflated; sometimes constricted along their length. Attached to rocks or floating in rock pools, brackish lagoons, and estuaries. Pacific and Atlantic coasts.

IRISH MOSS *Chondrus crispus*   Length up to 9in
Variable seaweed that branches repeatedly into broad, flat branches that look crinkly at the tips. Color forms include red, green, and brown. Attached by short stem to rocks on lower shore. Atlantic coast, N from New England.

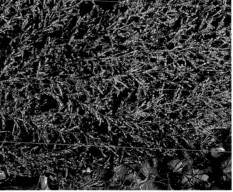

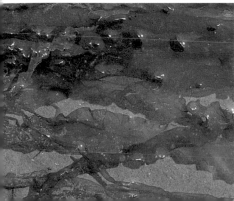

SEA LETTUCE *Ulva lactuca*   Length up to 1½ft
Delicate green and membranous seaweed. Grows attached to rocks on sheltered shores; often thrives in rock pools on upper and middle shores, even if detached from substrate. Widespread on both Pacific and Atlantic coasts.

GIGARTINA (TUFTED RED WEED) *Gigartina stellata*   Length up to 4in
A low-growing seaweed, fronds of which are flat, divided, and often curled; blades expand towards their tips where they are studded with short outgrowths. Grows attached to rocks on lower to middle shore. Atlantic, mainly N from NY.

BULL KELP *Nereocystis luetkeana*   Length up to 100ft
Impressive seaweed. A long stalk, attached by holdfast to submerged rocks, ends in air-filled float up to 6in across; suspended from this are straplike fronds. Sub-tidal zone; only the float is visible at surface. Pacific coast.

GIANT PERENNIAL KELP *Macrocystis* sp.   Length up to 200ft
The continent's largest seaweed. Entirely submerged but sometimes washed up on shore. A branching stalk is attached by holdfast to rock. Along its length are round floats from which 1ft-long blades arise. Widespread on Pacific coast.

WINGED KELP *Alaria* sp.   Length up to 10ft
Frond comprises broad blade up to 10in wide with a conspicuous midrib along its length. At base of main blade, smaller, narrower reproductive blades project from main stalk. Attached to rocks; lower shore. Pacific and NE Atlantic coasts.

SUGAR WRACK *Laminaria saccharina*   Length up to 5ft
A robust stalk up to 3ft long, attached to rocks by holdfast, gives rise to a broad blade with a ruffled margin. Sometimes forms dense stands in suitable locations. Lower shore and sub-tidal zone. N Pacific and N Atlantic coasts.

SEA PALM *Postelsia palmaeformis*   Length up to 1½ft
Distinctive seaweed with passing resemblance to a miniature palm tree. A robust stalk is anchored to rocks by holdfast and produces palm frondlike blades at tip. Exposed coasts on upper shore. Pacific coast, from BC to CA.

SEA STAGHORN *Codium fragile*   Length up to 3ft
Green seaweed that branches frequently and equally; branches are tubular and up to ½in in diameter with a spongy texture. Attached to rocks, pebbles or shells in sheltered waters on lower shore. Pacific coast; locally N Atlantic shores.

DULSE *Rhodymenia palmata*   Length up to 1ft
Edible seaweed with a texture like rubber. Frond is broad, sometimes divided in a finger-like manner, and usually dark red. Grows attached to rocks from lower shore into sub-littoral zone. Atlantic coast, from NY northwards.

YELLOW MOREL *Morchellus esculenta*   Height up to 1ft
Distinctive edible fungus, prized for its delicious flavor. Head pear-shaped to rounded and fawn colored; surface is honeycombed. Stem thick and white, swollen at base. Open woodland and grassy places. Widespread throughout North America.

FLUTED WHITE HELVELLA *Helvella crispa*   Height up to 8in
Has strangely convoluted and distorted cap resembling melted plastic. Cap is creamy white; usually slightly paler than stem which is grayish white and furrowed. Roadsides and grassy woodland. Widespread; absent from far N and hot, dry S.

SCARLET CUP *Sarcoscypha coccinea*   Up to 2in across
Colorful and distinctive fungus that grows as well-formed cups or bowls. Inner surface is bright scarlet and smooth. Outer surface is pale with a chalky texture. On part-buried wood (Jan–Apr). E and NW of North America.

ORANGE PEEL *Aleuria aurantia*   Up to 3in across
Distinctive fungus that comprises a wavy-edged, saucer-shaped disc. Upper surface is bright orange and smooth. Lower surface is grayish orange with a powdery texture. On bare ground (Jun–Oct). Widespread throughout North America.

SWAMP BEACON *Mitrula paludosa*   Height up to 1½in
Intriguing little fungus. Spore-producing head is rounded or club-shaped and bright yellow or yellow-orange. Borne on long, slender white stem. Wet habitats including among sphagnum moss and woodland puddles (Apr–Jul). Throughout North America.

PURPLE JELLY DROPS *Ascocoryne sarcoides*   Up to ½in across
Unusual fungus that comprises reddish purple jellylike blobs that are clustered together. In maturity, blobs become flat-topped. Grows on the bark of fallen deciduous trees and stumps (Sep–Nov). Widespread across North America.

BLACK JELLY DROP *Bulgaria inquinans*   Up to 1½in across
Each jellylike blob consists of a circular base the top of which is rounded, becoming flat-topped with age; brown at first but becoming black on upper surface. On bark of recently fallen oak and other trees (Sep–Oct). N of North America.

CARBON BALLS *Daldinia concentrica*   Up to 2in across
Forms hard, knobbly balls on bark of dead and dying branches of deciduous trees. Surface is usually shiny black and fungus is brittle. Concentric rings revealed in cross-section. Found all year. Widespread; absent from hot, dry southern parts.

CARBON ANTLERS *Xylaria hypoxylon*   Height up to 2in
Widespread and common woodland fungus. Flattened, antler-shaped stems arise from dead wood; they start off white but gradually blacken as they mature. Usually grows in clusters on stumps. Found all year. Throughout North America.

TREE-EAR *Auricularia auricula*   Up to 4in cross
Unusual gelatinous fungus. Partly translucent when seen against the light and often distinctly ear-shaped. Hollow of 'ear' faces down and back often has veinlike wrinkles. Mainly on deciduous branches (Oct–Jun). Throughout North America.

BLACK JELLY ROLL *Exidia glandulosa*   Up to 2in across
Strange fungus with fruit bodies that are shiny and gelatinous; these resemble blackened knobs of butter. Grows on the twigs and branches of deciduous trees. Found at any time of year except summer. Widespread throughout North America.

WITCHES' BUTTER *Tremella mesenterica*   Up to 4in across
Conspicuous jellylike fungus. Fruit body comprises a convoluted, brainlike mass that is bright yellow when fresh; darkens and hardens with age. On deciduous wood, usually on dead branches that have not yet fallen (Nov–Mar). Throughout North America.

CHANTERELLE *Cantharellus cibarius*   Height up to 4in
Prized edible fungus. Smells of apricots. Cap bright yellow; rounded at first, becoming funnel-shaped with age. Gill-like ribs run down tapering, short stem. Undisturbed woodland. Throughout North America but time of appearance varies with location.

STRAIGHT-BRANCHED CORAL *Ramaria stricta*   Height up to 3in
Stiffly upright, highly branched fungus. Warm buff color but often paler at tips of branches. Grows on rotting stumps and part-buried, decaying timber (Aug–Oct). Found in both coniferous and deciduous woodland. Widespread throughout North America.

COMMON FIBRE VASE *Thelophora terrestris*   Up to 2in across
Fruiting bodies are reddish brown fans that darken with age; in overlapping whorls or clusters. Surface is covered with radiating fibres that overhang edge as white margin. Grows on ground, usually under pines (all year). N of North America.

TREMBLING MERULIUS *Merulius tremullosus*   Up to 2in across
Fruiting body forms soft, gelatinous brackets that are usually roughly semicircular. Upper surface cloaked in woolly, whitish hairs; underside has pinkish orange pores. On decaying deciduous wood. Widespread throughout North America.

THIN-MAZE FLAT POLYPORE *Daedaleopsis confragosa*   Up to 6in across
Tough bracket fungus. Upper surface is concentrically zoned with brown and buff. Underside has white pores which bruise reddish and darken with age. Found on dead branches of deciduous trees. Widespread but absent from hot, dry parts of SW.

BEEFSTEAK POLYPORE *Fistulina hepatica*   Up to 6in across
Rubbery bracket fungus. Red when young, oozing bloodlike fluid; texture and color give it a passing resemblance to beefsteak. Bracket darkens with age. On oak trees (Aug–Oct). Widespread where host trees grow; absent from far N and S.

TINDER POLYPORE *Fomes fomentarius*   Up to 1ft across
Tough and rigid fungus that looks surprisingly like a hoof. Gray surface bears darker, horizontal ridges. In the past, used for tinder. Grows on birches and other deciduous trees. Widespread in N half of North America; absent from hot, dry S.

ARTIST'S CONK *Ganoderma applanatum*   Up to 2ft across
Large bracket fungus; roughly semicircular in outline, up to 1ft deep and 2in thick. Upper surface with knobbly, reddish brown concentric layers. Underside pale buff, easily bruising. On dead deciduous wood (all year). Throughout North America.

CHICKEN MUSHROOM *Laetiporus sulphureus*   Up to 2ft across
Fruiting bodies comprise leathery brackets, up to 2in thick. Upper surface sulfur-yellow; underside orange-yellow and covered with pores. Often grows in overlapping tiers. On deciduous trees (Jul–Nov). Widespread; absent far N and SW.

BIRCH POLYPORE *Piptoporus betulinus*   Up to 10in across
Fruiting bodies comprise semicircular brackets up to 2in thick. Upper surface is buffish brown; underside is white with tiny pores. Grows on birch trees, both living and dead. Widespread in N of North America wherever host trees are common.

TURKEY-TAIL *Trametes versicolor*   Up to 3in across
Brackets are broadly semicircular in outline, often with lobed margins. Upper surface zoned with many colors, ranging from buffish pink to black. Underside pale buff with fine pores. On decaying wood (all year). Throughout North America.

FUNGI

HAIRY PARCHMENT *Stereum hirsutum*　　　　Up to 2in across
Forms irregular tiers of thin, rubbery but tough brackets that have wavy margins. Upper surface grayish and hairy. Underside variable but usually orange-yellow. Grows on dead wood (all year). Widespread; absent from hot, dry S.

HORSE MUSHROOM *Agaricus arvensis*　　　　Height up to 4in
Robust edible fungus. Cap creamy white and up to 10in across; domed at first but flattening with age. Gills pale pink at first, maturing brown. Stem bears ring of 2 membranes. Grassy meadows (summer and fall in E; spring in W). Throughout North America.

MEADOW MUSHROOM *Agaricus campestris*　　　　Height up to 4in
Familiar edible fungus. Cap pale buffish brown, flattening with age. Gills pink at first but darkening with maturity. Flesh smells mushroomy. Stem has ring that is easily lost. Grassy places (mostly Aug–Dec). Widespread throughout North America.

PARASOL *Lepiota procera*　　　　Height up to 1½ft
Distinctive fungus. Cap is pale buff and marked with brown scales; egg-shaped when young but flattens with age. Gills white and stems brown with scaly patterns. Open, grassy places (Aug–Nov). E of North America. Similar species in W.

TAWNY GRISETTE *Amanita fulva*　　　　Height up to 5in
Distinctive fungus. Tawny brown cap is sometimes marked with radial streaks around the margin. Gills and flesh are white. Stem white, lacking a ring; grows from a saclike volva at base. Woodland (mainly Aug–Nov). Throughout North America.

FLY AGARIC *Amanita muscaria*　　　　Height up to 10in
Distinctive toadstool. Cap is red and covered with white flecks (remains of veil) that are washed off in heavy rain. Gills white and stem white with a ring and bulbous base. Woodland, usually under birch. E of North America.

DEATH CAP *Amanita phalloides*　　　　Height up to 4in
Highly poisonous fungus; sickly sweet smell. Cap tinged green. Gills and flesh white. White stem has ring; base surrounded by saclike volva. Woodland, both under conifers and broad-leaved trees (fall in E; winter in W). Absent far N and S.

BLUSHER *Amanita rubescens*　　　　Height up to 7in
Cap is pale buffish brown and covered with pinkish gray fragments of veil. Gills white. Stem has a ring and usually flushes pinkish buff, especially near the base. Mainly deciduous woodland (fall in E; spring in W). E US and CA.

ALCOHOL INKY *Coprinus atramentarius*　　　　Height up to 6in
Cap egg-shaped and furrowed; grayish white but soon blackening. Gills white, maturing black and liquefying. Stem tall and slim. Causes sickness if eaten with alcohol. Open woods; in clusters (fall in E; spring in W). Throughout North America.

SHAGGY INKY *Coprinus comatus*　　　　Height up to 1½ft
Distinctive fungus. At first, cap shrouds stem and is egg-shaped and whitish with shaggy fibres; expands with age and, with gills, blackens and liquefies. Grows on roadsides and other grassy places (mainly Aug–Nov). Throughout North America.

MICA CAP *Coprinus micaceus*　　　　Height up to 4in
Clump-forming fungus. Cap buffish yellow, darkest towards center and covered with glistening granules; these are lost with age and cap darkens generally. Gills white but blacken with age. On dead wood (mainly Jun–Nov). Throughout North America.

SEMI-OVATE PANEOLUS *Paneolus semiovatus*　　　　Height up to 4in
Distinctive fungus. Cap is pale creamy buff and shaped like the pointed half of an egg. Gills black and spotted. Stem tall, slim and same color as cap. Grows from horse dung (Jul–Oct). Widespread but local because of habitat requirements.

BAY BOLETE *Boletus badius* Height up to 6in
Cap is up to 4in across and color ranges from tan to buff; surface sticky when wet. Pores yellow but bruise bluish green. Flesh white but flushes blue when cut. Stem often tapers. Deciduous and coniferous woods (Aug–Nov). NE of North America.

RED-CRACKED BOLETE *Boletus chrysenteron* Height up to 4in
Distinctive fungus. Cap is buffish brown at first but soon cracks, especially around margins, revealing red flesh. Pores buffish yellow. Stem flushed red. Deciduous woods, especially under oak (mainly Jul–Nov). Widespread in North America.

KING BOLETE *Boletus edulis* Height up to 1ft
Prized edible fungus. Cap is up to 10in across, brown and often dimpled or lobed. Pores white at first, becoming creamy or yellow. Stem is fat and bulbous. Both deciduous and coniferous woodland (Jul–Oct). Widespread in North America.

PEPPERY BOLETE *Boletus piperatus* Height up to 4in
Cap is up to 4in across and orange-brown; shiny when dry, sticky when wet. Pores are orange-tan. Flesh stains yellow and tastes peppery. Stem is same color as cap. Woodland, mainly under conifers (mainly Aug–Nov). Widespread in North America.

COMMON SCABER STALK *Leccinum scabrum* Height up to 10in
Cap is up to 6in across, gray-brown and rounded. Pores off-white but bruise darker. Flesh white; does not discolor when cut. Stem tall, white, and covered with blackish scales. Under birch trees (Jul–Nov). Widespread throughout North America.

SLIPPERY JACK *Suillus luteus* Height up to 5in
Cap up to 3in across, chestnut-colored and covered with gluten which becomes slippery in wet weather. Pores dirty yellow and flesh whitish. Stem whitish at base, yellowish towards top. Under conifers (Sep–Nov). E of North America.

SILVERY-VIOLET CORT *Cortinarius alboviolaceus* Height up to 4in
Cap up to 2in across, whitish but tinged violet; bell-shaped at first but flattening with age. Gills bluish becoming brown and flesh bluish white. Stem is same color as cap, marked with fibrous lines. Woodland (Sep–Oct). Widespread in North America.

SCARLET WAXY CAP *Hygrophorus coccineus* Height up to 3in
Striking, bright red fungus. Cap 1–2in across; conical or rounded at first, expanding and flattening with age. Gills red but with yellow margins. Flesh reddish. Grassy woodlands (Aug–Nov). E of North America; locally in Pacific states.

POISON PAXILLUS *Paxillus involutus* Height up to 5in
Cap is up to 4in across and tawny brown; flattened then funnel-shaped but with margin inrolled. Gills brown and decurrent down brown stem. Woodlands, often under birch (Jul–Oct). Widespread throughout North America.

GRAYING YELLOW RUSSULA *Russula claroflava* Height up to 4in
Cap is up to 3in across, bright yellow and smooth; margins sometimes grooved. Gills and stem are off-white, becoming gray with age; flesh is white. Woodland, both coniferous and deciduous (Aug–Sep). Widespread in North America.

EMETIC RUSSULA *Russula emetica* Height up to 3in
Colorful, poisonous fungus. Cap is bright red, domed at first but flattened later; sticky and shiny when wet. Gills creamy white. Stem and flesh white. In conifer woodland on damp ground (Aug–Oct). Widespread in North America.

ORANGE-LATEX MILKY *Lactarius deliciosus* Height up to 3in
Cap is up to 3in across, buffish yellow but zoned with orange and greenish hues. Gills decurrent and pale pink, turning green with age or damage. Flesh yellowish when cut and milk orange. Conifer woodlands (Aug–Oct). Widespread in North America.

SCALY PHOLIOTA *Pholiota squarrosa*   Height up to 6in
Clump-forming fungus. Cap is up to 3in across, deep yellow and covered in dark brown scales; domed but flattening with age. Gills yellow. Stem has similar ground color and scales as cap. Woods, at base of trees (Aug–Oct). Throughout North America.

HONEY MUSHROOM *Armillaria mellea*   Height up to 6in
Cap is up to 4in across, brown and slightly scaly; domed at first but expanding and flattening with age. Gills pale buff. Stem brown and bears a ring. Woodland, growing on stumps or at tree bases (Aug–Nov). Widespread in North America.

VELVET FOOT *Flammulina velutipes*   Height up to 5in
Cap is up to 2in across, orange or yellow-buff, darker around margins. Gills yellowish. Stem tough and orange with velvet texture towards base. Deciduous woodland, on tree stumps (mainly late winter and early spring). Widespread in North America.

COMMON LACCARIA *Laccaria laccata*   Height up to 3in
Variable fungus. Cap usually orange-brown and irregularly rounded, often distorted. Gills pinkish buff and stem twisted, fibrous and same color as cap. Among leaf litter in woods and open places (Jul–Oct). Widespread in North America.

FAIRY RING MUSHROOM *Marasmius oreades*   Height up to 4in
Ring-forming fungus associated with lawns and short grassland. Cap is usually pale buffish tan but sometimes stained darker. Gills white and widely spaced. Flesh is white. Stem is same color as cap. Widespread (mainly Jul–Oct).

COMMON MYCENA *Mycena galericulata*   Height up to 4in
Clump-forming fungus. Cap up to 2in across and gray to brown with radiating lines towards margins; conical, flattening with age. Gills pinkish. Stem slender and same color as cap. Woodland, on tree stumps (mainly Jul–Dec). Throughout North America.

BLEEDING MYCENA *Mycena haematopus*   Height up to 4in
Clump-forming fungus. Conical cap up to 2in across, gray-brown with radiating lines towards margins. Gills whitish and stem slender and downy. All parts exude bloodlike fluid when damaged. On decaying tree stumps (Jul–Oct). Widespread in North America.

OYSTER MUSHROOM *Pleurotus ostreatus*   Up to 5in across
Bracket-shaped fungus with a rubbery texture. Cap up to ½in thick; color variable but usually dark gray or pale buff. Gills whitish and widely spaced; run down short lateral stem. Grows on deciduous trees (all year). Widespread in North America.

COLLARED EARTHSTAR *Geastrum triplex*   Up to 4in across
Extraordinary-looking fungus. Initially, fruit body resembles an onion. Outer layer then splits into 4–7 segments that fold back and eventually lift central orb off ground. Spores expelled via pore. Open woods (Aug–Nov). Widespread in North America.

GEM-STUDDED PUFFBALL *Lycoperdon perlatum*   Height up to 3in
The club-shaped fruit bodies are found in clusters. Fruit body off-white with dark spines when young; mature specimens are brown and wrinkled; spores expelled via terminal pore. On dead and part-buried decaying wood (Aug–Nov). Widespread in North America.

STINKHORN *Phallus impudicus*   Height up to 6in
Striking fungus. Seen initially as a soft, white ball, 2–3in across, from which phalluslike fruit body emerges. Stalk's oval tip is coated with spore-laden, stinking mucus on which flies feed. Rotten tree stumps (Jul–Oct). Widespread in North America.

PIGSKIN POISON PUFFBALL *Scleroderma citrinum*   Up to 4in across
Resembles old, cracked tennis ball. Fruit body brown with darker, flaky scales; expands and surface cracks with age showing paler inner layer. Mature fruit body splits irregularly to liberate spores. Woodland (Aug–Nov). Widespread in North America.

GLOSSARY

Abdomen: hind section of an insect's body; usually appears segmented

Accidental: not regularly occurring in an area; few records

Aestivation: dormancy observed in an animal during summer

Alien: species that is not native to a particular region but which has been introduced by man and has become naturalized

Annelid: a type of segmented worm

Annual: a plant that lives for a single growing season

Antennae: slender, paired sensory organs on the head of an insect or crustacean

Anther: pollen-containing structure in a flower, located on the end of the male reproductive structure, the stamen

Aperture: the opening of a snail's shell

Arboreal: tree-dwelling

Awn: bristle found in flowers of many grasses

Axil: angle where upper surface of a leaf meets the stem on a plant

Benthic: found on the floor of lakes, ponds, oceans and other bodies of water

Berry: fleshy fruit containing several seeds

Biennial: a plant that takes two years to complete its life cycle

Bivalve: mollusk whose shell comprises two halves

Body whorl: the last whorl of the spire of a snail

Bract: a small leaflike or scalelike structure beneath a flower

Bulb: fleshy, underground structure found in certain plants and comprising leaf bases and next year's bud

Bulbil: small, bulblike structure

Cap: structure seen in fungi under which spore-bearing structures, usually gills or pores, are suspended

Capsule: structure within which seeds are formed in flowering plants and spores develop in mosses and liverworts

Carapace: hard, upper surface of a crustacean's shell

Carpal: area on a bird's wing corresponding to the "wrist" joint

Caterpillar: larval stage of a butterfly or moth

Catkin: flowering structure of certain trees and shrubs

Caudal fin: the tail fin of a fish

Cephalothorax: fused head and thorax found in spiders

Cerci: paired appendages at hind end of an insect's body

Chiton: the primary component of the external skeleton of crustaceans and insects

Chlorophyll: green pigment found in plant tissue and essential for photosynthesis

Compound eye: eye structure typical of insects and some other invertebrates comprising numerous cells and lenses, not a single lens

Cone: structure bearing reproductive elements of conifers

Conifer: tree that bears its reproductive structures in cones

Cosmopolitan: usually found worldwide in suitable habitat

Crepuscular: active at dawn and dusk

Cryptic: colored to blend in, providing camouflage

Deciduous: woody plant that sheds its leaves in winter

Disc florets: small flowers found at the centre of the inflorescence of members of the daisy family

Diurnal: active during daylight

Dorsal: upper surface

Dorsal fin: one or more fins along the backbone of a fish, dolphin or whale

Elytra: the hard horny forewings of a beetle, which cover and protect the hindwings

Endangered: much reduced in number and could disappear in part or all of its range

Endemic: confined to a geographical area such as an island, state or country

Evergreen: plant that retains its leaves throughout the year

Exotic: usually refers to an alien or introduced species

Feral: having returned to the wild

Floret: small flower

Frond: leaflike structure found in some lower plants

Fruit: seeds together with their surrounding tissues

Gall: plant growth induced by another organism, often a gall wasp

Girdle: the oval band surrounding the plates of a chiton

Glume: stiffened bract found on a grass flower

Hemoglobin: red pigment in blood that absorbs oxygen

Holdfast: rootlike structure that anchors seaweeds to rocks

Hybrid: offspring from different parent species

Inflorescence: combination of a flower, its bracts and flowering stems

Insectivore: an organism that feeds on insects

Juvenile: newly fledged bird that has not yet acquired adult plumage

Lanceolate: lance-shaped

Larva: soft-bodied, pre-adult stage in the life-cycle of certain insects

Lateral line: a sensory organ along the side of a fish that senses pressure changes

Leaflet: small, separate segment of a leaf

Lek: communal display area used by certain bird species

Ligule: membranous leaf sheath found in grasses

Mantle: the tissue of a mollusk that secretes the shell

Melanic: showing dark pigmentation

Migrant: animal that spends the summer and winter in different areas

Moult: process seen in birds during which old feathers are lost and replaced by new ones

Mucus: slimy, viscous fluid secretion

Native: a naturally occurring species

Needle: narrow leaves found in conifers

Nocturnal: active after dark

Node: part of stem at which leaves arise

Nudibranch: a marine snail without a shell; also called a sea slug

Nut: dry and often hard fruit containing a single seed

Nymph: pre-adult stage in certain insects, notably bugs, which has some characters in common with the adult stage

Operculum: plate found in some mollusks and used to seal off the entrance to the shell

Ovate: roughly oval in outline

Ovipositor: egg-laying structure found at the tail-end of some female insects

Ovoid: egg-shaped

Palmate: leaf divided into lobes which fancifully resembles a hand

Palps: sensory appendages found around the mouth in insects and crustaceans

Parasite: organism that lives on or in another organism, relying on it entirely for its nutrition

Passage migrant: bird species seen mostly on migration and which does not necessarily breed in the region

Pectoral fins: a pair of fins behind and often below the head of a fish

Pelagic: living in the open ocean

Pelvic fins: a pair of fins to the rear but before the anal fin of a fish

Perennial: plant that lives for more than two years

Periostracum: the tough external covering of many mollusks' shells

Petal: often colourful inner row of structures surrounding reproductive part of a flower

Pinnate: leaf divided into more than three leaflets, these being arranged in pairs on either side of the leaf stem

Planarian: an unsegmented flatworm

Pollen: minute grains produced by anthers and containing male sex cells

Primaries: flight feathers located on the outer half of a bird's wing

Pronotum: hardened dorsal plate covering the thorax of an insect

Pupa: stage in an insect's life-cycle between the larva and adult; also called the chrysalis

Radula: the tongue of a snail, which has teeth to bore holes in shells or prey

Ray florets: small flowers found on the outer fringe of the inflorescence in flowers of the daisy family

Recurved: turned backwards in a curve

Rhizome: underground stem

Rosette: radiating arrangement of leaves

Runner: creeping stem that occurs above ground and may root at nodes or tip

Saprophyte: a plant that lacks chlorophyll and which gains its nutrition from decaying organic matter, such as fallen leaves

Secondaries: flight feathers located on the inner half of the wing of birds

Sepal: outer row of structures surrounding the reproductive part of a flower

Siphon: the tube through which water enters and leaves a mollusk

Sole: underside of the foot in mollusks

Spadix: upright spike of florets, found in arums

Spathe: large bract surrounding spadix in arums

Species: unit of classification defining animals or plants that are able to breed with one another and produce viable offspring

Speculum: species-specific patch of colour seen on ducks' wings

Spike: simple, branched inflorescence

Spikelet: inflorescence arrangement in grasses, sedges, and so on

Spire: the upper whorls of a snail shell; may be few or many

Spore: tiny reproductive body that disperses and gives rise to a new organism

Stamen: male reproductive structure of a flower

Steppe: *see* introductory section on Mediterranean habitats

Stigma: receptive tip of female part of flower, the style

Stipule: leaflike or scalelike structure at base of leaf stalk

Style: female reproductive structure of a flower

Subspecies: sub-division of a species, members of which are able to breed with other subspecies but seldom do so because of geographical isolation

Tendril: slender, modified leaf or stem structure which assists climbing in some plants

Thallus: unspecialized vegetative body of a lower plant

Thorax: middle section of an insect's body

Tragus: pointed inner ear outgrowth found in some bat species

Trifoliate: leaf divided into three sections

Umbel: umbrellalike inflorescence

Ventral: lower surface

Whorl: a 360 degree turn of a snail's shell

Zooplankton: the general term for all of the very small animals that swim or float at or near the water's surface

FURTHER READING

This book is an overview of some of the more widespread species, selected from the rich diversity of life on the North American continent. The lists below will enable readers to follow up any particular interests, and identify more accurately most species they are likely to encounter.

PETERSON NORTH AMERICAN FIELD GUIDES
This series includes the following volumes:

Animal Tracks
Atlantic Coast Fishes
Atlantic Seashore
Beetles
Birds of Eastern and Central North America
Birds of Texas
California and Pacific Northwest Forests
Coral Reefs of the Caribbean and Florida
Eastern Birds
Eastern Birds' Nests
Eastern Butterflies
Eastern Forests
Eastern Moths
Eastern Trees
Ecology of Eastern Forests in North America
Ecology of Western Forests
Edible Wild Plants of Eastern and Central North America
Feeder Birds of Eastern North America
Ferns and Their Related Families of Northeastern and Central North America
Freshwater Fishes
Insects of America North of Mexico
Mammals of North America, North of Mexico
Medicinal Plants and Herbs of Eastern and Central North America
Mexican Birds
Mushrooms of North America
Pacific Coast Fishes of North America
Pacific Coast Shells
Pacific States Wildflowers
Reptiles and Amphibians: Eastern and Central North America
Rocky Mountain and Southwest Forests
Rocky Mountain Wildflowers: Northern Arizona and New Mexico to British Columbia
Shells of the Atlantic and Gulf Coasts and the West Indies
Southeastern and Caribbean Seashores
Southwestern and Texas Wildflowers
Trees and Shrubs
Western Birds
Western Birds' Nests

Western Butterflies
Western Reptiles and Amphibians
Western Trees
Wildflowers of Northeastern and North-Central North America

NATIONAL AUDUBON SOCIETY FIELD GUIDES

This series includes the following volumes:

Birds: Eastern Region
Birds: Western Region
Butterflies
Fishes, Whales and Dolphins
Insects and Spiders
Mammals
Mushrooms
Reptiles and Amphibians
Seashells
Seashore Creatures
Trees: Eastern Region
Wildflowers of the Eastern Region
Wildflowers of the Western Region

NATIONAL AUDUBON SOCIETY REGIONAL NATURE GUIDES

Each Nature Guide covers one of North America's regional natural habitats, featuring trees, wildflowers, birds, mammals, and insects. Each guide is illustrated with colour photographs. This series includes the following volumes:

Deserts
Eastern Forests
Grasslands
Western Forests
Wetlands

NATIONAL AUDUBON SOCIETY REGIONAL FIELD GUIDES

This new series of comprehensive field guides covers flora, fauna, landscape, and climate of specific geographic regions of North America. This series contains the following volumes:

California
Florida
The Mid-Atlantic States
New England
The Pacific Northwest
The Rocky Mountain States
The Southeastern States
The Western States

GOLDEN GUIDES

Small, inexpensive, though remarkably comprehensive guides, which are mostly out of print, but are easily available in used bookstores. This series contains the following volumes:

Birds
Butterflies and Moths
Everglades National Park and Florida Keys
Fishes
Flowers
Insect Pests
Insects
Mammals
Non-flowering Plants
Pacific Northwest
Pond Life
Reptiles and Amphibians
Rocky Mountains
Sea Shells
Sea Shore
Spiders and Their Kin
Trees
Weeds
Whales and other Marine Mammals

SIERRA CLUB GUIDES TO THE NATIONAL PARKS

A series of five guides covering all 48 of America's national parks:

The Desert Southwest
The East and Middle West
The Pacific Northwest and Alaska
The Pacific Southwest and Hawaii
The Rocky Mountains

SIERRA CLUB NATURALIST'S GUIDES

A series of field guides that comprehensively describes the natural history of various ecologically distinct regions of North America:

The Deserts of the Southwest
The Middle Atlantic Coast
The North Atlantic Coast
The North Woods of Michigan, etc.
The Pacific Northwest
The Piedmont of Eastern North America
The Sierra Nevada
Southern New England
The Southern Rockies

MISCELLANEOUS

Abbot, R Tucker (1954) *American Seashells*, D Van Nostrand Co.,

Burton, John A (1999) *The Pocket Guide to Mammals of North America*, Prospero Books

Dunkle, Sidney W (2000) *Dragonflies through Binoculars: A Field Guide to Dragonflies of North America*, Oxford University Press

Glasserg, J (1999) *Butterflies through Binoculars*, Oxford University Press

Glasserg, J (1999) *Butterflies through Binoculars. The East*, Oxford University Press

Glasserg, J (1999) *Butterflies through Binoculars. Florida*, Oxford University Press

Griggs, Jack L (2002) *All the Birds of North America: American Bird Conservancy's Field Guide*, HarperCollins

Kays, Roland W, and Don E Wilson (2002) *Mammals of North America*, Princeton University Press

McClane, AJ (1974) *Freshwater Fishes of North America*, Henry Holt & Co., New York

McClane, AJ (1978) *Saltwater Fishes of North America*, Henry Holt & Co., New York

McGinnis, Samuel (1984) *Freshwater Fishes of California*, California University Press

Needham, James G, Minter J Westfall and Michael L May (2000) *Dragonflies of North America*, Scientific Publishers

Stupka, Arthur (1994) *Wildflowers in Color: A Field Guide to More than 250 Wildflowers of Eastern North America*, HarperCollins, Canada

USEFUL WEB ADDRESSES

GENERAL SITES
Amazing Environmental Organization WebDirectory
www.webdirectory.com
Claims to be the Earth's biggest environment search engine. Certainly a very useful website.

Canadian Wildlife Service
www.cws-scf.ec.gc.ca
A comprehensive government site.

www.eNature.com
A resource provided by the National Wildlife Federation, which contains online field guides and regional wildlife guides, and allows you to find your favorite US national parks and wildlife refuges.

National Audubon Society
www.audubon.org/states
The leading nature conservation organization with state chapters.

US Fish and Wildlife Service
www.fws.gov
The government wildlife agency, with a very comprehensive web site.

REPTILES AND AMPHIBIANS
Amphibian Information Website
www.mp2-pwrc.usgs.gov/amphibs
Searchable databases of literature references, researchers, and web sites dealing with amphibian conservation. The references database contains data only for North America.

North American Amphibian Monitoring Program
www.mp2-pwrc.usgs.gov/naamp
Part of a global effort to study and conserve amphibians.

Society for the Study of Amphibians and Reptiles
www.ukans.edu/~ssar
SSAR is an international herpetological society, recognized for having a diverse program of publications, meetings, and other activities of interest to herpetologists in zoos, museums, universities, and the general public.

FISH
The Native Fish Conservancy
www.nativefish.org
A really useful website for anyone interested in native freshwater fish.

MAMMALS
The American Society of Mammalogists
www.mammalsociety.org

BIRDS
American Ornithologists' Union
www.aou.org
The oldest and largest organization in the New World devoted to the scientific study of birds. Includes the authoritative Check-List of North American Birds.

BIRDNET
www.nmnh.si.edu/BIRDNET
The Ornithological Council's site with comprehensive information about North American ornithological resources.

Cornell Laboratory of Ornithology
www.birds.cornell.edu
Membership institute whose mission is to interpret and conserve the earth's biodiversity through research, education, and citizen science focused on birds.

PLANTS
Native Plant and Wildlife Organizations
www.tardigrade.org/natives/orgs.html
A useful site for finding out about plants of North America.

FUNGI
North America Mycologists Association
www.namyco.org

INDEX

PICTURE CREDITS

© Massachusetts Audubon Society 203c, 205f, 207a, 207b, 207d, 207g, 209c–e, 209g, 209k, 211b, 211c, 211i, 211k, 213d, 213e, 213g, 213i, 213j, 215a, 215b, 215d, 215g, 217a, 217d, 217f, 217g, 217h, 217j, 219f, 219h, 221h, 223a, 225b, 225d, 225j, 225k, 227b–d, 233b, 233h, 237j, 237k, 239b, 239f, 239h, 239i, 241b, 241d, 241b,241d, 243a, 243i, 243j, 249a, 249g, 249h, 249j, 253j, 255d, 255i, 257e, 257f, 257i, 259c, 263d, 267e, 267g–i, 269g, 269i, 273b, 273f–h, 275a, 275e, 277j, 279h, 279j–l, 281a, 281g, 283f, 283i, 285e, 285f, 291d, 291e, 291g, 293d, 293e, 293i, 293j, 295b, 295c, 295h, 295i, 295j, 297a, 297f, 297h, 299d, 307h
© Nature Photographers/SC Bisserot 115f, 115g, 119d, 121d, 127a–c, 129b–e, 129g, 131a, 131b, 131h, 133b, 133e, 135d, 135e, 137a, 141c, 145e, 145f, 177d, 187c, 187i, 200c, 275c, 283a, 309j
© Nature Photographers/Frank B Blackburn 211a, 215e, 241f, 289h, 317i, 321g
© Nature Photographers/Mark Bolton 225f
© Nature Photographers/LH Brown 99c
© Nature Photographers/Brinsley Burbidge 201j, 203d, 203g, 205b, 211d, 217e, 223j, 231e, 233c, 233d, 233g, 233l, 239c, 243c, 243h, 245j, 251i, 257c, 261g, 265g, 267f, 271h, 275d, 281e, 293a–c, 295a, 297c–e, 297g, 305h, 305j, 307c, 307e
© Nature Photographers/Robin Bush 59b, 215i, 263a, 269k, 279g, 289i, 299j, 305i, 321f
© Nature Photographers/NA Callow 161g
© Nature Photographers/Kevin Carlson 5, 37b, 37e, 39a, 73d, 75f, 75j, 77b, 91e, 97d, 99a, 99d, 99e, 99g, 99h, 99j, 101b, 103b, 103c, 103e, 103f, 103j, 105b–d, 109a, 109f, 111g, 113g, 131e, 209l, 221e, 229k, 235i, 263f, 263g, 269a
© Nature Photographers/Colin Carver 77g, 89e, 113j
© Nature Photographers/Hugh Clark 49b, 51j, 95c
© Nature Photographers/Andrew Cleave 16, 19 (bottom), 49a, 49c, 67a, 73e, 167f, 169h, 173f, 179a, 201a, 201b, 201d, 201f–i, 201k–l, 203a, 203e, 203f, 203h, 203j, 203k, 205a, 205c–e, 205h–j, 207c, 207h, 209a, 209i, 211j, 213b, 213c, 213f, 215c, 215f, 215h, 217k, 219d, 219g, 221b, 221c, 221d, 221f, 221g, 221j, 223g, 225g, 229a, 229g, 233a, 233f, 235h, 237c, 237f, 241g, 247j, 247k, 249b, 253a, 259g, 263c, 263e, 263h, 263i, 265i, 265j, 271e, 275b, 277e, 277h, 279a, 279c, 289f, 291c, 297j, 301h, 301j, 301l, 303c, 303h, 303j, 305b, 305d, 307f, 307j, 309k, 311a, 3111d, 311g, 311h, 313b, 313h, 317h
© Nature Photographers/Peter Craig-

Cooper 87i
© Nature Photographers/Ron Croucher 211f
© Nature Photographers/Andrew K Davies 303l
© Nature Photographers/David O Elias 287d, 315e
© Nature Photographers/Geoff du Feu 141b, 149c, 157c, 299i
© Nature Photographers/Michael Gore 28 (top), 75i
© Nature Photographers/Christopher Grey-Wilson 243f
© Nature Photographers/James Hancock 39f, 57b, 77e, 95d, 99b, 109l, 255b, 269d, 275f, 277i, 291h, 291i, 291k
© Nature Photographers/David Hawes 241i
© Nature Photographers/Michael Hill 69b, 77i, 83f, 85f
© Nature Photographers/Barry R Hughes 25, 63a, 79i, 89c
© Nature Photographers/Ernie A Janes 43e, 43f, 51a, 51d, 55c, 57d, 73a, 75e, 83d, 87h, 131d, 155a, 237d, 255e, 269b, 275i, 287a, 323h
© Nature Photographers/Richard J Mearnes 265a
© Nature Photographers/Lee Morgan 65d, 277f
© Nature Photographers/Philip J Newman 63c, 77h, 85e, 87b
© Nature Photographers/David Osborn 49d, 65f, 65h, 71g, 79j, 91c, 247d, 279b, 315g, 319i, 321a, 321h, 321l, 323f
© Nature Photographers/WS Paton 31h, 65a, 91g, 91j
© Nature Photographers/Nicholas Phelps-Brown 157d
© Nature Photographers/Nick Picozzi 26 (bottom), 37c
© Nature Photographers/David A Rae 207i, 223b, 239e, 297b
© Nature Photographers/John Reynolds 315a
© Nature Photographers/Tony Schilling 201e, 223c, 223d, 225a, 301g,
© Nature Photographers/Don Smith 39b, 77d, 93d, 97b, 97f, 101c, 101h, 123e, 195a, 195d, 309g
© Nature Photographers/Paul Sterry 4, 7, 13, 14, 15, 16, 18, 19 (top), 20, 21, 22, 23, 26 (top), 29, 37a, 37d, 37i, 39d, 45a, 45b, 45d, 45e, 45f, 47a, 47f, 51h, 59c, 59f, 59g, 61a, 61e, 63b, 63e, 63f, 63i, 65b, 65c, 65e, 65i, 65j, 67b, 67c, 67e, 67f, 67g, 67j, 69c–j, 71a–f, 71i, 71j, 73b, 73c, 73f–h, 73j, 73k, 75a, 75b, 79b, 79c, 81a–f, 81h, 81i, 83a, 83c, 83e, 83g–i, 85a–d, 85g–j, 87a, 87c–f, 87j, 89b, 89d, 89g–i, 91a, 91k, 93f, 93h, 93i, 95a, 97e, 97h, 101d, 107d, 107g, 107k, 109b, 109c, 109e, 109h, 109i, 111h, 113c,

ABOUT THE AUTHORS

Dr Gerard A. Bertrand has consulted on conservation issues in forty-five countries and has photographed wildlife in more than seventy countries. He has led birding and natural history trips for Massachusetts Audubon for the past twenty years. His primary current work is in preserving critical habitats for endangered bird species.

John Burton is author of numerous natural history books, including several field guides to mammals, reptiles and amphibians of Europe and North America. He has been running conservation organizations for more than twenty-five years and in 1989 founded the World Land Trust, which has helped purchase and protect more than 300,000 acres in Belize, the Philippines, Costa Rica, Brazil, Ecuador, and Argentina.

Paul Sterry is the author and photographer of *Complete British Wildlife* and *Complete Mediterranean Wildlife*. Trained as a zoologist, Paul has been a wildlife photographer for twenty years and regularly undertakes research expeditions.